The Living Spirit

Margaret Hebblethwaite is an Assistant Editor of *The Tablet*, the renowned international Catholic weekly, and is the author of numerous books including *Motherhood and God* (Geoffrey Chapman), *Way of St Ignatius: Finding God in all things* (HarperCollins), *Six New Gospels: New Testament women tell their stories* (Geoffrey Chapman), *Conversations on Christian Feminism* (co-authored with Elaine Storkey and published by HarperCollins) and *Stations of the Cross* (Hunt & Thorpe/Liguori).

She was married to the leading Vatican commentator and author, the late Peter Hebblethwaite, and she lives in Oxford.

The Living Spirit

*Prayers and Readings
for the Christian Year*

a *Tablet* anthology

edited by
Margaret Hebblethwaite

CANTERBURY
PRESS
Norwich

© in this compilation Margaret Hebblethwaite 2000

First published in 2000 by The Canterbury Press Norwich
(a publishing imprint of Hymns Ancient & Modern Limited
a registered charity)
St Mary's Works, St Mary's Plain
Norwich, Norfolk, NR3 3BH

British Library Cataloguing in Publication Data

A catalogue record for this book is available
from the British Library

ISBN 1-85311-330-1

Typeset by Rowland Phototypesetting,
Bury St Edmunds, Suffolk
Printed in Great Britain by
Biddles Ltd, Guildford and King's Lynn

Contents

Contents

Contents

Contents

Introduction

The Living Spirit is a popular feature for readers of *The Tablet*. It is a boxed column of spiritual readings, discreetly placed at the back of the paper and headed by the characteristic flying dove that appears on the cover of this volume. Sometimes there is a single passage, at other times a selection, whether of prose, or poetry, or prayers. Amidst the bustle of news from the Church around the world, the Living Spirit provides the reader with a space for meditation, according to the rhythm of the Church's year.

Over the nine years in which I have been overseeing this column, I have welcomed the discipline provided by the Church's calendar. The liturgical year is the spiritual air that we breathe weekly – even daily – through the lectionary. It gives us a balanced diet in which every aspect of our faith finds its appropriate place, saving us from the tyranny and smallness of our preoccupations of the moment.

The liturgical year reflects the seasons of waiting and penance, the measured pace of Jesus' ministry, the climaxes of joy and the exuberance of mission – and so carries us on the Church's back through what are known as the purgative, illuminative and unitive ways. And within its annual rhythm are also those leisurely periods known as Ordinary Time, when the Living Spirit column has wandered at will among spiritual texts on any subject.

The liturgical year is a precious tradition that links us with the memories of the past, holds us in communion in the present, and sets out a pattern for the future. It builds up a store of spiritual responses in us that can be drawn upon year after year after year as we live through the familiar cycle. As we remember the life of Jesus we draw on memories of memories that do not diminish with distance but rather grow, building up a spiritual tapestry that is the work of many hands.

Into the shape of the liturgical year slip also those more recent memories – the witness of saints and sinners who have made a mark on our lives, including a number of those who have died recently. And so it has felt natural to remember not only the canonized saints like John the Baptist and Stephen, Felicity and Perpetua, but also a few sisters and brothers who have gone to their rest in the last few years, and whose memory is still fresh in the Christian community: figures such as Pedro Arrupe and Mother Teresa, Cardinal Hume and Michael Hollings, Donald Nicholl and even Diana, Princess of Wales. To include these personalities from our own day is not to present them as saints but rather to reaffirm our affection for them, in a communion that stretches on both sides of the barrier of death.

Most of the entries in this anthology correspond to a single column of the Living Spirit, and nearly all the texts have appeared in *The Tablet* over the last five years. There are some exceptions – many of them texts commemorating women. It was only when I sat down and added up the number of male and female saints that I realized that twice as many men as women had been included. One can hardly ignore the great founding figures like St Peter and St Paul, St Francis and St Dominic, St Benedict and St Ignatius. But this anthology has made a conscious effort to restore the balance, rediscovering some powerful and far from subordinate figures who may appear in future rather than past *Tablet*s, women such as St Margaret of Scotland and St Brigit of Ireland, St Elizabeth of Hungary and St Clare of Assisi, St Angela Merici and St Joan of Arc – or, among the uncanonized, Josephine Butler and Florence Nightingale, Dorothy Day and Jean Donovan.

Of course many people will regret the omission of x or y, or feel quite unnecessary the inclusion of a or b. But the choice of people must in the end be a largely subjective though not unbalanced sample, without the slightest claim to definitive status.

More authoritative status, however, is claimed for the Church's year, so that the more important feasts have gathered material from up to three Living Spirit columns. The times of more intense prayer – Lent and the Easter season – have also received extra coverage, with a reading both for the Sunday and for the week, or even for every day of Holy Week and Easter Week.

I have also included a number of ecumenical dates, not only the Week of Prayer for Christian Unity but also the thematic Sundays like Homelessness Sunday, Harvest Festival or the National Sunday for Older People. Some Sundays will have two entries – for example, World Mission Sunday and the 29th Sunday of the year both appear, though in the year 2000 they coincide on 22 October. But Mothering Sunday is always the Fourth Sunday of Lent, so this receives only one entry.

The date of Easter varies every year, and with it all the other feasts that are calculated from it, from Ash Wednesday right up to the Immaculate Heart of Mary nearly four months later. Advent also varies in length, in such a way that there are always four Sundays before Christmas no matter what day of the week is 25 December. I have opted to place all moveable feasts in the position they will occupy in the year 2000, even though Easter is exceptionally late that year.

Subsequently the reader will need to make some adjustment for saints' days to fall into their correct position in each year's liturgical cycle. I considered this minor inconvenience to be preferable to constructing two separate annual schemes, forcing the reader to flit between moveable feasts and fixed dates.

A couple of oddities are worth mentioning. The Lent Fast Day organized by the Catholic aid agency CAFOD is normally the Friday of the 1st week of Lent. However, in the year 2000 that would fall on 17 March, St Patrick's day – not the best fast day for Catholics of Irish descent. So CAFOD have temporarily moved it to the following Friday, which being 24 March is the date of Archbishop Oscar Romero's death and a highly suitable day for remembering the world's poor.

Finally, Homelessness Sunday is a Sunday without a home: it wanders around trying to find a place to settle that belongs to no one else. In the year 2000 it will be celebrated on 30 January, but there is no guarantee that it will stay there.

Margaret Hebblethwaite

1st Sunday of Advent

The river of time sweeps on, but there, like a tree planted by the water, is our Lord Jesus Christ. He became human, willing to plant himself by the river of time.

If you feel yourself drifting down to the rapids, lay hold of the tree; if you are caught up in the love of the world, hold on to Christ. He for your sake entered into time, but he did not cease to be eternal.

St Augustine

When darkness had already fallen, we reached the climax – the reading of the Word of God. I will never forget the excitement of that moment, when a huge open Bible was carried in, held high above the head, and flanked by seven flaming torches and seven palm branches. As it came to the centre of the platform, it was greeted with a trimphantly declaimed speech of praise: here was the Bible that gives life and hope to the communities of God's people. I have never known the scriptures greeted with such enthusiasm.

Then there was the music: the crowd undulated with rows of singing, swaying people, each delegate with a little coloured flag of a Latin American country to wave in the air, and a couple of sticks (symbolising the wooden huts of the *favelas*) to clap in rhythm with the music. The favourite hymns rang out – which were to become so familiar over the next five days: 'We are a new people, living in unity, the seed of a new nation, Eh, eh!' 'Awake America, the hour has come to rise up!'

Finally the local bishop, Dom Mauro Morelli, drew our

attention through the evening blackness to a distant light of the famous, towering statue of Christ the Redeemer in Rio, visible even at this distance. 'His left hand is pointing over here, towards Duque de Caxias', he said. Duque de Caxias is considered one of the most violent areas in the world, and within Brazil it has the reputation of being the national cess-pit, for its street murders, drugs and prostitution. But Christ the Redeemer was telling us, 'That is where my heart is.'

From the report of the Seventh Interecclesial Assembly
of basic ecclesial communities

Dorothy Day,
29 November

L ater, in writing about Peter [Maurin], Dorothy put his idea in her own words: 'Every house should have a Christ's room . . . It is no use turning people away to an agency, to the city or the state or the Catholic charities. It is you yourself who must perform the works of mercy. Often you can only give the price of a meal, or a bed on the Bowery. Often you can only hope that it will be spent for that. Often you can literally take off a garment if it only be a scarf and warm some shivering brother. But *personally*, at a *personal sacrifice*, these were the ways, Peter used to insist, to combat the growing tendency on the part of the State to take the job which our Lord himself gave us to do.'

'We printed these essays,' Dorothy said of Peter's writings on houses of hospitality, 'and by mid-summer the *Catholic Worker* ceased to be just a newspaper but the voice of a movement.' The Fifteenth Street apartment had become a house of hospitality for men. But this male predominance did not last for long. An unemployed young woman, having read Peter's essays, visited Dorothy and 'demanded that we start such a house' for her – and 'at once.' So 'that very afternoon,' with money Dorothy begged from a friend, Mrs Porter Chandler, 'we rented our first apartment, moved in some beds and sheltered this one unemployed woman. Within a week we had a score of applicants at our doors . . . Since then . . . we have had rooms for women . . . We have never tried to think in terms of bigger houses, but have kept stressing the need for more and more shelters in Christian families as well as in parishes.' . . .

When fall came, Dorothy believed that she had found her vocation. Twenty thousand copies of the *Worker* were printed for the September issue. Granted that bundles were sent out pell-mell, the paper's growth was none the less phenomenal.

Why was this? Dorothy's energy and personality had something to do with it . . . Dorothy had, as her mother had said, a 'presence' about her, a controlled strength, unobtrusive but still a force. Without ever betraying the ordinary and usually unpleasant marks of assertiveness, she had a 'take charge' approach to things, and such was her poise, intelligence, and acumen that people were convinced immediately of the honesty and integrity of this plain but well-spoken woman.

William D. Miller
Dorothy Day: a biography

Dorothy Day died on 29 November 1980

C. S. Lewis,
29 November

Our lifelong nostalgia, our longing to be reunited with something in the universe from which we now feel cut off, to be on the inside of some door which we have always seen from the outside, is no mere neurotic fancy, but the truest index of our real situation. And to be at last summoned inside would be both glory and honour beyond all our merits and also the healing of that old ache.

And this brings me to the other sense of glory – glory as brightness, splendour, luminosity. We are to shine as the sun, we are to be given the Morning Star. I think I begin to see what it means. In one way, of course, God has given us the Morning Star already: you can go and enjoy the gift on many fine mornings if you get up early enough. What more, you may ask, do we want?

Ah, but we want so much more – something the books on aesthetics take little notice of. But the poets and the mythologies know all about it. We do not want merely to *see* beauty, though, God knows, even that is bounty enough. We want something else which can hardly be put into words – to be united with the beauty we see, to pass into it, to receive it into ourselves, to bathe in it, to become part of it.

That is why we have peopled air and earth and water with gods and goddesses and nymphs and elves – that, though we cannot, yet these projections can, enjoy in themselves that beauty, grace, and power of which Nature is the image. That is why the poets tell us such lovely falsehoods. They talk as if the west wind could really sweep into a human soul; but it can't. They tell us that 'beauty born of murmuring sound' will pass into a human face; but it won't. Or not yet.

For if we take the imagery of Scripture seriously, if we believe that God will one day *give* us the Morning Star and cause us to *put on* the splendour of the sun, then we may surmise that both the ancient myths and the modern poetry, so false as history, may be very near the truth as prophecy.

At present we are on the outside of the world, the wrong side of the door. We discern the freshness and purity of morning, but they do not make us fresh and pure. We cannot mingle with the splendours we see. But all the leaves of the New Testament are rustling with the rumour that it will not always be so. Some day, God willing, we shall get *in*.

C. S. Lewis
'The Weight of Glory'

C. S. Lewis was born on 29 November 1898

Etty Hillesum,
30 November

The jasmine behind my house has been completely ruined by the rains and storms of the last few days, its white blossoms are floating about in muddy black pools on the low garage roof. But somewhere inside me the jasmine continues to blossom undisturbed, just as profusely and delicately as ever it did. And it spreads its scent round the house in which you dwell, oh God. You can see, I look after you, I bring you not only my tears and my forebodings on this stormy, grey Sunday morning, I even bring you scented jasmine. And I shall bring you all the flowers I shall meet on my way, and truly there are many of those. I shall try to make you at home always. Even if I should be locked up in a narrow cell and a cloud should drift past my small barred window, then I shall bring you that cloud, oh God, while there is still the strength in me to do so. I cannot promise you anything for tomorrow, but my intentions are good, you can see.

12 July 1942

I shall allow the chain of this day to unwind link by link, I shall not intervene but shall simply have faith. I shall let you make your own decisions, oh God. This morning I found a buff envelope in my letter box. I could see there was a white paper inside. I was quite calm and thought, 'My call-up notice, what a pity, now I won't have time to try repacking my ruck-sack.' Later I noticed that my knees were shaking. It was simply a form to be filled in by the staff of the Jewish Council.

28 July 1942

All I wanted to say is this: the misery here is quite terrible and yet, late at night when the day has slunk away into the depths behind me, I often walk with a spring in my step along the barbed wire, and then time and again it soars straight from my heart – I can't help it, that's just the way it is, like some elementary force – the feeling that life is glorious and magnificent, and that one day we shall be building a whole new world. Against every new outrage and every fresh horror we shall put up one more piece of love and goodness, drawing strength from within ourselves. We may suffer, but we must not succumb. And if we should survive unhurt in body and soul, but above all in soul, without bitterness and without hatred, then we shall have a right to a say after the war. Maybe I am an ambitious woman: I would like to have just a tiny little bit of a say.

3 July 1943

Etty Hillesum
Etty: a diary 1941–43

Etty Hillesum died in Auschwitz 30 November 1943

Jean Donovan,
2 December

'She was the same Jeannie, but very alone, kind of desperate. She had seen an awful lot of pain, she had experienced the death of very dear friends, and she was afraid. She was afraid to get close to other people, to know that same kind of pain again.

'She was almost shell-shocked. She would have to speak very fast, and she so needed somebody to listen to her. We talked for hours actually. Some things were very simple – about her ... simple and ordinary. About her desire to marry, to have a child, to nurse a child, to enjoy what she perhaps thought of as ordinary, living your life. She had been asked to get married and she was trying to make that decision. But she had so many things before her, it was very difficult for her. I honestly think, that as much as she would have liked to get married, she knew she couldn't go back to something that she'd left behind ... and really she'd left that person behind. That person, meaning herself, more than the one she loved ...

'She talked to those of us at Maryknoll for hours on end, trying to explain what the recent events were like; the numbers of deaths; the kinds of oppression. When she found out how little coverage Salvador was getting in the press, and how misrepresented it was, she could not remain silent for any misrepresentation. She contacted different government officials and friends and family.

'She had made her decision to go back. I argued with her quite a bit about it, because there was no question, she couldn't live as she was without being killed. We talked about it a lot. I said, "What difference does it make if you go down there and you get killed? You're just one other person that's killed down there." She knew she could go to Los Angeles and work with the refugees – and all the good she would do by doing that. But it wasn't enough. Something more was calling her.

'Death was not so much of a fear as was torture. That was a terror for her. One of the last things she said was, "I just hope I'm not found on a ditch bank with all the markings of torture . . . " So I don't know . . . the bravery . . . the bravery came in saying yes. She didn't know when it was going to happen, she just knew. We all did. We all knew. Because Jeannie wouldn't run from a situation. She wouldn't leave people who needed her because it was dangerous. She was a person who walked out on a limb. To stay there was to die.'

Gwen Vendley
in Ana Carrigan, *Salvador Witness:*
The Life and Calling of Jean Donovan

Jean Donovan was killed in El Salvador on 2 December 1980

Migrants Day,
3 December

During Advent 1981 I visited a church in San Salvador to find 460 women, children and disabled men who had been staying there, in dark, cramped, musty squalor for almost four years. They had been eating, sleeping and 'living' there, too afraid to leave for fear of being shot by army-backed death squads.

In those terrible conditions, I met a newly-born baby. He was named Oscar, after Archbishop Oscar Romero. Feeding Oscar and the whole community was difficult, because church workers who were supporting these refugees were often targeted by the death squads. CAFOD was helping the local diocese to provide essential food supplies.

Whilst I was there, a delivery of beans and corn arrived. I watched the people carefully count out one in ten of the sacks and put them to one side. When I asked them what they were doing, one of the women told me: 'It is tragic here, but there are people outside far worse off than we are. So we are putting this aside to be taken to the ones who can't get into a refuge like this.'

Through CAFOD contacts, we managed to persuade the Nicaraguan government to take the people as refugees, and after considerable negotiation a group of nuns and priests accompanied the refugees to the airport, where they were safely put on a plane.

The group settled happily in a rural area of Nicaragua for several years, but with the end of the civil war in El Salvador, they have now returned home. They have called their new community Nueva Esperanza, meaning 'New Hope'. With

newly-built houses, a community health centre and a school –
where 14-year-old Oscar is in the top grade – the community
is thriving, thanks to the help of CAFOD supporters.

Julian Filochowski
Letter to CAFOD supporters

We want to place special emphasis on being with rather
than doing for. We want our presence among refugees
to be one of sharing with them, of accompaniment, of walking
together along the same path. In so far as possible, we want
to feel what they have felt, suffer as they have, share the same
hopes and aspirations, see the world through their eyes. We
ourselves would like to become one with the poor and
oppressed peoples so that, all together, we can begin the search
for a new life.

Jesuit Refugee Service

2nd Sunday of Advent
(Bible Sunday)

L et us now happily dwell upon the ways of his visible coming: *Behold*, says the Bride, *He comes leaping upon the mountains, skipping over the hills* (Song of Songs 2:18). You see him coming, O beautiful one, but you do not see where he rests in the midday. For she said: *show me, O thou whom my soul loves, where you lie in the midday* (Song 1:16). Resting he feeds the angels for all eternity. But do you not know, O beautiful one, that your Vision *is become wonderful to you: it is high, and you cannot reach to it* (Psalms 138:6); but look, he has come forth from his holy place, and he has begun and will restore you to health, and in his coming we shall see him who, while feeding his angels, could not be seen before.

Look, he comes, leaping upon the mountains, skipping over the hills. In place of mountains and hills understand patriarchs and prophets, and as he came leaping and skipping, read in the book of the generation of Jesus: *Abraham begot Isaac: and Isaac begot Jacob* and so on. From these mountains came forth the Root of Jesse, from which, according to the prophet, *there came forth a Rod*, and from there *a flower shall rise up*, upon which the Spirit of the Lord shall rest (Isaiah 11:1).

And the same prophet says: *Behold a virgin shall conceive, and bear a son, and his name shall be called Emmanuel, which is interpreted, God with us* (Matthew 1:23). For he whom he first refers to as a flower, the same he here calls Emmanuel; and that which he before calls a rod (*virga*), he here speaks of as the Virgin.

From this I believe it to be evident that the Mother of God is this Rod, and her son Jesus the Flower. A Flower accordingly is the son of the Virgin; a flower *white and ruddy, chosen out of thousands* (Song of Songs 5:10); a flower *upon which the angels desire to look* (1 Peter 1:12); a Flower whose fragrance restores the dead to life; and a *Flower of the field*, and not of the garden. For the field flowers without human help, it is sown by no man, unbroken to the spade, nor made rich with soil. So has flowered the womb of the Virgin; so has the inviolate, the pure flesh and blood of Mary, as a field, brought forth this flower of eternal beauty; whose perfection shall see no corruption, whose glory shall be forever unfading.

St Bernard

Immaculate Conception,
8 December

According to the hymn we sing at Vespers on all her feasts, Mary is distinguished by her graciousness among women – among so many virgins and mothers on whom God has also bestowed the grace of gentleness, yet whose very gentleness is at the same time their power and strength. But all that is both virginal and maternal Mary, the second and spiritual Eve, possesses to an exceptional degree.

We are told that gentleness is the summing up of all the Christian virtues; it consists, above all, of patience and kindness; of respect and love for souls, indeed for all animate being; since one who is gentle is gentle towards all living things. And this, because in its root it derives from harmony with the will of God under all its forms, a tender acquiescence in all that is. It is also the primary requisite for all who long to clarify and liberate their inward vision. There is no contemplative life without infinite patience; light only penetrates souls at rest. Tranquillity is the first disposition necessary, then, if the depths of the soul are to become translucent. The art of contemplating divine truths is the art of remaining still.

Gentleness is the quality of a forgiving and merciful soul, and is inseparable from true intellectual insight. When the mind is purified and sees all beings in their proper light, it cannot but be confident and loving. St John of the Cross has remarked with great insistence how essential kindness is for all interior progress. Our vocation is truly virginal and a mirror of Mary's. She had no need to condemn the world; it was the world that broke its strength against her graciousness.

A Carthusian
The Prayer of Love and Silence

Praying with Mary

Rejoicing with you,
grieving with you,
Mary, graced by God –
Love's Mystery did come to you –
of our race we deem you most blessed,
save but the Blessed One,
the Child who came to birth in you.

Woman holy,
trembling at the Presence of the Angel,
willing the rare and marvellous exchange,
in the darkness holding the Unseen,
bearing forth the Word made flesh for
   Earth's redeeming,
hold to your heart our world,
and pray for humankind,
that we with you be bearers of the Christ,
through this and all our days,
and at the last.

Jim Cotter

Human Rights Day,
10 December

We pray for those who have been exiled from their native land, refugees, who have been forced to leave behind their heritage and possessions, their families and their friends, and those who have had to begin life anew in a foreign culture and among strangers.

Lord, let justice run down like rivers.

We pray for those who are discriminated against on grounds of their race or sex, who offer the gifts of their presence, culture and personality, but find them despised or rejected.

Lord, let justice run down like rivers.

We pray for those who at this moment are being tortured in their bodies or in their minds because of the convictions they hold so dear, that their pain may be eased and that the peace of God may bring them release even in the midst of suffering.

Lord, let justice run down like rivers.

We pray for all rulers and those who hold positions of authority in the state and in all the powerful institutions of our society that they may use their power for good and not for evil, that the rights of men and women may no longer be abused.

Lord, let justice run down like rivers.

We pray for all whose basic needs for food, shelter, clothing and healing are not met. Stir up the consciences of peoples and governments, to re-arrange the world's unjust systems; teach us all to live more simply, that others may simply live.

Lord, let justice run down like rivers.

We pray for the nations of the earth that you in your mercy will save them from their folly and humankind from its sin, that people will be set free from vindictiveness and fear, that forgiveness will replace revenge, that none shall be in bondage to another and none shall hold another country in contempt, and you alone will be worshipped all over the earth.

Lord, let justice run down like rivers.

From a Human Rights Day service

L oving God,
  open our hearts,
so that we may feel the breath and play of your spirit.
Unclench our hands
so that we may reach out to one another,
and touch and be healed.
Open our lips
that we may drink in the delight and wonder of life.
Unclog our ears
to hear your agony in our inhumanity.
Open our eyes,
so that we may see Christ in friend and stranger.
Breathe your Spirit into us,
and touch our lives with the life of Christ,
    Amen.

Out of the Darkness: paths to inclusive worship

The Universal Declaration of Human Rights was signed on
10 December 1948

Thomas Merton,
10 December

T he secret of the Advent mystery is then the awareness that
I begin where I end because Christ begins where I end. In
more familiar terms: I live to Christ when I die to myself.

I begin to live to Christ when I come to the 'end' or to the
'limit' of what divides me from my fellow human beings: when
I am willing to step beyond this end, cross the frontier, become
a stranger, enter into the wilderness which is not 'myself',
when I do not breathe the air or hear the familiar, comforting
racket of my own city, when I am alone and defenceless in the
desert of God.

Thomas Merton
Seasons of Celebration

In Louisville, at the corner of Fourth and Walnut, in the centre
of the shopping district, I was suddenly overwhelmed with the
realization that I loved all those people, that they were mine
and I theirs, that we could not be alien to one another even
though we were total strangers. It was like waking from a
dream of separateness, of spurious self-isolation in a special
world, the world of renunciation and supposed holiness. The
whole illusion of a separate holy existence is a dream . . .

This sense of liberation from an illusory difference was such
a relief and such a joy to me that I almost laughed out loud.
And I suppose my happiness could have taken form in the

words: 'Thank God, thank God that I *am* like other men, that I am only a man among others.' . . .

I have the immense joy of being *man*, a member of a race in which God himself became incarnate. As if the sorrows and stupidities of the human condition could overwhelm me, now I realize what we all are. And if only everybody could realize this! But it cannot be explained. There is no way of telling people that they are all walking around shining like the sun . . .

At the centre of our being is a point of nothingness which is untouched by sin and by illusion, a point of pure truth, a point or spark which belongs entirely to God, which is never at our disposal, from which God disposes of our lives, which is inaccessible to the fantasies of our own mind or the brutalities of our own will. This little point of nothingness and of *absolute poverty* is the pure glory of God in us. It is so to speak his name written in us, as our poverty, as our indigence, as our dependence, as our sonship. It is like a pure diamond, blazing with the invisible light of heaven.

Thomas Merton
Conjectures of a Guilty Bystander

Thomas Merton died on 10 December 1968

3rd Sunday of Advent

R emember Lord
the sick among your people:
heal them
in your compassion.
Remember Lord
the fruits of the earth:
bless them
and keep them without loss.
Remember Lord
the down-coming of the rains
and bless them.
Remember Lord
the seeds and fruits of every year:
bless them
and make them abundant.
Remember Lord
the safety of your human family and beasts.
Remember Lord
the afflicted and distressed.
Remember Lord
the poor and oppressed:
have pity on them
and make them the
dwelling place of the Holy Spirit. Amen.

from the Ethiopian Prayer of the Covenant

Like the seed that grows into a tree,
Open our eyes to the new vision as
Green leaf sprouts awaken to blue sky;
Nurture us in the sunlight and rain of your truth;
Make us strong like the tall tree with leafy branches
Mothering those who need protection from
The storms of poverty and injustice.
Oh Holy Spirit, make us one with you;
Deepen our roots in nature, history and culture
And breathe into us your healing power
To reach beyond the barriers of division and
Create a New Community of love and peace.

Marion Kim, Korea

Lord of Light
Shine on us
Let us share
in your love

King of Kings
Enlighten us
Help us tell
your Good News

Prince of Peace
Be our light
Show us how to
love one another

Emmanuel
Illuminate us
Light our candle
in this still night

Holli Ball

St John of the Cross, 14 December

If I had to choose a patron saint for those who work with or suffer AIDS I would choose St John of the Cross. He was a man of humble origin whose childhood was one of poverty and pain. His adolescent years were spent as a carer in the company of people dying from sexually transmitted disease. Those hard formative years led John into religious life as a Carmelite where he met and came to revere and love St Teresa of Avila.

The highest moment of his life came when it was darkest, when he was imprisoned and at least mentally tortured by his religious brothers. As a reformer he was too radical for them and perhaps too loving. In that dark night of the soul he opened himself to the Lord and found love. It was during that year when he was shred of every human dignity that the John of Pain became the John of Ecstasy. It was in the healing darkness of that prison that John found the embrace of the God of love, and poured out his ecstasy in love poems that can only find their match in God's own passionate love poem in the Bible, the Song of Songs.

I think the secret to a full life is found in Our Lord's advice to his disciples. When they asked Jesus to teach them to pray he advised them to begin by going into their little room. The saints hasten to tell us that he was not speaking of a room with walls and a ceiling, but of that space within each one of us that is secret to ourselves – where our thoughts are, where our feelings are. Secret to ourselves ... *and to God*. The God who created us and holds us in being is there within us, trying to give to each one of us, personally, the message to which the whole of creation and every religion is trying to give a voice.

That message is clear for every man, woman and child to hear: 'I love you!' It is the Lord who speaks, and no conditions or 'ifs' are attached. Whatever we may say of ourselves, or other people may say of us, that warm love of God is there within every one of us and is permanent. If we could find the courage to accept that love and to respond to it in kind, it would overflow. We would be transformed and, like St John of the Cross, would be empowered to transform our world and restore it to hope.

Bishop Victor Guazzelli

World AIDS Day is 1 December

4th Sunday of Advent
(Expectant mothers)

It moves one's heart to think:
   Nine months before I was born
  there was a woman who loved me deeply.
She did not know what I was going to be like,
   but she loved me
   because she carried me in her womb.
And when she gave me birth,
   she took me in her arms
   because her love was not just beginning –
   she conceived it along with me.

A mother loves –
and that is why abortion is so abhorrent:
A mother who aborts
is unfaithful to the love that she should have
   (like God in eternity)
before her child is born.

God is the exquisite likeness
of a mother with child.
God bore me in his womb
   and loved me and destined me
   and already thought of my days
   and of my death.
What will happen to me doesn't matter to me;
God already knows it.

Let us not be afraid, brothers and sisters.
   We are living through difficult and uncertain days.

We do not know if this very evening
we will be prisoners
or murder victims.
We do not know
  what the forces of evil will do with us.
But one thing I do know:
  even those who have disappeared after arrest,
  even those who are mourned in the mystery of an
  abduction,
are known and loved by God.
If God allows these disappearances
it is not because he is helpless.
He loves us,
  he keeps on loving.

He loves our history too, and he knows
where the ways of our land's redemption will lead.
We do not lose hope in this great truth.
This is the true treasure of God's reign:
  hope, faith, prayer,
  the intimate force that joins one to God.
Let us pray for this.

Oscar Romero
The Violence of Love

Christmas Eve,
24 December

It was a night in winter.
Our house was full, tight-packed as salted herrings –
So full, they said, we had to hold our breaths
To close the door and shut the night-air out!
And then two travellers came.
They stood outside
Across the threshold, half in the ring of light
And half beyond it. I would have let them in
Despite the crowding – the woman was past her time –
But I'd no mind to argue with my husband,
The flagon in my hand and half the inn
Still clamouring for wine. But when trade slackened,
And all our guests had sung themselves to bed
Or told the floor their troubles, I came out here
Where he had lodged them. The man was standing
As you are now, his hand smoothing that board.
He was a carpenter, I heard them say.
She rested on the straw, and on her arm
A child was lying. None of your creased-faced brats
Squalling their lungs out. Just lying there
As calm as a new-dropped calf – his eyes wide open,
And gazing round as if the world he saw
In the chaff-strewn light of the stable lantern
Was something beautiful and new and strange.
Ah well, he'll have learnt different now, I reckon,
Wherever he is. And why I should recall
A scene like that, when times I would remember
Have passed beyond reliving, I cannot think.

It's a trick you're served by old possessions;
They have their memories too – too many memories.
Well, I must go in. There are meals to serve.
Join us there, Carpenter, when you've had enough
Of cattle-company. The world is a sad place,
But wine and music blunt the truth of it.

Clive Sansom
'The Witnesses: The Innkeeper's Wife'

He who was the Son of God, for you has become the Son of man, so that you who were children of men, might become the children of God. What was he; what became he? What were you; what have you become? He was the Son of God. What did he become? The Son of man. You were the sons of men. What have you become? Children of God.

St Augustine

Christmas Day,
25 December

It is the joy of the resurrection, of the Christ who is present through his conquest of death and decay which enters our hearts at Christmas. This recognition that it can only be the risen Christ whom we encounter seems strange and wrongly timed, yet the atmosphere of the liturgy drives us to make the connection. For this is above all else the day of light.

The collects for the Midnight Mass of Christmas and for the Easter Vigil have a close, almost uncanny resemblance. 'You have made this night holy with the splendour of Jesus Christ our Light.' 'You have brightened this night with the radiance of the Risen Christ.' Both nights are referred to as 'holy night' and the readings of each liturgy focus on light and glory . . .

To see the centrality of the symbol of light as common to both incarnation and resurrection is to see how inseparable are the Christmas and Easter mysteries. Together they constitute the basic framework of God's activity in and beyond history and time, as they form the heart of Christian faith and hope. Without Easter, Christmas has no point; without Christmas, Easter has no meaning. Both incarnation and resurrection have significance because in these events God is glorified in the flesh. The flesh becomes the source of light, the raw material of glory . . .

The light of Christ is a persistent light. It shines through the most powerfully oppressive darkness, shines in the midst of devastation, disaster and upheaval, yet without explaining them, justifying them, or making sense of them. The gospel of incarnation and resurrection is not the answer to a set of questions. It is a persistent and defiant light. And its persistence is paradoxical. For the truth of the gospel of incarnation and resurrection is paradoxical. For the truth of the gospel of incarnation and resurrection stands in contradiction to, and seems to be contradicted by, the realities of the world in which there is still no room and where the dead bodies pile up, inexplicably, meaninglessly . . .

Is the light of Christ, then, no more than an illusory comfort, a false reassurance that all is well when in fact all is clearly unwell in the 'demented inn' of the world? Certainly religious light is often of this illusory kind. But the gospel of incarnation and resurrection cannot be preached in an authentic and truthful way unless it faces the terrible reality of homelessness and meaningless death.

It is these two realities which provide the only possible material context for the light of Christ. For it is as the homeless unwanted Christ of Bethlehem and as the naked condemned Christ of Golgotha that the light shines with its strange persistence and its baffling power to draw people to its shining, enabling them to become dynamic agents in the historical process, lights in the world.

Kenneth Leech
The Independent

T he feast day of your birth resembles you, Lord,
Because it brings joy to all humanity.
Old people and infants alike enjoy your day.
Your day is celebrated from generation to generation.
Kings and emperors may pass away,
And the festivals to commemorate them soon lapse.
But your festival will be remembered till the end of time.
Your day is a means and a pledge of peace.
At your birth heaven and earth were reconciled,
Since you came from heaven to earth on that day

You forgave our sins and wiped away our guilt.
You gave us so many gifts on your birthday:
A treasure chest of spiritual medicines for the sick;
Spiritual light for those that are blind;
The cup of salvation for the thirsty;
The bread of life for the hungry.
In the winter when trees are bare,
You gave us the most succulent spiritual fruit.
In the frost when the earth is barren,
You bring new hope to our souls.
In December when seeds are hidden in the soil,
The staff of life springs forth from the virgin womb.

St Ephraim the Syrian

O ur Saviour's birth in the flesh is an earnest, and, as it were, beginning of our birth in the Spirit. It is a figure, promise, or pledge of our new birth, and it effects what it promises. As he was born, so are we born also: and since he was born, therefore we too are born. As he is the Son of God by nature, so are we sons of God by grace; and it is he who has made us such. This is what the text says; he is the 'Sanctifier', we the 'sanctified'. Moreover, he and we, says the text, 'are all of one'. God sanctifies the angels, but there the Creator and the creatures are not of one. But the Son of God and we are of one.

John Henry Newman
'The Mystery of Godliness'

M y mouth will speak the praise of the Lord ... He is great as the day of the angels is great and small as the day of men, the Word of God before all time, the Word made flesh at a suitable time. Maker of the sun, he is made under the sun. Disposer of all ages in the bosom of the Father, he consecrates this day in the womb of his mother. In him he remains, from her he goes forth. Creator of heaven and earth, he was born on earth under heaven. Unspeakably wise, he is wise speechless. Filling the world, he lies in a manger. Ruler of the stars, he nurses at his mother's bosom. He is both great in the nature of God and small in the form of a servant, but in such a way that his greatness is not diminished by his small-ness, nor his smallness overwhelmed by his greatness. For he did not desert his divine works when he took to himself human parts. Nor did he cease to reach from end to end mightily, and to order all things sweetly (Wisdom 8:1), when, having put on the infirmity of the flesh, he was received into the Virgin's womb, not confined therein. Thus the food of wisdom was not taken away from the angels, and we were to taste how sweet is the Lord.

O food and bread of angels, the angels are filled by you, are satisfied by you, but not to the point of satiety. They live by you; they have wisdom by you. By you they are blessed. Where are you for my sake? In a mean lodging, in a manger. For whom? He who rules the stars sucks at the breast. He who speaks in the bosom of the Father is silent in the mother's lap. But he will speak when he reaches a suitable age, and will fulfil for us the gospel. For our sakes he will suffer, for us he will die. As an example of our reward, he will rise again. He will ascend into heaven before the eyes of his disciples, and he will come from heaven to judge the world. Behold him lying in the manger; he is reduced to tininess, yet he has not lost anything of himself. He has accepted what was not his, but he remains what he was. Look, we have the infant Christ; let us grow with him.

St Augustine
Sermons on Christmas

On this night, as we Christians have done every year for twenty centuries, we recall that God's reign is now in this world and that Christ has inaugurated the fullness of time. His birth attests that God is now marching with us in history, that we do not go alone, and that our aspiration for peace, for justice, for a reign of divine law, for something holy, is far from earth's realities. We can hope for it, not because we humans are able to construct that realm of happiness which God's holy words proclaim, but because the builder of a reign of justice, of love, and of peace is already in the midst of us.

Oscar Romero

St Stephen,
26 December

Not only do we at the feast of Christmas celebrate at once
Our Lord's birth and his death: but on the next day we
celebrate the martyrdom of his first martyr, the blessed
Stephen. Is it an accident, do you think, that the day of the
first martyr follows immediately the day of the birth of Christ?
By no means. Just as we rejoice and mourn at once, in the
birth and in the passion of Our Lord; so also, in a smaller
figure, we both rejoice and mourn in the death of martyrs. We
mourn, for the sins of the world that has martyred them; we
rejoice, that another soul is numbered among the saints in
heaven, for the glory of God and for the salvation of men.

Beloved, we do not think of a martyr simply as a good
Christian who has been killed because he is a Christian: for
that would be solely to mourn. We do not think of him simply
as a good Christian who has been elevated to the company of
the saints: for that would be simply to rejoice: and neither our
mourning nor our rejoicing is as the world's is. A Christian
martyrdom is never an accident, for saints are not made by
accident. Still less is a Christian martyrdom the effect of a
man's will to become a saint, as a man by willing and contriving
may become a ruler of men. A martyrdom is always the design
of God, for his love of men, to warn them and to lead them,
to bring them back to his ways. It is never the design of man;
for the true martyr is he who has become the instrument of
God, who has lost his will in the will of God, and who no
longer desires anything for himself, not even the glory of being
a martyr. So thus as on earth the Church mourns and rejoices
at once, in a fashion that the world cannot understand; so in

heaven the saints are most high, having made themselves most low, and are seen, not as we see them, but in the light of the Godhead from which they draw their being.

I have spoken to you today, dear children of God, of the martyrs of the past, asking you to remember especially our martyr of Canterbury, the blessed Archbishop Elphege; because it is fitting, on Christ's birth day, to remember what is that peace which he brought; and because, dear children, I do not think I shall ever preach to you again; and because it is possible that in a short time you may have yet another martyr, and that one perhaps not the last. I would have you keep in your hearts these words that I say, and think of them at another time. In the Name of the Father, and of the Son, and of the Holy Ghost. Amen.

T. S. Eliot
Murder in the Cathedral

St John the Evangelist,
27 December

He who is the first principle and pattern of all things, came to be the beginning and pattern of human kind, the firstborn of the whole creation. He who is the everlasting light, became the light of men; he, who is the life from eternity, became the life of a race dead in sin; he, who is the Word of God, came to be a spiritual Word, 'dwelling richly in our hearts', an 'engrafted Word, which is able to save our souls'; he, who is the co-equal Son of the Father, came to be the Son of God in our flesh, that he might raise us also to the adoption of sons, and might be the first among many brethren.

John Henry Newman
'The Mystery of Godliness'

There came, at a predetermined moment, a moment in
    time and of time,
A moment not out of time, but in time, in what we call
    history: transecting, bisecting the world of time, a moment
    in time but not like a moment of time,
A moment in time, but time was made through that
    moment: for without the meaning there is no time, and
    that moment of time gave the meaning.
Then it seemed as if men must proceed from light to light, in
    the light of the Word,
Through the Passion and Sacrifice saved in spite of their
    negative being;

Bestial as always before, carnal, self-seeking as always
   before, selfish and purblind as ever before,
Yet always struggling, always reaffirming, always resuming their
   march on the way that was lit by the light.

T. S. Eliot
Chorus from 'The Rock'

The incorporeal, incorruptible and immaterial Word of God entered into our own situation, even though he previously was not far distant. No part of creation was deprived of him and he always filled all things since he existed together with his Father. But he came down to us on account of his benevolence and appeared among us. Seeing how all were liable to death, he had mercy on our race and compassion on our weakness. He came to the aid of our corruption and did not stand for the domination of death, in order that what had been created might not perish and that the Father's work on behalf of man might not be in vain. He took a body to himself which was in no way different from our own. For he did not wish simply to dwell in a body nor did he want only to seem to be a man. Had he only wanted to appear to be a man he could have appeared by means of a better body. But he took our own.

St Athanasius

Holy Innocents,
28 December

Mary and Joseph, having duly received warning, had to flee to Egypt – a long journey along desert roads which even today are difficult for people to traverse by land in spite of modern means of communication. They had to retrace the steps taken by their forefathers in going out of Egypt. Mary would therefore have had to suffer the trials of this journey in the hot sun with an infant baby ... The holy family were political exiles fleeing their country to safeguard the life of their child.

Her action is a common phenomenon that people engaged in radical liberation movements have to face today, as we have seen in the case of the political exiles. She experienced the hatred, the jealousy and the venom of the political rulers of the day. She felt the brutality and savagery of the soldiers who carried out the behests of Herod. From the birth of her son Jesus, she was involved in the political issues of the day. Even if she did not herself choose to have it that way.

Herod preferred to kill the innocent children rather than see a threat to his power. He did not enquire into the type of kingdom the new Messiah would install. Political power generally reacts thus nervously, violently, cruelly, and oppressively. Even today the powerful react thus. The rich are afraid that the children of the poor humans will take their thrones and privileges.

Thus the enormous effort of the rich to plan the families of the poor, instead of reforming themselves and their wasteful ways. Hence the Herodian approach of the rich who propagate the compulsory sterilization of the poor women and men, and compel them to situations where aborting a child may seem a necessity. The murder of the innocents by Herod was a proto-type of the way the rich and the powerful deal with the poor whom they consider a threat to their privileges.

Mary experienced this hatred and cruelty in her own life. She had to face it bravely, sadly and even cunningly. Her approach was a mature, courageous one of a woman who knew her mind . . .

In the flight into Egypt she was a refugee and an exile in Egypt. The family returned to the land where the Jews had been slaves for several centuries. Joseph had to be a migrant worker, a non-national to whom the most menial tasks are given even in our own day.

Hence, for many years, Mary along with Joseph would have experienced tribulations by being foreign workers in Egypt. In this too, she experienced personally the problems which many of the under-privileged people even in the rich countries have to face. They are the 'Third World' inside the rich countries . . . It is a pity that the popular devotions to Mary do not recall her in these experiences (of the incarnation, the presentation, the flight and exile into Egypt) as a poor, courageous woman. She foreshadows the trials and struggles of women of our time too.

Tissa Balasuriya
Mary and Human Liberation

I t is surely right and meet thus to celebrate the death of the Holy Innocents: for it was a blessed one. To be brought near to Christ, and to suffer for Christ, is surely an unspeakable privilege; to suffer anyhow, even unconsciously. The little children whom he took up in his arms were not conscious of his loving condescension; but was it no privilege when he blessed them? Surely this massacre had in it the nature of a sacrament;

it was a pledge of the love of the Son of God towards those
who were included in it.

John Henry Newman

All hail! ye infant martyr flowers,
  Cut off in life's first dawning hours:
As rosebuds, snapped in tempest strife,
When Herod sought your Saviour's life.

You, tender flock of lambs, we sing,
First victim slain for Christ your King:
Beneath the Altar's heavenly ray,
With Martyr Palms and Crowns ye play.

For their redemption glory be,
O Jesu, Virgin-born, to Thee!
With Father, and with Holy Ghost,
For ever from the Martyr Host.

Prudentius

The reign of God is here and we are invited to enter. The
door is a humble and hidden Messiah whose moving force
is the power of God, totally directed to the life about to be
born . . . to liberate, to give growth, to render fruitful. Human
violence and power cannot compare with this quiet force, nor
can they further it . . . for they are marked with the sign of
death. This quiet, life-giving force, we call it Love.

Pierre Claverie, Bishop of Oran, Algeria
(assassinated August 1996)

L et us accept to sacrifice for others, especially at this time: to help refugees and displaced persons to find a home; to help them to rebuild and repair their damaged houses; to give them seeds and clothing; to share the little we have with them. For it is only when we lack love that we find nothing to share with others.

Joachim Ruhuna,
Archbishop of Gitega, Burundi
(assassinated September 1996)

O ne cannot wait for conditions to be easy in order to act. And so, people of good will must never be disheartened when faced with the sudden unleashing of violence. In the midst of it all, the seed sown in the soil of our heart slowly germinates. When God becomes a child, he knows that there is no better way for him to express himself than through the weakness of that child. This is love telling us that it comes unarmed.

Christophe Munzihirwa,
Archbishop of Bukavu, Zaire
(assassinated October, 1996)

L ast weekend I took part in another celebration which included an all-night vigil under the stars. It took place in a remote village, until a couple of years ago totally abandoned, called El Mozote (The Thistle) . . . On 11 December 1980 these soldiers surrounded the village, separated the men, women and children, and then systematically murdered each group in turn, slaughtered all the animals and set fire to the houses . . . Of the 143 skulls exhumed in the *convento* (sacristy and priest's room) by the Argentine Forensic Anthropology Unit, all but twelve turned out to be those of children under twelve years of age.

The people gathered throughout the day . . . and Rufina Amaya, one of the very few who escaped, once again told her harrowing story:

Then I heard one of my children crying. My son, Cristino, was crying, 'Mama Rufina help me! They're killing me! They killed my sister! They're killing me! Help me!' I did not know what to do. They were killing my children. I knew that if I went back there to help my children, I would be cut to pieces. But I couldn't stand hearing it, I couldn't bear it. I was afraid that I would cry out, that I would scream, that I would go crazy. I prayed to God to help me. I promised God that if he helped me I would tell the world what happened here.

The exhumed remains were placed on seven coffins which remained open all night for those present to pray and meditate in front of them. Many of us did so in tears. Just before first light, we closed the coffins and carried them in a candlelight procession to be buried on either side of the simple monument of a family holding hands in front of a large cross.

Michael Campbell-Johnston

O God, you have dealt very mysteriously with us. We have been passing through deep waters, our feet were well-nigh gone. But though you slay us, yet will we trust in you ... They are gone from us ... You have reclaimed the lent jewels. Yet, O Lord, shall I not thank you now? ... I thank you for the blessing of the last ten years, and for all the sweet memories of these lives ...

Archibald Campbell Tait

Between 11 March and 8 April 1856 Tait and his wife lost five of their six daughters through scarlet fever

Josephine Butler, 30 December

In the afternoon I had been getting ready for a dinner party. Eva, who was now six years old, ran in to show me something she had just found. She was all childish joy; 'Mummy, mummy, look what I've got here!'

I remember my answer with shame. 'Run along, Eva dear, and don't bother me with your chatter – I can see your caterpillar later, dear. Mummy is busy getting ready to go out.' Her mood changed completely and she left me, looking sad and disconsolate.

When we returned later that evening, the children ran eagerly to meet us across the upstairs landing. Eva shouted to us and missed her footing on the bannister. She tumbled headlong over it and landed on the stone floor below, right at her father's feet. Even now, many years later, I can hardly bear to write about it. It was pitiful to see her helpless in her father's arms, her little head drooping on his shoulder, and her beautiful golden hair all stained with blood, falling over his arm. My baby died a few hours later in her father's arms.

I had to struggle through that terrible Valley of the Shadow, that dark passage through which some toil only to emerge into a hopeless and final denial of divine goodness. George and I locked ourselves into separate cocoons of grief, and had to learn to talk to each other all over again. It seemed we were destined to be sojourners with no fixed abode, and that was a relief in a way. Cheltenham held no more charms for us, and we were glad to be called north, when George was offered the post of Principal of Liverpool College. But our lives were changed for ever, and I knew that God had asked the ultimate of me.

I became possessed with an irresistible desire to go forth and find some pain keener than my own, to meet with people more unhappy than myself, and to say, as I now knew I could, to afflicted people: 'I understand, I too have suffered.'

Even more than ever I despised the broken and desultory education of women, the barring of public life and professions to them, and lives divested of any real and important purpose. I was delighted when my cousin, Charles Birrell, who was a Baptist preacher, invited me to visit the huge workhouse at Brownlow Hill in Liverpool. Though my friends, and my husband's colleagues, advised against it, I prepared to visit this vast and forbidding institution. The conditions were appalling, with thousands of people huddled together without proper food and in totally insanitary conditions.

I insisted on visiting the Bridewell, home of destitute women and girls, and was led to the sheds where the women picked oakum. With bare hands, for no tools were provided, the women sat on the floor and unpicked tarred ropes, which made the oakum used to caulk the hull planks of wooden ships. Their fingers were scarred and bleeding, and I sat down on the floor and started to work with them. At first they mocked me. Everything about me made me a figure of fun to them . . .

When I look back on those early visits now, I wonder at my naivety. We were far from wealthy amongst our peers – but my clothes must have spoken of undreamed wealth to the women in the Bridewell. I asked if any of them could read. One woman said she could – sort of – so I asked if she could memorize some Bible verses for my next visit . . .

There was a stony and hostile silence at first when I returned. When I think about it now, I wonder that I did not realize the truth – that these poor, lost women had far more to give me than merely reciting Bible verses to please me.

Anna Briggs
Not Counting the Women and Children – a life of Josephine Butler

Josephine Butler died on 30 December 1906

New Year's Eve,
31 December

L et us bid farewell to the old year thankfully so that it may become what it ought to be, the gift of the grace of God. For God has given us all the days of this year. And if we have truly accepted them as gifts of his love – and it is always within our power to do this – they have been blessed days, days of grace and salvation.

We must never think of ourselves so sullenly, wearily, sceptically and morosely that this brooding actually becomes a mistrustful way of thinking about God himself. If we were only to say that we have been poor, failures, burdened, weary, afraid, that we have been adequate neither to our life nor to God's call, then we would perhaps have said something true. But if as Christians we were to say no more than this about ourselves and our past year, we should be unjust to God. Has he not preserved us in his grace? Has he not repeatedly given us the blessed Body of his Son? Is not his Holy Spirit in our hearts? Have we not after all borne God's burden through the year, though perhaps only with difficulty and groaning under it? Has God's grace not done good to others even through us? . . .

For that matter we cannot say that the good that we did not find difficult to do was no true goodness in the eyes of God; and it is not even necessarily true that we have often or mostly omitted the good which we found difficult, except when it was forced from us by God through the hardships of life. Have we not resigned ourselves even after some grumbling and protest to much that we found hard, and accepted it? And that means, even if we do not very explicitly realize it, that we have accepted

God, because it is only possible calmly to accept what is deadly by reaching out to true unlimited life.

But because by God's grace it was what it was as we lived through it, because despite everything it was more God's gracious deed in us than our failure, we can bless it, we must and may do so. We can take leave of this year gratefully and entrust it to the grace and love of God, the love of the God who is eternity and who preserves for us for our eternity what we are taking our leave of today and tomorrow. What we give in gratitude, God receives in grace, and what is so accepted by him is redeemed and made holy, blessed and set free. And so it remains for eternity: a year of ours which is saved and acquired for ever.

Karl Rahner
'Spiritual Balance-Sheet of a Year'

God of all time,
who makes all things new,
we bring before you the year now ending.
For life full and good,
for opportunities recognized and taken,
for love known and shared,
we thank you.

Where we have fallen short,
forgive us.
When we worry over what is past,
free us.

As we begin again
and take our first few steps into the future,
where nothing is safe and certain,
except you,
we ask for the courage of the wise men
who simply went and followed a star.

We ask for their wisdom,
in choosing to pursue the deepest truth,
not knowing where they would be led.
In the year to come, God of all time,
be our help and company.
Hold our hands as we journey onwards
and may your dream of *shalom*,
where all will be at peace,
be our guiding star.

Francis Brienen

And I said to the man who stood at the gate of the year: 'Give me a light that I may tread safely into the unknown.'
And he replied:

'Go out into the darkness and put your hand into the hand of God. That shall be to you better than light and safer than a known way.'

So I went forth, and finding the hand of God, trod gladly into the night. And he led me towards the hills and the breaking of day in the lone East.

M. Louise Haskins
The Gate of the Year

Jubilee, 1 January

B lessed are you, Lord,
  Father in heaven,
who, in your infinite mercy,
stooped down to us in our distress
and gave us Jesus, your Son, born of a woman,
to be our Saviour and friend, our brother and redeemer.
We thank you, good Father,
for the gift of the Jubilee Year;
make it a time of favour for us,
the year of a great return to the father's house,
where, full of love, you await your straying children
to embrace them in your forgiveness
and welcome them to your table,
in their festive garments.

> *We praise you, Father, forever!*

Father most merciful,
during this Holy Year
may our love for you and for our neighbour
grow ever stronger:
may Christ's disciples promote justice and peace;
may they proclaim the Good News to the poor;
and may the Church our Mother direct her love
especially to the little ones and the neglected.

> *We praise you, Father, forever!*

Father of justice,
may the Great Jubilee be the fitting time
for all Catholics to rediscover

the joy of living by your word
and obeying your will;
may they know the goodness of fraternal communion,
as they break bread together
and praise you in hymns and inspired songs.

We praise you, Father, forever!

Father, rich in mercy,
may the holy Jubilee be a time of openness,
of dialogue and encounter,
among all who believe in Christ
and with the followers of other religions:
in your immense love,
be bountiful in mercy to all.

We praise you, Father, forever!

O God, Almighty Father,
as we make our way to you,
our ultimate destiny,
may all your children experience
the gentle company of Mary most holy,
image of purest love,
whom you chose to be Mother of Christ and Mother of the Church.

We praise you, Father, forever!

To you, Father of life,
eternal source of all that is,
highest good and everlasting light,
be honour and glory, praise and thanksgiving,
with the Son and with the Spirit,
for ages unending. Amen.

Pope John Paul II
Prayer for the third year of preparation
for the Great Jubilee

G od of all ages, Lord of all time,
  you are the Alpha and the Omega,
the origin and goal of everything that lives,
yet you are ever close to those
who call on you in faith.

We look with expectant joy
to the Jubilee of your Son's coming among us,
two thousand years ago.
We thank you for the years of favour
with which you have blessed your people.

Teach us to share justly the good things
which come from your loving hand;
to bring peace and reconciliation
where strife and disorder reign;
to speak out as advocates
for those who have no voice;
and to rejoice in a bond of prayer and praise
with our sisters and brothers throughout the world.

When Christ comes again in glory
may he find us alive and active in faith,
and so call us to that Kingdom
where, with you and the Holy Spirit,
he is God, to be praised, worshipped and glorified,
both now and for ages to come. Amen.

CAFOD Millennium Prayer

L et there be
respect for the earth,
peace for its people,
love in our lives,
delight in the good,
forgiveness for past wrongs,
and from now on a new start.

Millennium Resolution prepared by
Churches Together in England

G enerous God, you created this world for all to share,
Unclench our hands to let go of the greed which
robs the poor,
   Unclog our ears to hear the agony of all who cry for
justice,
   Unbind our hearts to recognize those who are oppressed
by debt,
   Open our lips to proclaim jubilee in our own time and
place,
   May our care be thorough and our solidarity active,
   May this community be a sign of hope,
   For now is the favourable time. Amen.

Jubilee prayer
St Michael's Parish, Liverpool 6

World Day of Prayer for Peace, 1 January

The hatred which divides nation from nation,
race from race, class from class,
Father, forgive.

The covetous desires of people and nations
to possess what is not their own,
Father, forgive.

The greed which exploits the work of human hands,
and lays waste the earth,
Father, forgive.

Our envy of the welfare and happiness of others,
Father, forgive.

Our indifference to the plight of the imprisoned, the
homeless, the refugee,
Father, forgive.

The lust which dishonours the bodies
of men, women, and children,
Father, forgive.

The pride which lead us to trust in ourselves
and not in God,
Father, forgive.

Be kind to one another, tenderhearted,
forgiving one another, as God in Christ forgave you.

Prayer from the Litany of Reconciliation,
used daily in Coventry Cathedral

Y ou have called us to be one,
   to live in unity and harmony,
and yet we are divided:
race from race,
faith from faith,
rich from poor,
old from young,
neighbour from neighbour . . .
O Lord, by whose cross all enmity is brought to an end,
break down the walls that separate us,
tear down the fences of indifference and hatred;
forgive us the sins that divide us,
free us from pride and self-seeking,
overcome our prejudices and fears,
give us courage to open ourselves to others;
by the power of your Spirit make us one.

> Opening worship of the sixth assembly of
> the World Council of Churches, Vancouver 1983

G od our Father, Creator of the world,
   please help us to love one another.
Make nations friendly with other nations;
make all of us love one another like brothers and sisters.
Help us to do our part to bring peace in the world
and happiness to all people.

> Prayer from Japan

FREE US FROM EVIL!
As we recite these words from Christ's prayer, it is very difficult to give them a meaning different from opposition to what is against peace, destroys it, threatens it. So let us pray:

Free us from war, from hatred, from destruction of human lives!

Do not let us slay! Do not permit the use of means which are at the service of death and destruction . . .

FREE US FROM EVIL!

Father in heaven, Father of life and Giver of peace . . . How meaningful are Jesus Christ's words: 'Peace is my farewell to you, peace is my gift to you; I do not give it to you as the world gives peace' (John 14:27). In this dimension of peace, the deepest dimension which Christ alone can give.

It is fullness of peace rooted in reconciliation with God himself . . .

We implore this peace for the world . . . for all people, for all nations, of differing languages, cultures and races. For all continents . . .

Peace is indispensable.

Pope John Paul II
Prayers and Devotions

Mary, Mother of God,
1 January

I seek your grace, Oh Mary my Mother!
You are the fruit of Anna and Joachim.

You are a vine tree
Oh Mary!

You are like the alphabet.
You gave birth to the gospel.
You gave us the Cross.

You are like the heavens.
You gave birth to the Son.
You gave us the Saviour.

You are like a banquet.
You gave birth to the star.
You satiate the hungry.

You are like the tabernacle.
You gave birth to the altar.
You gave the heavenly.

You are like the cloud.
You gave birth to the Eucharist.
You gave us health.

You are like fragrance.
You gave birth to the Saviour.
You heal the sick.

You are like the East.
You gave birth to thunder.
You clothe the ragged.

You are the bride of the Father.
You are the mother of the Son.
You are the dwelling of the Holy Spirit.

You bless those who eat
The body of your Son and
Drink the blood of your Son.

Ancient Ethiopian hymn

1st week of the year

All being is from God.
    This is not simply an arbitrary and tendentious 'religious' affirmation which in some way or other robs being of autonomy and dignity. On the contrary, the doctrine of creation is, when properly understood, that which implies the deepest respect for reality and for the being of everything that is.

The doctrine of creation is rooted not in a desperate religious attempt to account for the fact that the world exists. It is not merely an answer to the question of how things got to be what they are by pointing to God as a cause. On the contrary, the doctrine of creation as we have it in the Bible and as it has been developed in Christian theology (particularly in St Thomas) starts not from a *question about being* but from a *direct intuition of the act of being*. Nothing could be further from a merely mechanistic and causal explanation of existence. 'Creation' is then not merely a pat official answer to a religious query about our origin.

One who apprehends being as such apprehends it as an act which is utterly beyond a complete scientific explanation. To apprehend being is an act of contemplation and philosophical wisdom rather than the fruit of scientific analysis. It is in fact a gift given to few. Anyone can say: 'This is a tree; that is a man.' But how few are ever struck by the realization of the real import of what is really meant by *is?*

Sometimes it is given to children and to simple people (and the 'intellectual' may indeed be an essentially simple person, contrary to all the myths about him – for only the stupid are disqualified from true simplicity) to experience a direct intuition of being. Such an intuition is simply an immediate grasp of one's own inexplicable personal reality in one's own incommunicable act of existing!

One who has experienced the baffling, humbling, and liberating clarity of this immediate sense of what it means to *be* has in that very act experienced something of the presence of God. For God is present to me in the act of my own being, an act which proceeds directly from his will and is his gift. My act of being is a direct participation in the Being of God. God is pure Being, this is to say he is the pure and infinite act of total reality. All other realities are simply reflections of his pure act of being, and participations in it granted by his free gift.

Thomas Merton
Conjectures of a Guilty Bystander

Epiphany, 6 January

At Christmas we celebrate the coming of the Magi, or wise men, who came to offer their gifts to the infant Jesus. Some believe that these men came from Persia; Fr Heras made out a case for their coming from India; but it does not really matter where they came from. They represent the 'Gentiles', the 'pagans', in other words the other religions of the world. May we not see in these wise men the representatives of the other religions who bring their gifts to Christ and which the Church today is called to receive in his name?

Could we not say that the Hindus offer the gift of gold, of interior religion, of the pure heart in which is found the presence of God? The Muslim can be seen to offer the gift of frankincense, the incense of the prayer of adoration, of worship which the Muslims offer five times daily to the one supreme God. The Buddhist can be seen to offer the gift of myrrh, the symbol of suffering and death, the sign that this world is passing away and that our destiny lies beyond the grave with the risen Christ.

Bede Griffiths
'The Gifts of the Magi'

It is from the Asian sages that Jerusalem hears the good news (Matthew 2:2–3). It is through them that God reveals to God's own people in Jerusalem that the Divine is present in Christ. It is their enquiry that provokes the priests to read the scriptures for further light.

Aloysius Pieris

There is a famous Russian folk tale of the old babushka, or grandmother, who was visited on the eve of Epiphany by the three Wise Men, and invited by them to journey to Bethlehem to find the Prince of Peace. But the night was icy, the wind was fierce and Babushka was old. Sadly she let them go on alone. But the next day she set off visiting poor children in her country, with gifts to keep them warm and fed. And when she grew weary she heard the voice of the Wise Men ringing in her ears, 'Further on, Babushka, further on.' Always she is journeying to find the Prince of Peace . . . in her own way, her own context.

The famous pilgrimage described by the German writer Hermann Hesse, in his novel *Journey to the East*, told of a great pilgrimage breaking up and the travellers returning home disillusioned, asking what had happened to the dream, only to find that the pilgrimage did not require a physical leaving of home for exotic shrines: *the challenge lay on the doorstep.* Only they had never seen it before.

Mary Grey

God of gold, we seek your glory:
    the richness that transforms our drabness into colour,
    and brightens our dullness with vibrant light;
    your wonder and joy at the heart of all life.

God of incense, we offer you our prayer:
    our spoken and unspeakable longings,
    our questioning of truth,
    our search for your mystery deep within.

God of myrrh, we cry out to you in our suffering:
    the pain of all our rejections and bereavements,
    our baffled despair at undeserved suffering,
    our rage at continuing injustice:
    and we embrace you, God-with-us,
    in our wealth, in our yearning, in our anger and loss.

Jan Berry

May Jesus Christ, the king of glory, help us to make the right use of all the myrrh that God sends, and to offer to him the true incense of our hearts; for his name's sake. Amen.

Johann Tauler

I realized that I had joined a pilgrimage to the East, seemingly a definite and single pilgrimage – but in reality, in its broadest sense, this expedition to the East was not only mine and now; this procession of believers and disciples had always and incessantly been moving towards the East, towards the home of light. Throughout the centuries it had been on the way, towards light and wonder, and each member, each group, indeed our whole host and its great pilrimage, was only a wave in the eternal stream of human beings, of the eternal strivings of the human spirit towards the East, towards home. The knowledge passed through my mind like a ray of light and immediately reminded me of a phrase which I had learned during my novitiate year . . . It was a phrase by the poet Novalis, 'Where are we really going? Always home!'

Hermann Hesse
The Journey to the East

'Like me,' she [Helena, the mother of Constantine] said to them [the Magi], 'you were late in coming. The shepherds were here long before; even the cattle. They had joined the chorus of angels before you were on your way. For you the primordial discipline of the heavens was relaxed and a new defiant light blazed amid the disconcerted stars.

'How laboriously you came, taking sights and calculating, where the shepherds had run barefoot! How odd you looked

on the road, attended by what outlandish liveries, laden with
such preposterous gifts!

'You came at length to the final stage of your pilgrimage
and the great star stood still above you. What did you do?
You stopped to call on King Herod. Deadly exchange of com-
pliments in which began that unended war of mobs and magis-
trates against the innocent!

'Yet you came, and were not turned away. You too found
room before the manger. Your gifts were not needed, but they
were accepted and put carefully by, for they were brought with
love. In that new order of charity that had just come to life,
there was room for you, too. You were not lower in the eyes
of the holy family than the ox or the ass.

'You are my especial patrons,' said Helena, 'and patrons of
all latecomers, of all who have a tedious journey to make
to the truth, of all who are confused with knowledge and
speculation, of all who through politeness make themselves
partners in guilt, of all who stand in danger by reason of their
talents.

'Dear cousins, pray for me,' said Helena, 'and for my poor
overloaded son. May he, too, before the end find kneeling-
space in the straw. Pray for the great, lest they perish utterly.
And pray for Lactantius and Marcias and the young poets of
Trèves and for the souls of my wild, blind ancestors; for their
sly foe Odysseus and for the great Longinus.

'For his sake who did not reject your curious gifts, pray
always for all the learned, the oblique, the delicate. Let them
not be quite forgotten at the throne of God when the simple
came into their kingdom.'

Evelyn Waugh
Helena

Baptism of the Lord, 9 January

The Lord Jesus came to baptism, and willed to have his body washed with water.

Perhaps some one will say 'He who is holy, why did he wish to be baptized?' Pay attention therefore! Christ is baptized, not that he may be sanctified in the waters, but that he himself may sanctify the waters, and by his own purification may purify those streams which he touches. For the consecration of Christ is the greater consecration of another element.

For when the Saviour is washed, then already for our baptism all water is cleansed and the fount purified, that the grace of the washing may be administered to the peoples that come after. Christ therefore takes the lead in baptism, so that Christian peoples may follow after him with confidence.

I understand the mystery: for the column of fire went first through the Red Sea, that the children of Israel might tread the hazardous journey without fear; and it, itself, went first through the waters, so that for those coming after it, it might prepare a way to pass. Which event, as the Apostle says, was a symbol of baptism. Clearly baptism in some sort of way has been carried out when the cloud overshadowed the men, and the wave bore them.

But the one who performed all these things was still the same Lord Christ, who as he then went before the children of Israel in a pillar of fire, now by baptism goes before Christian peoples in the pillar of his body. This is the very pillar I maintain which then supplied light to the eyes of those who followed, and who now furnishes light to the hearts of believers; who then in the waves of the sea made firm the pathway, and now in the washing strengthens the footprints of faith.

St Maximus of Turin

A stream flows
       whispering inside me;
Deep within me it says:
   Come to the Father.

St Ignatius of Antioch

Today the Holy Spirit floats over the waters in the form of a dove, so that by this sign it might be known that the world's universal shipwreck has ceased, as the dove had announced to Noah that the world's flood had subsided. Nor does this dove carry a branch of the old olive, but it pours the whole richness of the olive on the head of the author of the new anointing, in order to fulfil what the prophet foretold: 'Therefore God, your God, has anointed you with the oil of gladness above other kings.'

St Peter Chrysologus

Lord, you have shown me
       what I must suffer.
As a dove descending,
   offering me food that is sweet,
So I know that you have called me.

Philip of Heraclea

2nd week of the year

The changing of water into wine at the wedding of Cana, is the foundation of all that is to follow; in the words of St John it 'manifested his glory', his power over nature, which could turn one substance into another. From earliest times it has also been interpreted spiritually, and it is certainly in accordance with the mind of St John himself to see in it more than the gracious gesture of Christ using his divine power to relieve the embarrassment of his host. The beginning of the signs of Jesus is a miracle of change: what had been mere water in the Old Dispensation is turned into the wine 'that rejoices the heart of men' in the new era. The age of legal ceremonial is past, the new age of grace has begun, involving a radical transformation of all things. In the hands of the incarnate Word life will be sacramentalized; the humdrum will be charged with new meaning; water and wine, bread and oil will be made into vehicles of the divine life for men.

Now a strange trait of this first miracle of transformation is that Christ did not do it on his own initiative. It was suggested to him by his Mother. The other evangelists, St Matthew and St Luke, had recorded the human birth of Christ from the Virgin; St John could presuppose that his readers knew this and, in his prologue, he concentrated on the eternal birth of the Logos in the mystery of the inner divine life. But the Synoptists had been silent about Mary's part in her Son's public life: according to the disciple in whose care she spent the last years of her life, it was she who launched him, as it were, on his 'career' by asking him to use his miraculous powers. Many interpretations have been given of the dialogue between Mother and Son on this occasion, of his first apparent refusal and almost immediate compliance with her wish. Whatever

the exact significance of the difficult words: 'Woman, what is
that to me and to thee? My hour is not yet come' (John 2: 4),
the main point is clear: as Mary brought Jesus into the world,
so she gives him to the world when it is time for him to leave
her to teach and do miracles. Again only John will show her,
at the last stage of Christ's earthly life under the Cross, once
more giving her Son to the world, and this time in the most
painful but also the most efficacious way when, according to
the prophecy of Simeon, her own heart was pierced by the
sword, and both her Son's mission and her own began to
embrace the whole earth.

It is true that John, like the other evangelists, kept Mary in
the background; the time had not yet come fully to reveal her
place in the plan of Redemption. But it was reserved to him,
the contemplative among the disciples, to show her at the two
crucial points in her Son's life, when water was changed into
wine, and death into life.

Hilda Graef
The Light and the Rainbow

3rd week of the year

In the beginning, God made the world:
Made it and mothered it,
Shaped it and fathered it;
Filled it with seed and with signs of fertility,
Filled it with love and its folk with ability.
All that is green, blue, deep and growing,
God's is the hand that created you.
All that crawls, flies, swims, walks or is motionless,
God's is the hand that created you.
All that speaks, sings, cries, laughs or keeps silence,
God's is the hand that created you.
All that suffers, lacks, limps or longs for an end,
God's is the hand that created you.
The world belongs to the Lord,
The earth and its people are his.

Let us give thanks.
Let us give thanks
for the continuity of the universe;
for the sun rising day by day,
and the moon rising night by night;
for all the life with which we share this planet;
for the interactions and connections that bind us to it,
and the elements of which all is composed.
Let us give thanks
for the flow of human history;
for the events that have shaped and moulded us
and all our sisters and brothers;
for those who question that history;
for those who unearth the stories of the vanquished,

the oppressed, the forgotten, the unrecorded.
Let us give thanks
for those who have provided inspiration and hope;
for prophets and martyrs and poets;
thinkers and preachers and healers;
for those who have linked thought and action;
for reformers and rebels and strikers.

We do not understand, eternal God,
the ways of your Spirit in the lives
of women and men.
She comes along secret paths to
take us unawares.
She touches us in joy and sorrow
to make us whole.
She hides behind coincidence to
lead us forward and
uses our human accidents as occasions
for influence.
We do not understand but
we welcome her presence and
rejoice in her power.

St Hilda Community
The New Women Included: a book of services and prayers

Week of Prayer for Christian Unity, 18–25 January

Appointed by our churches and under the guidance of the Holy Spirit we declare that this, the broadest assembly of British and Irish Churches ever to meet in these islands, has reached a common mind. We are aware that not all Christians are represented amongst us but we look forward to the time when they will share fully with us.

We came with different experiences and traditions, some with long ecumenical service, some for whom this is a new adventure. We are one band of pilgrims. We are old and young, women and men, black and white, lay and ordained and we travelled from the four corners of these islands to meet at Swanwick in Derbyshire. There we met, we listened, we talked, we worshipped, we prayed, we sat in silence, deeper than words. Against the background of so much suffering and sinfulness in our society we were reminded of our call to witness that God was in Christ reconciling the world to himself. We affirmed that this world with all its sin and splendour belongs to God. Young people called on us to be ready to sort out priorities so that we could travel light and concentrate on our goal. Driven on by a gospel imperative to seek unity that the world may believe, we rejoiced that we are pilgrims together and strangers no longer.

We now declare together our readiness to commit ourselves to each other under God. Our earnest desire is to become more fully, in his own time, the one Church of Christ, united in faith, communion, pastoral care and mission. Such unity is the gift of God . . .

This is a new beginning. We set out on our further pilgrimage ready to take risks and determined not to be put off by 'dismal stories'. We resolve that no discouragement will make us once relent our avowed intent to be pilgrims together. Leaving behind painful memories and reaching out for what lies ahead, we press on towards the full reconciliation in Christ of all things in heaven and on earth, that God has promised in his kingdom.

Final declaration
Swanwick meeting of the
Inter-Church process
(September 1987)

L ord God, we thank you
  For calling us into the company
Of those who trust in Christ
And seek to obey his will.
May your Spirit guide and strengthen us
In mission and service to your world;
For we are strangers no longer
But pilgrims together on the way to your kingdom. Amen.

The Pilgrims' Prayer

M ay he leave behind to his bride, the Church, his own
  robe as a token of her inheritance – a many-coloured robe, both seamless and woven from top to bottom, many-coloured because of the many distinct ways of life found within it and seamless because of the indivisible unity of her indestructible love. 'Who,' he asked, 'will separate me from the love of Christ?' Hear in what way she is many-coloured: 'There are varieties of gifts, but the same Spirit; and there are varieties of service but the same Lord'. Then, having enumerated the different gifts of grace as the various colours by which the robe is

known to be many-coloured, in order to show that it is seamless and woven from top to bottom the Apostle adds, 'These
are inspired by one and the same Spirit, apportioning to each
one individually as the Spirit wills. Love has been poured into
our hearts through the Holy Spirit, who has been given to us.'

Therefore, do not let the robe be divided, but let the Church
be allotted it whole and complete by hereditary right, as was
written concerning her, 'The queen stands on your right in
golden clothing, encircled with diversity.' And so different
people receive different gifts, one this, another that; in short
every language, sex, age and condition; in every place and in
every time.

St Bernard

Creator of rainbows,
come through the closed doors
of our emotions, mind and imagination;
come alongside us as we walk,
come to us at work and worship,
come to our meetings and councils,
come and call us by name,
call us to pilgrimage.

Wounded healer,
out of our disunity
may we be re-membered,
out of the pain of our division
may we see your glory.
Call us from present
preoccupation
to future community,

Spirit of Unity,
challenge our preconceptions,
enable us to grow in love and understanding,

> accompany us on our journey together,
> that we may go out with confidence
> into your world as a new creation –
> one body in you,
> that the world may believe.

Kate McIlhagga
Encompassing Presence

Today there are many stratagems and endeavours to unify Christendom. We fail to succeed because it has not yet been established for what purpose we want to be one.

Jesus long ago designated the overriding reason for unity: 'May they be one that the world may believe' (John 17:21). Too many of us live very comfortably even though the world is made up of unbelievers. Their salvation is not our passion. Therefore our plans for unity fail.

A little girl got lost in a huge wheat field, where the wheat was taller than her. Her parents called in the neighbours to help in the search, but in vain, though they shouted and used torches. Finally, on the third day the father said to the towns-people, 'Let's all join hands and go through the field in a line.' In no time the child was found. Behind the operation was a common purpose: the child had to be found.

Do we love the world with all our heart? Would we be very unhappy if all but a few were lost? Of what denomination were the people this father gathered to seek his child? It would be foolish to ask the question. He gathered all who shared his burden and were willing to help. This is what Jesus meant by being one.

An Israeli army unit risked its life to save the Jews hijacked in a plane that was forced down in Uganda. When the rescue plane was on its way home, soldiers and passengers sang together in Hebrew Psalm 133: 'Behold, how good and pleas-ant it is for brethren to dwell together in unity.' What were the religious convictions of the rescuers? Who knows? They belonged to a nation that had experienced the loss of many innocent victims and were united in their determination to prevent the killing of more Jews. They had a single purpose. Therefore unity was established.

Untold millions have gone to the grave without salvation because of our divisiveness. Think in these terms and your unity with all who desire to see souls saved will be established.

Several men sitting in a boat observed one of their number boring a hole beneath his seat. 'Why are you doing that?' one of his companions enquired. 'It's none of your business,' he replied. 'I'm boring the hole under *my* seat.'

The water entering through 'his' hole would swamp the whole boat with all its passengers.

Unity would be greatly served if Christians realized what obsolete and often petty questions divided them.

Richard Wurmbrand
The Total Blessing

4th week of the year

In those days, the Christ of Corcovado, in the city of San Sebastian de Rio de Janeiro, trembled and was revitalized. What was cement and stone became body and blood.

He extended his arms, wanting to embrace the city and the world, he opened his mouth and said:

'I feel sorry for you, millions and millions of sisters and brothers, the smallest and most defenceless of my flock expelled from the land, alone, hidden in the jungle, living piled on top of each other on the outskirts of the cities, so many fallen along the way without a single Samaritan to offer you help.

'Blessed are you, the poor and hungry, the hurt and the desperate. Your virtues and vices matter little. What matters most is that you are oppressed, victims of a perverse society. My Father, who is the giver of life, holds you in his heart . . .

'Woe to you, the powerful, who have sucked the blood of the workers for more than 500 years . . . You will not be judged by me or by my father, but by those you have victimized. Look at their faces! Remember their features. They will be your judges . . .

'Blessed is the great Latin American homeland . . . Observe the thickets and the prickly grass, the giant mountains and the immense Amazon, the swift rivers and the deep valleys, the wild animals and the innumerable birds. They all are your brothers and sisters . . . Blessed are you, indigenous peoples of the Americas, my first witnesses in the fertile lands of the Abia Yala. Your cities, your pyramids, your long trails, your rituals, the sun and the moon that you venerated, are signs of the true God, of God both near and far, of the God the giver of all life . . .

'Woe to those who subjugated you, who destroyed your

cultures, who grabbed up your flowers, who overturned your altars, who confused your knowledge and who imposed their doctrines day and night with the violence of the sword and the cross . . .

'Blessed are the base communities where you, the poor, are brought together in faith and life to celebrate my name, you give happiness and strength to the reasons for living and struggling . . . Blessed are those who wait with tears for the great dawn of liberation, fruit of divine grace and human struggle, because your eyes will see the rays of the sun of justice. Blessed are those of good will, who are fed by the internal fire and believe in the dream of a new world.'

After speaking these words of admonition, consolation and promise, Christ became stone once again with his arms outstretched and his heart open.

All of us should know that we are within the reach of his arms to feel free and trapped in his heart because we are all loved eternally. And that is how it was yesterday, is today and will be tomorrow in the sun and rain, in wind and at night, for ever and ever. Amen.

Leonardo Boff
Sermon on the Mount of Corcovado

St Francis de Sales,
24 January

If some strict duty keeps you from being present in person at the celebration of this sovereign sacrifice, try at least to transport your heart to it and assist at Mass by your spiritual presence. Sometime during the morning go in spirit into the church, if you cannot do so otherwise, unite your intention with that of all Christians, and in the place you are make the same interior acts that you would make if you were really present in church at the offering of Holy Mass.

Look into your heart and behold how generous it is. As bees can never remain upon anything decayed but only among flowers, so also our heart finds rest solely in God and no creature can ever satisfy it. Think deeply on the dearest and strongest affections that have filled your heart up to now and judge truthfully whether they were not full of worry and unrest, tormenting thoughts and demanding cares in the midst of which your poor heart was wretched.

Our heart, alas! runs after creatures. It eagerly seeks them, thinking that they will satisfy its desires. As soon as it has obtained them, it sees that it is all to do over again and that nothing can satisfy it. God does not will that our heart should find a place of rest, any more than did the dove that went out from Noah's ark, so that it may return to himself from whom it came. Ah! what natural beauty is there in our heart! Why then do we detain it against its will in the service of creatures?

Is it possible that I could have been loved, so tenderly loved, by my Saviour that he should think of me in particular even in all these little events by which he has drawn me to himself? How much then must we love and cherish them and turn them all to our own profit! How sweet this is! God's loving heart has thought of Philothea, loved her, and brought her countless means of salvation, so many that it would seem there had been no other soul in the world for him to think of.

The sun shines upon a certain spot on the earth and gives it no less light than if it shone nowhere else and shone only for that place. In the very same manner Our Lord thinks about all his beloved children and gives them his care. He thinks of each of them as though he did not think of all the others.

'He loved me,' says St Paul, 'and delivered himself for me.' He says 'for me alone,' as if he had done nothing for the rest. Philothea, these words should be engraved upon your soul so that you may rightly cherish and nourish a resolution that has been so precious to the Saviour's heart.

St Francis de Sales
Introduction to the Devout Life

St Angela Merici,
27 January

Let them hold this as most certain: that they will never be abandoned in their needs. God will provide for them wonderfully. They must not lose hope. How many lords, queens and other great persons there are who, with the many riches and possessions they have, will not be able to find true relief in some extreme need; and yet these little ones, poor as they are, will find consolation and comfort.

Also, tell them that now I am more alive than I was when they saw me in the flesh, and that now I see them and know them better. And can and want to help them more. And that I am continually among them with my Lover, or rather ours, the Lover of us all, provided they believe and do not lose heart and hope. And so, especially for those you see disconsolate, doubtful and faint-hearted, enlarge the scope of the promises, which will not go unfulfilled. Tell them that they should long to see me not on earth, but in heaven, where our love is. Let them set their hopes on high and not on earth. Let them have Jesus Christ for their only treasure, for there also will be love, which is to be sought not here in this world, but above.

Next I beg you that you willingly hold in consideration and have engraved on your mind and heart all your dear daughters, one by one; not only their names, but also their condition, and character, and their every situation and state. This will not be difficult for you if you embrace them with an ardent charity.

For you can see that natural mothers, even if they had a thousand sons and daughters, would have them wholly fixed in their hearts, all and each one separately, because this is how

real love works. Indeed it seems that the more children they
have, the more their love and care for each one grows. How
much more spiritual mothers can and should do this, since
spiritual love is beyond comparison much more powerful than
natural love.

Therefore, my most loving mothers, if you love these dear
daughters of ours with a burning and passionate charity, it
will be impossible for you not to have them all depicted individually in your memory and in your heart.

In this matter I do not want you to seek outside advice; you
decide, only among yourselves, according as charity and the
Holy Spirit will enlighten and inspire you, directing everything
towards the good and spiritual benefit of your dear daughters,
as much to urge and move those who are already in [the Com-
pany] to greater love and obligation to do good, as to attract
still others to it. For this is the real purpose, agreeable to God,
of almsgiving and kindness, that by means of them the creature
is drawn away from evil and vice, and led to virtue and good
behaviour, or at least to greater spiritual benefit. Indeed, in
this way people are so to speak won over and obliged and
compelled to do the very thing one wants.

Because just as, for example, if a girl takes and accepts
some present and gift from some worldly stranger, she remains
obliged to gratify the wishes of that person, and it seems that
she is no longer able to say no, so, neither more nor less, by
gifts and alms people are drawn and somehow compelled to
do good; and thus they remain almost bound to do good.
Follow this road and you cannot go wrong.

St Angela Merici
Counsels and *Testament*

St Thomas Aquinas,
28 January

G odhead here in hiding, whom I do adore
  Masked by these bare shadows, shape and nothing
  more,
See, Lord, at thy service low lies here a heart
Lost, all lost in wonder at the God thou art.

Seeing, touching, tasting are in thee deceived;
How says trusty hearing? that shall be believed;
What God's Son has told me, take for truth I do;
Truth himself speaks truly or there's nothing true.

On the cross thy godhead made no sign to men;
Here thy very manhood steals from human ken:
Both are my confession, both are my belief,
And I pray the pray'r made by the dying thief.

I am not like Thomas, wounds I cannot see,
But can plainly call thee Lord and God as he:
This faith each day deeper be my holding of,
Daily make me harder hope and dearer love.

O thou our reminder of Christ crucified,
Living bread the life of us for whom he died,
Lend this life to me then: feed and feast my mind,
There be thou the sweetness man was meant to find.

Bring the tender tale true of the pelican;
Bathe me, Jesus Lord, in what thy bosom ran
Blood that but one drop of has the world to win
All the world forgiveness of its world of sin.

Jesus whom I look at shrouded here below,
I beseech thee send me what I thirst for so,
Some day to gaze on thee face to face in light
And be blest forever with thy glory's sight. Amen.

St Thomas Aquinas
Adoro te devote
transl. Gerard Manley Hopkins

M ost merciful God, let me ardently desire what pleases you, prudently seek, truly learn, and faithfully fulfil all to the praise and glory of your name. Order my day so that I may know what you want me to do, and for my soul's good, help me to do it. Let me not be elated by success nor cast down by failure, neither puffed up by the former, nor depressed by the latter. I want only to take pleasure in what draws me to you, only to grieve for what displeases you. I want neither to please nor fear to displease anyone but you.

St Thomas Aquinas
'Prayer before a picture of Christ'

Homelessness Sunday

Communicating with homeless people all over Britain reminds me of the vulnerability and fragility of human life. We are broken people but often we hide our fragmented condition behind our outer appearances. It can be disguised with a smile or wrapped up with an attraction to materialism. But when you are homeless, your misfortune is exposed to the whole of society and you are at the mercy of others for help. We can bandage each other's wounds if our minds are open to the plight of those who suffer. We can heal each other's sores. This gives birth to a regeneration, an energy which gives hope. But so often I see people wanting to be helped and no one is there. Hence they live out their lives in isolation and confusion.

Mark is still struggling with a heroin addiction. He lives in central London and at night he sleeps in a doorway near Oxford Street. His gaunt face and pale complexion remind me of the chemical substance that eats away at his flesh. Drugs block out the pain of the past and prevent him from facing the reality of the present moment. He's only nineteen.

John sleeps in a urinated cardboard box. He has spent the last eight years living on the streets of London. His face is cut and it exhibits one black eye. Earlier on in the day he was caught up in a fight over a can of cider. At the age of 38 the doctors don't give him much longer to live as his kidneys are packing up.

I have walked with those who have lost the power to live. I have stared into the faces of the young who slowly lose the will to fight on. I have held the scarred hands of the addicts and have seen the perspiration on their foreheads as they run from the drug pusher. I have stood at the graveside of the homeless alcoholic and have listened to young women cry as they speak of the degradation of selling their bodies for sex.

I ask myself why? Yet when I ponder more deeply, these are the people who have revealed God to me. Beneath the scars of their human existence, their warm hearts and humble spirits have welcomed me. Their lives were not in vain.

Jim McCartney
Edges magazine

H oly Child of Bethlehem,
      whose parents found no room in the inn;
   we pray for all who are homeless . . .

Holy Child of Bethlehem,
   rejected stranger;
   we pray for all who are lost, alone;
   all who cry for loved ones . . .

Holy Child of Bethlehem,
   in you the Eternal was pleased to dwell;
   help us, we pray, to see the divine image
   in people everywhere.

David Blanchflower

5th week of the year

Our deepest fear
   is not that we are inadequate
Our deepest fear is that we are
  powerful beyond measure.
It is our light, not our darkness,
  that most frightens us.
We ask ourselves
Who am I to be brilliant,
  gorgeous, talented and fabulous?
Actually who are you *not* to be?
  You are a child of God.
Your playing small doesn't save the world.
There's nothing enlightened about shrinking
  so that other people won't feel insecure
  around you.
We were born to make manifest
  the glory of God
  that is within us.
It's not just in some of us
  it's in *everyone*.
And as we let our light shine
We unconsciously give other people
  permission to do the same.
As we are liberated from our own fear
  our presence automatically liberates others.

Attributed to Nelson Mandela

I vow to you, my friends of earth,
All worldly things above,
Entire and whole – yet broken
The service of my love:
The love that dares to question,
The love that speaks its name,
That flowers still in barren ground,
Yet hides no more for shame,
The love that struggles through the pain
And whispers in the night,
Yet shares its secret with the world
To bring the truth to light.

This *is* that other country
We heard of long ago,
When called to be the spies of God
Where milk and honey flow:
A world where hurts find healing,
Where all th'oppressed run free,
Where friends who have been sore betrayed
Each other truly see:
It is our earth, transfigured, new,
Where wars and hatred cease,
Where spy and friend walk hand in hand
In Christ our Lover's Peace.

Jim Cotter
Prayer in the Morning

Mary Ward,
30 January

I was abstracted out of my whole being, and it was shown to me with clearness and inexpressible certainty that I was not to be of the Order of St Teresa, but that some other thing was determined for me, without all comparison more to the glory of God than my entrance into that holy religion. I did not see what the assured good thing would be, but the glory of God which was to come through it, showed itself inexplicably and so abundantly as to fill my soul in such a way that I remained for a good space without feeling or hearing anything, but the sound, 'Glory, glory, glory'.

There was a Father that lately came into England whom I heard say that he would not for a thousand of worlds be a woman, because he thought a woman could not apprehend God. I answered nothing, but only smiled, although I could have answered him, by the experience I have of the contrary. I could have been sorry for his want – I mean not want of judgement – nor to condemn his want of judgement, for he is a man of very good judgement; his want is in experience. It was a wise speech of the Queen of Spain, when she had brought the Teresians into some part of Spain, and much commended them, some went of curiosity to see them, and after they had seen them said they were not such as they expected. She answered: 'If you look upon them as saints you shall find them women; but if you look upon them as women, you will find them saints.' So we may say of men, if we look upon them as prophets we shall see their imperfections, but if we look upon them as men, we shall see them far otherwise.

O Parent of parents, and Friend of friends . . . without entreaty, thou tookest me into thy care and by degrees led me from all else, that at length I might see and settle my love on thee. O happy begun freedom, the beginning of all my good.

He was very near me and within me, which I never perceived him to be before. I was moved to ask him with great confidence and humility, what I came to know – to wit, *what he was*. I said, 'My God, what art Thou?' I saw him evidently and very clearly go into my heart and by little and little hide himself.

Mary Ward
in Lavinia Byrne, *Mary Ward: A Pilgrim Finds Her Way*

Mary Ward died on 30 January 1645

St Brigit of Ireland,
1 February

Now, of her father's wealth and property, whatsoever her hands would find or would get, Brigit used to give to the poor and needy of the Lord. Wherefore her father became displeased with her and desired to sell the holy Brigit. He went with her in a chariot, and said: 'Not for honour or for reverence to thee art thou carried in the chariot; but to take thee to sell thee, that thou mayst grind at the quern of Dunlaing, son of Enna, king of Leinster.'

When they came to the king's fortress, Dubthach went in, and left his sword near Brigit in the chariot. And a leper came to Brigit, and besought her to bestow something upon him. Brigit handed him her father's sword. Said Dubthach to the king when he had come inside, 'Wilt thou buy my daughter from me?'

'Wherefore sellest thou thine own daughter?' said Dunlaing.

'Not hard to say. She is selling my wealth and bestowing it on wretched worthless men.'

'Let her be brought to us that we may see her,' said Dunlaing.

Dubthach went for her, and when he came to the chariot he saw not his sword. He asked Brigit what she had done with it. 'I gave it,' said she, 'to a poor man who came to beg of me.'

Dubthach was mightily enraged with her for having given the sword away. When Brigit came before the king, he said, 'Why dost thou steal thy father's property and wealth, and what is worse, why hast thou given the sword away?'

Then said Brigit: 'The Virgin's Son knoweth if I had thy power, with all thy wealth, and with all thy Leinster, I would give them all to the Lord of the Elements.'

Said the king to Dubthach, 'It is not meet for us to deal with this maiden, for her merit before God is higher.' Thus was Brigit saved from bondage.

Everything that Brigit would ask of the Lord was granted her at once. For this was her desire: to satisfy the poor, to expel every hardship, to spare every miserable man ... She was simple towards God: she was compassionate towards the wretched: she was splendid in miracles and marvels: wherefore her name among created things is Dove among birds, Vine among trees, Sun among stars.

adapted from *The Lives of the Saints from the 'Book of Lismore'*

Presentation of the Lord,
2 February

Time will not suffice for us to recount the virtues of all the saints, so let us consider for the moment the last of the righteous men of old. Whom do I mean? Simeon, whose name is given in the gospel according to Luke. He stands both first and last, being the last to live under the law and the first to live by grace. In observance he was a Jew, in thanksgiving a Christian; by training he was a lawyer, but by knowledge of God an ambassador.

This Simeon, whose story has just been read to us, was plucked from the ill-fame of the Pharisees like a rose from thorns, and became the first to win renown through the gift of grace. Because of his righteousness God revealed to him, while he was still in the body, that he would not depart this present transitory life until his own arms had enfolded Life Eternal, our Lord Jesus Christ. Simeon the righteous, who before the incarnation had longed to see the Lord, saw him incarnate, recognized him, and took him in his arms. Then he cried for release from the prison of his body, calling as a servant on the Lord of all who appeared as a child, in the words you have just heard: 'Now, Lord, you let your servant go in peace as you promised, for my eyes have seen your salvation.'

I have seen, allow me to leave, do not keep me here. Let me depart in peace, do not keep me in distress. I have seen, let me go: I have seen your glory, seen the angels dancing, the arch-angels praising you, creation leaping for joy, a way made between heaven and earth. Now let me depart, do not keep me here below.

Do not let me see the insolence of fellow Jews, the crown

of thorns being plaited, a slave beating you, or a spear being thrust into you: do not let me see the sun darkened, the moon fading, the elements altered; do not let me see you broken on a cross, the rocks split asunder, the veil of the temple rent. The elements themselves will not endure this audacity, and will share in the suffering of the Lord. 'Now, Lord, you let your servant go in peace as you promised, for my eyes have seen your salvation, which you have prepared in the sight of all the nations.'

Timothy of Jerusalem

As we stand in the temple and hold the Son of God and embrace him, let us pray to almighty God and to the child Jesus that we may be found worthy of discharge and departure to better things, for we long to speak with Jesus and embrace him. To him be glory and power for ever and ever. Amen.

Origen

Pedro Arrupe,
5 February

How I wish I were in a better condition for this meeting with you! As you see, I cannot even address you directly. But my general assistants have grasped what I want to say to everyone.

More than ever, I now find myself in the hands of God. This is what I have wanted all my life, from my youth. And this is still the one thing I want. But now there is a difference: the initiative is entirely with God. It is indeed a profound spiritual experience to know and feel myself so totally in his hands . . .

My call to you today is that you be available to the Lord. Let us put God at the centre, ever attentive to his voice, ever asking what we can do for his more effective service, and doing it to the best of our ability, with love and perfect detachment. Let us cultivate a very personal awareness of the reality of God . . .

From our young people I ask that they live in the presence of God and grow in holiness, as the best preparation for the future. Let them surrender to the will of God, at once so awesome and so familiar.

With those who are at the peak of their apostolic activity, I plead that they do not burn themselves out. Let them find a proper balance by centring their lives on God, not on their work – with an eye to the needs of the world, and a thought for the millions who do not know God or behave as if they did not. All are called to know and serve God. What a wonderful mission has been entrusted to us: to bring all to the knowledge and love of Christ!

On those of my age I urge openness: let us learn what must be done now, and do it with a will . . .

For myself, all I want is to repeat from the depths of my heart:

Take O Lord, and receive, all my liberty, my memory, my understanding and my whole will. All I have and all I possess – it is all yours, Lord: you gave it to me; I make it over to you: dispose of it entirely according to your will. Give me your love and your grace, and I want no more.

Pedro Arrupe

Pedro Arrupe died on 5 February 1991

6th week of the year

O Jesus, Son of God, who was silent before Pilate, do not let us wag our tongues without thinking of what we are to say and how to say it.

Irish prayer

May the roads rise to meet you, may the wind be always at your back, may the sun shine warm upon your face, the rains fall soft upon your fields, and until we meet again may God hold you in the hollow of his hand.

Irish blessing

May the roof above never fall in,
May we below never fall out.

Irish grace

Lord, be with us this day,
Within us to purify us;
Above us to draw us up;
Beneath us to sustain us;
Before us to lead us;
Behind us to restrain us;
Around us to protect us.

Our God, God of all men,
God of heaven and earth, seas and rivers,
God of sun and moon, of all the stars,
God of high mountain and lowly valleys,
God over heaven, and in heaven, and under heaven.
He has a dwelling in heaven and earth and sea and in all
    things that are in them.
He inspires all things, he quickens all things.
He is over all things, he supports all things.
He makes the light of the sun to shine,
He surrounds the moon and the stars,
He has made wells in the arid earth,
Placed dry islands in the sea.
He has a Son co-eternal with himself . . .
And the Holy Spirit breathes in them;
Not separate are the Father and the Son and Holy Spirit.

St Patrick

St Scholastica,
10 February

Once a year Scholastica, the sister of St Benedict, who had been dedicated to God from her youth, used to visit her brother. The man of God would go down to meet her in a house belonging to the monastery not far from the gate.

One day she paid her usual visit and her brother joined her with some disciples. They spent the whole day praising God and talking of sacred things, and then, as the light began to fail, they had a meal together. Their conversation went on till quite late, and the nun said to her brother: 'Please do not leave me tonight: let us go on until morning talking about the joys of heaven.' 'Whatever are you saying, sister?' he replied. 'I cannot possibly stay out of the monastery.'

At her brother's refusal, the nun joined her hands on the table, laid her head on them and prayed to almighty God. As soon as she raised her head, a violent storm broke out with thunder and lightning, and such a downpour of rain that St Benedict, and the brethren accompanying him, could not set foot outside the door of the place where they had been sitting. 'God forgive you, sister,' he said. 'What have you done?' She replied: 'I asked you, but you would not listen; I asked my God and he did listen. Set off now, if you can: leave me and return to your monastery.'

But now he who would not remain of his own free will had to do so against his will; and so it happened that they spent the whole night talking together about spiritual things to their mutual benefit. That the woman should have prevailed over the man is not surprising, for since, as St John says, God is love, it was only right that the one who loved more should be able to achieve more.

Three days after this, as the man of God was standing in his cell looking up at the sky, he saw his sister's soul, in the form of a dove, leave her body and enter the gates of heaven. He rejoiced at her great glory, thanking God with hymns of praise. Then he sent brethren to bring her body to the monastery and place it in the tomb he had prepared for himself.

So it came that just as their hearts had always been united in God, so also their bodies shared a common grave.

St Gregory the Great
'Dialogues'

World Day for the Sick,
11 February

The Millennium Dome is at the moment, a huge and fascinating building site. The structure is being upheld by several cranes – like supports in an outward-leaning circle, giving the appearance of a massive crown.

My parents were both in Greenwich Hospital from Christmas until now. My mother died in May, my father is still there. From the windows of their respective wards was a perfect view of the Dome; very close too. As I jotted down the following, I was sitting with the view of the Dome on my left, and my slowly dying mother on my right.

I sit and watch helplessly, as the one who gave me life struggles to breathe. I sense an outside edge beyond all edges. The paralysed body, which can only move to breathe, paralyses me with helpless love. Are you in there somewhere?

I kiss the cold forehead, and I see her crown of thorns.

On another ward, my father lies quietly staring out of the window. His octogenarian mind has sought sanctuary in the comfort of the past. His ramblings are at once imaginative and heart breaking – he sees the Dome not as the future, but as part of a past mental tapestry of which only he knows the meaning. I see the outside edge of a soul in misery. Are you in there deep down?

I kiss his bewildered forehead; the thorns pierce my being.

From both, I look around in desperation for meaning; for life – then I focus through the window to that vast, futuristic crown; not of thorns but of cranes, concrete and steel; ingenious engineering. Above all, I see enthusiasm for a future; I see life, continuity, evolution.

Frail human beings completing their span fill this hospital. They all had a future once too. Trying to remain optimistic, I search for a purpose in all this suffering. I look across the roofs at that much-debated edifice and hope desperately that the whole of existence isn't just a superficial nonentity within a hollow crown.

Then I ponder on the crown of thorns. It singled out its wearer from the crowds, leaving him alienated and alone; yet it was the beginning of his journey to a crown of shared glory.

An hour after writing this, my mother died. It was an experience for which there are no words. I can only say that I thank God for it. When I eventually left the hospital with my brother, the sky was fairly dark and the Dome was floodlit for the workmen. The red warning lights on the top of each crane flickered like jewels against the twilight.

Through my immense sorrow, I was aware of an overwhelming sense of death, life; past, future; pain, glory – eventually everything comes full circle.

I look again to that crown, now shrouded in a rush-hour city smog, and I wonder how many of the millennium generations will be allowed their full-circleness.

Elaine Kennedy
Edges magazine

7th week of the year

At every moment
   you stand at the threshold
   of God's eternity.
On the one side
   there is God's Eternal Now.
On the other side
   there is the totality of human endeavour
   from the beginning of creation
   to its consummation
   seeking to cross the limit.
Every human effort
   is not just a part of this totality,
   but a symbol and representative
   of the whole.
Scientists tell us
   that every atom
   is not merely a part
   of the visible universe,
   but a symbol, a miniature
   and a valid representative
   of the sum total of things.
In like manner,
   even the simplest human action
   has a validity and definitiveness
   of its own and has a potentiality
   for vast consequences.
It is true, through God's mercy,
   mistaken actions are repairable.
But that does not take away
   anything from the decisive nature

and the earth-shaking importance
of every single good deed.
This awareness fills you
with an awful sense of responsibility.
It also fills your heart with unlimited happiness,
'while you wait with joyful hope
for the coming of our Saviour,
Jesus Christ'.
Human desires
are of universal dimensions.
You like to reach out in all directions,
to be with everyone in every place
and be involved with everything.
This is clearly impossible.
What, however, gives you a grip
into the immense universe
and the entire course of history
is your present moment
and your present task.
Your faithful use of the present moment
and your fidelity to today's task
makes you plug your 'now'
into God's 'Eternal Now'.
And with that you achieve
the impossible mentioned above:
you can be truly with everyone
in every place
and be involved with everything.
Time and space disappear.
You can link yourself
with every godly event
in any period of history.
You can carry God's love
to anyone in any part of the world.

Thomas Menamparampil
A Path to Prayer

St Valentine,
14 February

What love is this of thine, that cannot be
        In thine infinity, O Lord, confined.
Unless it in thy very person see
    Infinity and finity conjoined?
    What! hath thy Godhead, as not satisfied,
    Married our manhood, making it its bride?

Oh matchless love! Filling heaven to the brim!
    O'errunning it: all running o'er beside
This world! Nay, overflowing hell, wherein,
    For thine elect, there rose a mighty tide!
    That there our veins might through thy person bleed,
    To quench the flames that else would on us feed.

Oh! that thy love might overflow my heart!
    To fire the same with love: for love I would.
But oh! my straightened breast! my lifeless spark!
    My fireless flame! What chilly love and cold!
    In measure small! In manner chilly! See!
    Lord, blow the coal: thy love enflame in me.

                                        Edward Taylor

We must not forget that if earthly love has in the vulgar
    mind been often degraded into mere animal passion, it
still remains in its purest sense the highest mystery of our
existence, the most perfect blessing and delight on earth, and

at the same time the truest pledge of our more than human nature.

If we do a thing because we think it is our duty, we generally fail; that is the old law which makes slaves of us. The real spring of our life, and of our work in life, must be love – true, deep love – not love of this or that person, or for this or that reason, but deep human love, devotion of soul to soul, love of God realized where alone it can be – in love of those whom he loves. Everything else is weak, passes away; that love alone supports us, makes life tolerable, binds the present together with the past and future, and is, we may trust, imperishable.

Max Müller

'I love and love not: Lord, it breaks my heart
    To love and not to love.
Thou veiled within thy glory, gone apart
    Into thy shrine which is above,
Dost thou not love me, Lord, or care
    For this mine ill? –

'I love thee here or there,
    I will accept thy broken heart – lie still.'

Christina Rossetti

Education Day
(3 Sundays before
1st Sunday of Lent)

The whole process of education has a spiritual context. The pursuit of knowledge begins with a sense of awe at the mystery of existence. The very idea of universal education is rooted in our sense of the sanctity of the individual. Secularize education and you diminish it. You diminish its power for children; you diminish the dignity of our teachers; you diminish the value of education as an end in itself . . .

There is no such thing as spirituality in the abstract. Our great religious emotions need a language in which they are expressed, or they cannot be expressed. Our languages *are* our several religious traditions, and we need to learn them just as we learn languages if we are not to be condemned to an inarticulate life of emotional under-development.

These would be reason enough for the importance of religious education at any time. But there is a third reason, which is of our time. Never before have human beings been challenged as our children are challenged, to live in a world of rapid and bewildering change: economic, political, and technological. They have lost what most people at most times have had: a set of stable expectations. Almost everything that makes us what we are has become vulnerable to sudden and unforeseen rupture: our job, our relationships, our human and natural environment.

At such a time we owe it to our children to give them what Alvin Toffler calls 'personal stability zones'. And of these none is more powerful than a sense of rootedness in a living tradition that links us to our ancestors and to our collective past and future. We need to teach our children to hear the sound of eternity in the midst of change.

I speak on behalf of a people which for nearly four thousand years has lived on the precipice of instability, never knowing when the next expulsion or persecution would come. How did Jews survive? By obeying the Bible's command to teach our faith diligently to our children; by predicating our entire continuity on religious education. You defend a country by armies. But you defend a civilization by schools.

No culture can survive change without faith. From today, and for the sake of our children, I hope that the voice of faith will speak more loudly in our culture.

Jonathan Sacks
The Chief Rabbi

8th week of the year

To the world it seems foolish that we delight in poor food, that we relish rough and insipid bulgur; possess only three sets of habits made of coarse cloth or old soutanes, mend and patch them, take great care of them and refuse to have extra; enjoy walking in any shape and colour of shoes; bathe with just a bucket of water in small bathing rooms; sweat and perspire but refuse to have a fan; go hungry and thirsty but refuse to eat in the houses of the people; refuse to have radios or gramophones which could be relaxing to the racked nerves after the whole day's hard toil; walk distances in the rain and hot summer sun, or go cycling, travel by second-class tram, or third-class over-crowded trains; sleep on hard beds, giving up soft and thick mattresses which would be soothing to the aching bodies after the whole day's hard work; kneel on the rough and thin carpets in the chapel, giving up soft and thick ones; delight in lying in the common wards in the hospital among the poor of Christ when we could easily have private cabins; work like coolies at home and outside when we could easily employ servants and do only the light jobs; relish cleaning the toilets and dirt in the Nirmal Hriday and Shishu Bhavan as though that was the most beautiful job in the world, and call it all a tribute to God. To them we are wasting our precious life and burying our talents. Yes, our lives are utterly wasted if we use only the light of reason. Our life has no meaning unless we look at Christ in his poverty.

Cheerfulness and joy was Our Lady's strength. This made her a willing handmaid of God, her Son, for as soon as he came to her she 'went in haste'. Only joy could have given her the strength to go in haste over the hills of Judaea to do the work of handmaid to her cousin.

So with us too; we like her must be true handmaids of the Lord, and daily after Holy Communion go in haste, over the hills of difficulties we meet in giving whole-hearted service to the poor. Give Jesus to the poor as the handmaid of the Lord.

Mother Teresa of Calcutta

Michael Hollings, 21 February

Look at the crucifix and see there the Lord in agony, dying. Sometimes as you look, you will see how he is joined by a loved one, he too in agony, dying. On the Cross I see now Christ, then the loved one. Sometimes on entering the ward, I saw Christ lying there, struggling for a life that was slowly ebbing away. When I saw you, Michael, sick in bed I thought of Christ in agony. Every time I glanced at the crucifix, I thought of you, agonizing in pain, dying. It is a lonely business, dying, till we remember that God is everywhere and God is love. That makes all the difference. We can then pray with peace of mind what Christ prayed on the Cross, 'Into thy hands, Lord, I commend my spirit.'

Few of us are called to suffer as you did, to make up – in that strange phrase of St Paul's – whatever is wanting in the suffering of Christ. Not many of us are called as you were to undergo the agony of being publicly humiliated. It is good that it is the Lord alone who looks into our hearts and knows our secret struggles, how we have striven to be for him what all of us in our better moments would wish to be. You, Lord, judge us according to our deeds, you know the good we have done, you see the motives that drove us to serve you. You, Michael, were his servant and a good one too. You served him, and remarkably so, in the poor and distressed, in those for whom no one else would care. Your door was always open for those who needed you, and your heart too.

You can look back, Michael, on your life with pride. Your war record would be the boast of any man; your care for students at London and Oxford put many of them in your debt; those you guided to the priesthood over the years learned from you what demands will be made on devoted and selfless priests and what joys can be discovered; the people of Southall and Bayswater had in you a leader who stood for what was decent and right in a multi-cultural and multi-faith society.

The sharing of yourself in your many books reached persons who only knew you through your writing, and were greatly helped and inspired. The simplicity of your life-style and the long hours of prayer gave you a remarkable pastoral zeal and spiritual energy.

Stop, stop – I hear you say – do not overstate my virtues or exaggerate my achievements. Do not give to others any excuses not to pray for me. I was as frail as any other human being, I hear you say. True, Michael, you had the weaknesses of your strengths, as we all do; yes, you had your faults and shortcomings. Who has not? In any case, you cannot ask me to list these here – *de mortuis nihil nisi bonum*. It is fashionable in our day to try to cut down to size those who in life were bigger than ourselves, we like too to belittle those with whom we do not agree. We can be very mean-spirited. That is not for us today.

So Michael, I shall sing of your strengths, rejoice in the good that you did. Today we salute greatness in a man, we celebrate holiness in a priest, we admire a devoted shepherd. The rest I leave in the hands of God, the gentle judge of those who made him their first concern. You did precisely that, Michael. You made God your first concern. We mourn you now.

There will be tears in your family and among those to whom you meant so much. They will pray for you as you would wish. Now as I look at the crucifix, I see you passing from it to a new life, risen in Christ.

Cardinal Basil Hume
Funeral homily

Michael Hollings died on 21 February 1997

If you take my advice you will try to get a certain amount of time alone with yourself. I think when we are alone we sometimes see things a little bit more simply, more as they are.

Sometimes when we are with others, especially when we are talking to others on religious subjects, we persuade ourselves that we believe more than we do. We talk a great deal, we grow enthusiastic, we speak of religious emotions and experiences. This is, perhaps, sometimes good.

But when we are alone we see just how much we really believe, how much is mere enthusiasm excited at the moment. We get face to face with him, and our heat and passion go, and what is really permanent remains. We begin to recognize how very little love we have, how very little real pleasure in that which is alone of lasting importance.

Then we see how poor and hollow and unloving we are; then, I think, we also begin to see that this poverty, this hollowness, this unloving void, can be filled only by him who fills all in all. To get alone – to dare to be alone – with God, this, I am persuaded, is one of the best ways of doing anything in the world . . .

If we are ever to be or to do anything, if we are ever to be full of deep, permanent, rational enthusiasm, we must know God. If we are ever to know each other, we must know him first . . .

I believe that we do most for those whom God has begun to teach us to love, not by constantly thinking of their goodness, their grace, their simplicity, but by never thinking of them apart from God, by always connecting their beauty and purity with a higher beauty and a higher purity, by seeing God in them. Let us learn to make every thought of admiration and love a kind of prayer of intercession and thanksgiving. Thus human love will correct itself with, and find its root in, divine love. But this we can do only if we are willing to be alone with him.

Forbes Robinson
Letters to his Friends

St David,
1 March

There is no frontier between two worlds in the Church;
The Church militant upon earth is the same
As the Church triumphant in heaven.
And the saints are in this Church which is two in one.
They come to worship with us, our small congregation,
The saints, our oldest ancestors,
Who built Wales on the foundation
Of the Cradle, the Cross and the Empty Tomb;
And they go out from it as of old to tread their customary
    ways
And to evangelize Wales.
I have seen David going from county to county like God's
    gypsy
With the Gospel and the Altar in his caravan;
And he came to us in the Colleges and schools
To show us what is the purpose of learning.
He went down to the bottom of the pit with the miners
And cast the light of his wise lamp onto the coal face;
At the steel works he put on the spectacles and the short
    grey overall
And showed the Christian being purified like the metal in
    the furnace;
And he led the industrial people to his disreputable Church.
He carried his Church everywhere
Like a body, having life, mind and will
Doing things small and great.
He brought the Church into our homes,
Put the Sacred Vessels on the kitchen table,

And took bread from the pantry and cheap wine from the
    cellar,
And stood behind the table like a tramp
So as not to hide from us the wonder of the sacrifice.
And after the Communion we had a talk round the fire,
And he spoke to us of God's natural Order,
The person, the family, the nation and the society of
    nations,
And the Cross which keeps us from turning any of them
    into a god.
He said that God has fashioned our nation
For his own purpose,
And its death would be a breach of that Order . . .
We besought his pardon, his strength and his keenness,
And told him, before he left us,
To give the Lord Jesus Christ our poor congratulations,
And to ask Him whether we might come to him
To praise him for ever in Heaven,
When comes that longed-for moment
That we have to say Good Night to the world.

D. Gwenallt Jones
St David

Women's World Day of Prayer
(1st Friday of March)

Our Father Who Art in Heaven

Inside, Alejandra talks of her nine brothers and sisters. Holding on to the bars of the women's cell, a child, born inside, peers out. He knows no other room. People's fathers, people's mothers, their sons, daughters and friends are here. Made in the image of God. They reach their hands out for some variety in their monotonous, claustrophobic lives, starving for food, some of them, but all of them starving for life.

Hallowed Be Thy Name

There are calendar pictures on the grimy walls alongside shockingly gaudy pictures of the Sacred Heart – their images, not ours, as if to say, 'I may appear diminished, but my God is still mine, you can't take him away from me'.

Thy Kingdom Come

The rooms are as the concrete cages of a zoo. We look through the bars at the human life within – fifteen people in a space the size of my bedroom, but there are no beds and there is no door to close at night, only the gate which is always locked. This is the only ground their feet will touch until they leave.

Thy Will Be Done As It Is In Heaven

We hold the hands which reach through the bars and listen and talk. Laughter is release and attention is medicine. For a split second we can set some captives free.

Give Us This Day Our Daily Bread

We come with sacks of bread for the prisoners. Relatives need to be local and willing if the prisoners here are to eat. They used to bring rice, but the stoves 'used too much electricity' and were taken away.

And Forgive Us Our Trespasses

They brought it upon themselves! In without trial, unable to afford the bribe, some of these people wait over a year for their release. How can we walk past the frightened or the infirm who beg on the streets and direct the judgement away from ourselves?

As We Forgive Those Who Trespass Against Us

Where is the bitterness in their eyes as we walk away, freely, as we talk about tomorrow as if it will be different from today?

And Lead Us Not Into Temptation But Deliver Us From Evil

As our God appeared on the Cross before us, naked, weak and loving, so need we be before the people of this place. Don't let us suffocate the pale flames of lives behind bars with the temporariness of our sympathy and the self-satisfaction of our gestures. In their sickness and loneliness, by their tears and smiles, they open our blind eyes. *Amen*

Alison Evans
writing about
Cochabamba, Bolivia

I believe in you God
Who created woman and man in your own image
Who created the world
And gave both sexes the care of the earth.

I believe in Jesus
Child of God Chosen of God
Born of the woman Mary
Who listened to women and liked them.
Who stayed in their homes
Who discussed the Kingdom with them
Who was followed and financed
By women disciples.

I believe in Jesus
Who discussed theology with a woman at a well
And first confided in her his messiahship
Who encouraged her to go and tell
Her great news to the city.

I believe in Jesus who healed
A woman on the Sabbath
And made her straight
Because she was a human being.

I believe in Jesus
Who thought of pregnancy and birth
With reverence
Not as punishment
As a wrenching event
A metaphor for transformation
Born again
Anguish – into – joy.

I believe in Jesus
Who spoke of himself
As a mother hen
Who would gather her chicks
Under her wing.

I believe in Jesus
Who appeared first to Mary Magdalene
Who sent her with the bursting message
GO AND TELL . . .

I believe in the wholeness
Of the Saviour
In whom there is neither
Jew nor Greek,
Slave nor free,
Male nor female
For we are all one in salvation.
Amen.

The Women's Creed

When the hour comes,
you shall change my desert into a waterfall,
you shall anoint my head with fresh oil
and your strength shall overcome
my weakness.

You shall guide my feet into your footsteps
and I will walk the narrow path
that leads to your house.

You shall tell me when
and where
I will walk your path
totally bathed in joy.
In the meantime,
I ask you, Lord, you who awaken
in the most intimate place in my soul
the feast of Life!
That of the empty tomb!
That of the victorious Cross!

Let your voice mistaken as the gardener's
awaken my hearing every morning
with news that's always fresh:
'Go and tell my brothers
that I have overcome death,
that there is a place for everyone,

there where the New Nation is built.
There,
where neither earth, love or joy
can be bought or sold,
where wine and milk
are shared without money
and without price.'

Julia Esquivel
Threatened with Resurrection

One stayed behind,
   Magdalene. Was it tears that made her blind?
She told us later that she had to stay
Close to the place where her beloved lay.
So she was first to meet him,
To undo the traitor's kiss and greet him.
We thought it right
She should be chosen for delight.
But, when she told the men,
Incredulous, as of us, they jeered and then
Ran off to see for themselves.
The rest is told.

But just remember: men recount the story,
We women were the first to see the glory.

Joan Smith
Celebrating Women

Sunday for the Unemployed
(Sunday before 1st Sunday of Lent)

That night, when I recorded my voice for a final greeting to the diocese, it was the only time in eight years when I cried, and cried bitterly!

Then the tribulations in Saigon, the arrest; I am led back to my first diocese in Nhatrang, in the hardest captivity, so close to bishop's residence. Morning and evening in the darkness of my cell I hear the bells of the Cathedral where I spent eight years, and they tear at my heart; at night I hear the waves of the sea in front of my cell . . .

Many times I was tempted, tormented by the fact that I am 48 years old, the age of maturity; I have worked as a bishop for eight years, I have acquired much pastoral experience, and here I am isolated, inactive, separated from my people . . .

One night, I heard a voice prompting me from the depths of my heart: 'Why do you torment yourself so? You have to distinguish between God and God's works. Everything you have done and want to continue doing . . . all these are excellent works, God's works, but they are not God! If God wants you to abandon all these works, putting them in his hands, do it immediately, and have confidence in him. God will do it infinitely better than you; he will entrust his works to others who are much more capable than you. You have chosen God alone, not his works!'

While I find myself in the prison of Phu-Khanh, in a cell without windows, it is extremely hot; I am suffocating; I feel my lucidity lessen bit by bit until I am unconscious; at times the light is left on day and night, at times it is always dark; it is so humid that mushrooms grow on my bed. In the darkness

I saw a hole in the bottom of the wall (to let the water run
out): so I spent one hundred days on the ground, putting my
nose in front of the hole so as to breathe.

To choose God and not God's works: God wants me here
and nowhere else.

When the communists load me into the hull of the ship
Hai-Phong with another 1500 prisoners to be transported
north, seeing the desperation, the hate, the desire for revenge
on the faces of those held under arrest, I share their suffering,
but immediately this voice calls out to me again: 'Choose God
and not God's works,' and I say to myself: 'In truth, Lord,
here is my cathedral.'

Archbishop Nguyen Van Thuan
Five Loaves and Two Fish

St Perpetua and St Felicity,
7 March

Arrested were some young catechumens: Revocatus and Felicitas (both servants), Saturninus, Secundulus, and Vibia Perpetua, a young married woman about twenty years old, of good family and upbringing. She had a father, mother, two brothers (one was a catechumen like herself), and an infant son at the breast. The following account of her martyrdom is her own, a record in her own words of her perceptions of the event.

'Then my brother said to me, "Dear sister, you already have such a great reputation that you could ask for a vision indicating whether you will be condemned or freed." Since I knew that I could speak with the Lord, whose great favours I had already experienced, I confidently promised to do so. I said I would tell my brother about it the next day. Then I made my request and this is what I saw.

'There was a bronze ladder of extraordinary height reaching up to heaven, but it was so narrow that only one person could ascend at a time. Every conceivable kind of iron weapon was attached to the sides of the ladder: swords, lances, hooks, and daggers. If anyone climbed up carelessly or without looking upwards, he/she would be mangled as the flesh adhered to the weapons. Crouching directly beneath the ladder was a monstrous dragon who threatened those climbing up and tried to frighten them from ascent.

'Saturninus went up first. Because of his concern for us he had given himself up voluntarily after we had been arrested. He had been our source of strength but was not with us at the time of the arrest. When he reached the top of the ladder he turned to me and said, "Perpetua, I'm waiting for you, but be careful not to be bitten by the dragon." I told him that in the name of Jesus Christ the dragon could not harm me. At this the dragon slowly lowered its head as though afraid of me. Using its head as the first step, I began my ascent.

'At the summit I saw an immense garden, in the centre of which sat a tall, grey-haired man dressed like a shepherd, milking sheep. Standing around him were several thousand white-robed people. As he raised his head he noticed me and said, "Welcome, my child." Then he beckoned me to approach and gave me a small morsel of the cheese he was making. I accepted it with cupped hands and ate it. When all those surrounding us said "Amen," I awoke, still tasting the sweet cheese. I immediately told my brother about the vision, and we both realized that we were to experience the sufferings of martyrdom. From then on we gave up having any hope in this world.'

The day of their victory dawned, and with joyful countenances they marched from the prison to the arena as though on their way to heaven. If there was any trembling it was from joy, not fear. Perpetua followed with quick step as a true spouse of Christ, the darling of God, her brightly flashing eyes quelling the gaze of the crowd. Felicitas too, joyful because she had safely survived child-birth and was now able to participate in the contest with the wild animals, passed from one shedding of blood to another: from midwife to gladiator, about to be purified after child-birth by a second baptism.

The Martyrdom of Perpetua

Ash Wednesday

Whether I fly with angels, fall with dust,
    Thy hands made both, and I am there;
Thy power and love, my love and trust,
    Make one place ev'rywhere.

George Herbert

When the signs of age begin to mark my body (and still more when they touch my mind); when the ill that is to diminish me or carry me off strikes from without or is borne within me; when the painful moment comes in which I suddenly awaken to the fact that I am ill or growing old; and above all at that last moment when I feel I am losing hold of myself and am absolutely passive within the hands of the great unknown forces that have formed me; in all those dark moments, O God, grant that I may understand that it is you (provided only my faith is strong enough) who are painfully parting the fibres of my being in order to penetrate to the very marrow of my substance and bear me away within yourself.

Pierre Teilhard de Chardin
Le Milieu Divin

I've been giving more thought to the immortality of the soul. Plainly its immortality derives from the fact that the monad (that is to say the world) has gathered itself into a definitive centre *in us*. But by what sign do we recognize that this organic phenomenon has taken place? Obviously by our power of

reflection and idealization. But – and I become more and more
convinced of it – there is another sign. If the person did not
continue, then our inner and most priceless work would
become vain, we wouldn't have sufficient motive for action,
and the prospect of death would be intolerable. The double
burden of (1) our action, the human task, to be pursued, and
(2) the prospect of death, can only be countenanced for a
conscious, reflective being if the soul is immortal. In this way
immortality and reflections go hand in hand, not only by meta-
physical or physical necessity but by moral necessity. A universe
in which reflection were to appear without immortality would
be not only absurd but, which is almost more serious, hateful.

Pierre Teilhard de Chardin
Letters to Léontine Zanta

'By the sweat of your face
   you shall eat bread
until you return to the ground,
   for out of it you were taken;
you are dust,
   and to dust you shall return.'

Genesis 3:19

Meditation on the third station of the cross:
Jesus falls for the first time

Eat dirt.
   We all like to see the mighty fallen
Don't we?
So, here's God in the dust.

Except,
Crumpled and tumbled beneath his cross,

He resembles nothing so much
As a child.

Grown-ups don't fall down, do they?
Well, not often.
Not unless they are
Drunk;
Crippled;
Down and out;
Mugged;
Starved;
Queer-bashed;
Frail;
Raped;
Stoned;
Or
Plain suicidal.

He's there in all those of course.

Dear Jesus of the gutter I cannot forget
It was Roman feet you saw,
Ready to kick you onwards.
Just as later, your sisters and brothers
Would see jack-boots
In Auschwitz.

So,
It's hard to watch you squirm,
Debased,
Degraded,
Filthy,
Beneath your cross.

But where and how else could we understand
Your solidarity
With
The dispossessed?

Sylvia Sands

I n meat and drink be thou scarce and wise. Whiles thou eatest and drinkest, let not the memory of thy God that feeds thee pass from thy mind; but praise, bless, and glorify him in ilka morsel, so that thy heart be more in God's praising than in thy meat, that thy soul be not parted from God at any hour. . . .

Doubtless the virtue of charity surpasses without comparison all fasting or abstinence, and all other works that may be seen; and oft it happens that he that before men is seen least to fast, within, before Christ, is more fervent in love.

Richard Rolle

D id you ever hear his whisper who offered you the pleasant bread of temptation when God had bidden you tread the lonely wilderness of self-denial with its hard stones and heart-emptying hunger? Why forbid yourself one harmless indulgence? What harm will it do? Be a little kinder to yourself. You need not give up the spirit in order to mind the flesh a little. The bread will help you over the stones. Stop cutting off that right hand; at least leave three fingers on it; do not maim yourself; you can have the hand and the Kingdom. . . .

Did you ever heed that voice of the Tempter? Did you ever take the matter into consideration instead of felling him with a pebble from the brook of God, the divine Word? Ah me, for the saints of God who are pinioned and powerless, because of some secret compact with the adversary of souls; the redeemed of the Lord who are bondsmen because they allow themselves some little gratification about which they are not sure, about which they cannot be happy!

R. W. Barbour

1st Sunday of Lent

B ecause of their one attachment to the food and fleshmeat they had tasted in Egypt, the children of Israel were unable to get any taste out of the delicate bread of angels – the manna of the desert, which, as Scripture says, contained all savours and was changed to the taste each one desired. Similarly the spirit, still affected by some actual or habitual attachment or some particular knowledge or any other apprehension, is unable to taste the delights of the spirit of freedom.

The reason is that the affections, sentiments, and apprehensions of the perfect spirit, because they are divine, are of another sort and are so eminent and so different from the natural that their actual and habitual possession demands the annihilation and expulsion of the natural affections and apprehensions; for two contraries cannot co-exist in one subject.

Hence, that the soul pass on to these grandeurs, this dark night of contemplation must necessarily annihilate it first and undo it in its lowly ways by putting it in darkness, dryness, conflict, and emptiness. For the light imparted to the soul is a most lofty divine light which transcends all natural light and which does not belong naturally to the intellect.

St John of the Cross
The Dark Night

Lord, am I losing my mind?
Or is this what you want?
It would not matter, except that I am alone, I am alone.
You have taken me far, Lord; trusting I followed you,
And you walked by my side.
And now, at night, in the middle of the desert,
Suddenly you have disappeared.
I call, and you do not answer.
I search, and I do not find you.
I left everything, and now am left alone,
Your absence is my suffering.
Lord, it is dark.

Lord, are you here in my darkness?
Where are you, Lord?
Do you love me still?
Or have I wearied you?
Lord, answer,
Answer.
It is dark.

Michel Quoist

1st week of Lent

L ord Christ,
help us to have the courage and humility to name our
  burdens
and lay them down
so that we are light to walk across the water
to where you beckon us . . .

The memory of hurts and insults,
driving us to lash out,
to strike back
We name it
and we lay it down.
Our antagonism against those
whose actions, differences, presence,
threaten our comfort or security
We name it
and we lay it down . . .

We do not need these burdens,
but we have grown used to carrying them,
have forgotten what it is like to be light.

Beckon us to lightness of being,
for you show us it is not unbearable.
Only so can we close the distance
Only so can we walk upon the water.

It is so.

Blessed are you, Lord Christ, who makes heavy burdens light.

Kathy Galloway, Iona Community

We grieve and confess
  that we harm and have been harmed,
to the third and fourth generations,
that we are so afraid of pain
that we shield ourselves from being vulnerable to others,
and refuse to be open and trusting as a child . . .

O God of Wholeness, we rest in you . . .
You listen with us to the sound of running water,
you sit with us under the shade of the trees of our healing,
you walk once more with us in the garden in the cool of the
  day,
the oil of your anointing penetrates the cells of our being,
the warmth of your hands touches us kindly, steadies us and
  gives us courage.
O God of Wholeness, we rest in you . . .

We have injured your love:
  Binder of wounds, heal us.
We stumble in the darkness:
Light of the world, transfigure us.
We forget that we are your home:
Spirit of God, dwell in us.

O God of Joy, we rejoice in you . . .
You run to meet us like a welcoming friend,
you laugh with us in the merriment of heaven,
you feast with us at the great banquet,
Clown of clowns, Fool of fools,
the only Entertainer of Jesters.
O God of Joy, we rejoice in you . . .

Jim Cotter
Prayer at Night's Approaching

St Patrick's Day,
17 March

Prayer of St Patrick

May the strength of God pilot us.
May the power of God preserve us.
May the wisdom of God instruct us.
May the hand of God protect us.
May the way of God direct us.
May the shield of God defend us.
May the host of God guard us
against the snares of the evil one
and the temptations of the world.
May Christ be with us
Christ above us
Christ in us
Christ before us.
May your salvation, O Lord, be always ours
This day and for evermore.

Prayer of Thanksgiving

For those who throughout the years have laboured for reconciliation, for those who have put their lives at risk in the
cause of peace, for those who have ministered the gospel in all
Churches, for them all we give you thanks. Their heroic courage and their persistent endeavour have filled us with new
courage.

The Lord's Prayer (adapted out of the Troubles in Northern Ireland)

Our Father, who art in Heaven, hallowed be thy name. Thy Kingdom come. Thy will be done, on earth as it is in Heaven. Give us this day our daily bread. And forgive our trespasses, as we have forgiven those who trespass against us. For if we haven't, there isn't much point going any further. But if we have then we dare ask for two great favours: to be delivered from all evil and to learn to live together in peace. *Go naofar D'ainm.* For thine is the Kingdom, the Power and the Glory for ever and ever. Amen.

A Prayer for Continued Peace in Ireland

Lord Jesus Christ,
You are the way of peace,
Come into the brokenness of this land
With your healing love.
Help us to be willing to bow before you
In true repentance
And to bow to one another
In real forgiveness.
By the fire of your Holy Spirit
Melt our hard hearts and consume
The pride and prejudice
Which separate us from each other.
Fill us, O Lord, with your perfect love
Which casts out fear,
And bind us together in that unity
Which you share with the Father
And the Holy Spirit forever. Amen.

Prayers for peace in Northern Ireland

2nd Sunday of Lent

Epiphany at the Bay of Bengal

Words won't take you very near, my love,
But somehow I would have you know
How I have been transfigured.

Rapt and speechless on the seashore
I've sat many times before,
but this was otherwise.

Time melted:
I can't place when the world split open
And I fell inside.
One moment I was, as you know me,
Vague and moony and alone
Then suddenly I saw, and knew
What I had only read before
That all's one
And ripeness is all.

Hurt with awe
I loved and sang
And mutely cried
As the waves washed my feet in moonlight.

In that persistent moment
The whole world hung against my heart.
Sharp and beautiful,
It drove home deep inside me.
Once pierced, there's no forgetting.

Over and gone now,
But still the buried ache
Coaxes out a prayer
Not to be healed of that wound,
Never to relent from offering
The hard love that suffers into flower.

Michael Woodward

The transfiguring of pain, of knowledge, and of the world is attested in centuries of the experience of Christians. It comes neither by an acceptance of things as they are nor by a flight from them, but by that uniquely Christian attitude which the story of the transfiguration represents. It is an attitude which is rooted in detachment – for pain is hateful, knowledge is corrupted, and the world lies in the evil one – but which so practises detachment as to return and perceive the divine sovereignty in the very things from which the detachment has had to be. Thus the Christian life is a rhythm of going and coming; and the gospel narrative of the ascent of Hermon, the metamorphosis and the descent to a faithless and perverse generation, is a symbol of the mission of the Church in its relation to the world . . .

Confronted as they are with a universe more than ever terrible in the blindness of its processes and the destructiveness of its potentialities, human beings must be led to the Christian faith not as a panacea of progress nor as an other-worldly solution unrelated to history, but as a gospel of transfiguration.

Michael Ramsey
To Believe is to Pray

2nd week of Lent

When I was growing up I used to spend my summers in my grandfather's home in Kilkenny, Southern Ireland. My father was part of a very large family indeed and it would not be unusual to find myself as just one of thirty or thirty-five grandchildren there. If the evenings were wet we would all sit round in a circle, and my grandfather would recite stories of his life. One of those stories has remained with me ever since.

About thirty years ago now, my grandfather travelled to New York to nurse my ill uncle, Jim. He spent about three months there, but for him it was a massive step, to move from a quiet rural farm to the fast moving city. He never really adjusted to the roads moving in a different direction, or to buildings that stretched as far as the eye could see, to bright lights or strange noises.

One day, late in the evening, he travelled into New York to do some shopping, but when walking back to catch the bus everything went dark, pitch black in fact. It took him a few moments to realize that there had been a power cut, and there he was stranded in the middle of the city. There he was sur-rounded by children wailing, women crying, horns beeping – a torrent of confusion and chaos. My grandfather stood trem-bling – how could he possibly cross a road safely without the help of traffic lights? And yet the longer he remained there the more the risk of being attacked increased.

It was then that someone took his arm, and asked where he lived. My grandfather replied giving the name of the street. The man began to lead him into the chaos. They walked up and down subways, safely crossed roads, passed by all signs of danger. When at last they arrived my grandfather said:

'I don't understand. How have you been able to walk through all this?'

'But this is what I do every night,' the man replied.

You see, he was blind. And being blind he was unaffected by the darkness and the panic, and continued safely home as usual . . .

If you like Jesus is the blind man, leading the despairing from their situation of turbulence and chaos, and fright, to their home which is a place of peace, happiness and fulfilment and of knowing him . . . So I suppose the central message of all this is one of trust, of grasping into the dark, and hoping on when no hope remains. To the world, following a crucified messiah, the lowest of the low, and proclaiming him to be God himself may seem incredible. Even as incredible, I imagine, as following a blind man.

Clare Brennan

Lent Fast Day

Live slowly, think slowly, for time is a mystery.
Never forget that love requires always
that you be the greatest person you
are capable of being.

Be grateful for the manifold
dreams of creation
and the many ways of the unnumbered peoples.

Be grateful for life as you live it
and may a wonderful light
always guide you on the unfolding road.

                                        Ben Okri
                                        Nigeria

Come Lord,
do not smile and say
you are already with us.
Millions do not know you,
and to us who do,
what is the difference?
What is the point of your presence
if our lives do not alter?
Change our lives,
shatter our complacency.
Make your world our life's purpose.
Take away the quietness
of a clear conscience.

Press us uncomfortably.
For only thus
is that other peace made,
your peace.

                    Dom Helder Camara
                              Brazil

L ead us from death to life,
  from falsehood to truth.
Lead us from despair to hope,
from fear to trust.
Lead us from hate to love,
from war to peace.
Let peace fill our hearts,
our world, our universe.
Let us dream together
pray together,
work together,
to build one world
of peace and justice
for all.

                    Satish Kumar
                          India
            All from *They shall not rob*
                      us of hope

I t was agreed in December 1974 that, after twenty years at
  Worth and ten at Downside, I should go to Peru. I, who for
so long had preached the needs of the Third World, could
hardly say, whatever the state of my love life, that I did not
want to go. Whether the abbot or the headmaster (whom I
had not kept in ignorance of my wandering course) thought a

new start was what I needed, I do not know, but certainly there was need for change in our Peruvian jungle monastery and at forty-five I was not too old to take part. 'Did I want to go?' That is not a question one should ask me . . .

What is happening is that I am gradually stepping back into the real world again, with all its struggle between people, and I realize that what I have avoided for so long, the purpose for which I built the craft in the first place, has a name and is something many of us stylish intellectual people hate so much. It is *poverty*.

It is not a Third World I step into willingly. Too many names buzz through my head: Shakespeare, Arbuthnott, Knowles, Downside, Worth, Dominic, those two special women friends. But bit by bit, I am going to step into this world and leave the rest behind. If necessary, I may have to leave a wreck on the shore, perhaps with a few survivors. I wonder whether I can ever return to those shells, those so English structures, I left behind those years ago?

I have taken off my sixteenth-century monastic costume because I cannot meet poor men, ordinary men in a real world, dressed like a sober character in *Star Wars*. . . This is not the time to finger the theological frets, not the time to dawdle amid flying buttresses, nor the time to waste polishing up the intellectual fingernails of the public-school rich. A monastic life that does not have the compassion to share with the poor man, with Jesus of Nazareth, is a medieval sham. I know that our Benedictine prayer must be remade out of a common experience of poverty, out of a new need for music and joy amid hunger. In the end the poor men, the Nazarenes, will do it themselves without much help from us, the rich; but it is a great honour to get near to Christ, to see him at his wood, to watch him sweat and to hear the hammer on the nails.

So you love being in Peru? No; it's awful.

Fabian Glencross
in *A Touch of God: eight monastic journeys*

L ord, you are the light of the world.
Give light to those who walk in darkness
And guide our feet in the ways of peace.
Lord, you are the light of the world.
Forgive us when we deny the light,
ignoring the cries of the poor,
the despair of those homeless;
Give light to those who walk in darkness
And guide our feet in the ways of peace.
Lord, you are the light of the world.
Forgive us when we shut our eyes to the light,
when we are fearful and forget to trust you;
when we go our own way:
Give light to those who walk in darkness
And guide our feet in the way of peace.
Lord, you are the light of the world.
Forgive us when we refuse to light a candle in the darkness,
when we harden our hearts towards our sisters and brothers;
when we refuse to bring them into your light.
Give light to those who walk in darkness
And guide our feet in the way of peace.

The mystery of your love:
The unthinkable, unutterable
unbearable mystery of your love;
The sweetness of your mercy:
The impossible sweetness of your mercy;
The beauty of your holiness:
The harmony and symmetry,
the dazzling radiance of your holiness;
The generosity of your grace:
The unstinting, unsparing,
giving of your grace;

The tenderness of your compassion:
  The balm, the loveliness of your compassion.
    Lord, how can we not love you
    more than all the rest?

Barbara d'Arcy
The Trampled Vineyard: worship resources on Housing and
Homelessness

Oscar Romero,
24 March

What of these last hundred years, as violent as any in history, which have produced more Christian martyrs than any other century? Next summer ten empty niches on the west front of the Abbey at Westminster will be filled with statues of those who have borne that ultimate witness amidst injustice, genocide and tyranny. Among them will be . . . Oscar Romero of San Salvador, gunned down at his morning Mass in 1980.

The question poses itself, again and again; what generates such eagerness to kill? What is it in the Christian witness that so troubles the men of power that they seek so cruelly to extirpate it? Can it be the message of the Scriptures, and their great injunction to recognize that the power of a Creator God is greater than that of Man; that the justice of men must be ultimately subject to the justice of God; and that having come a first time, to be born among the powerless, the Christ will come again in glory to judge both the living and the dead? Is it that even in the darkest recesses of the mind of the tyrant there is no place to hide from that all-seeing eye which, knowing of every fledgling that falls from the nest, has no difficulty in knowing what dreadful deeds are done in even the most secret of places? . . .

It is no coincidence that the martyrs of our time are increasingly found in what we call the Third World, where poverty and political oppression go often hand in hand; where the poor are poor beyond our ordinary experience, and where the Christian mission is no longer associated with colonial domination but is identified with the needs of the poor. Across the developing world, their hunger and thirst is not simply for food and fresh water, but for the justice that springs ever clear from the rock of God's righteousness. Small wonder, then, that among the prime targets of the death squads are those Christians who minister in the shanty towns and impoverished villages.

Terence Morris

A rchbishop Romero represents the parable of the rich man and Lazarus for our world today. Archbishop Romero through his option for the poor stands for Lazarus. He is the embodiment of all the poor and oppressed of the Third World . . .

He has died and has certainly been received into the bosom of Abraham.

He will not come back to us from the dead. But as he himself said, if he is killed he will rise up in the people of El Salvador. In fact, he will rise up in all the people of the Third World – the Third World abroad and the Third World in our own midst.

If we want to honour Archbishop Romero, there is only one way to do so – by listening to the voice of these people. For us today they are the voice of Moses and the prophets.

If we refuse to listen to their voice, which is the voice of God, we who make up the First World have no hope of becoming 'free'.

Our presence here tonight is a sign of hope. It is a sign that we want to listen, that we want to become free.

Kevin Kelly

Archbishop Oscar Romero was killed on 24 March 1980

Annunciation, 25 March

Lord, within me there is a new spark of life that even death cannot extinguish. I should be glad, Lord, yet I am afraid of what is to be. With this new life you have given me the gift of motherhood. Help me to be grateful, Lord, for this gift that you have given me is denied to many women. You have chosen me to be the mother of this child, yet I wish it had never happened. Help me to say like Mary: 'Be it done to me.'

Althea Hayton
Prayer in Pregnancy

The solemnity of the Lord's annunciation providentially interrupts the days of our Lenten observance, so that we are able to refresh ourselves with spiritual joy in the midst of the physical austerities which weigh so heavily on us. Having been humbled by penitential sorrow, we are now encouraged by the announcement of the one who takes away the sins of the world. This is just what Scripture says: 'Grief makes the heart heavy, but a kind word makes it glad.'

It is indeed a kind word, a reliable word in which you can believe, this gospel of our salvation which the angel sent by God announced to Mary on this day. It is a joyful word which day utters to day, the angel to the Virgin, concerning the incarnation of the Word. It promises a son to the Virgin, and at the same time pardon to sinners, redemption to captives, release to the imprisoned, life to those in the grave.

Guerric of Igny

The titles of Mary are many
and it is right that I should use them:
she is the palace where dwells
the mighty King of Kings;
not as he entered her did he leave her,
for from her he put on a body and came forth.
Again, she is the new heaven,
in which there dwells the King of Kings;
he shone out in her and came forth into creation,
formed and clothed in her features.
She is the stem of the cluster of grapes,
she gave forth fruit beyond nature's means,
and he, though his nature bore no resemblance to hers,
put on her hue and came forth from her.
She is the spring, whence flowed
living water for the thirsty,
and those who have tasted its draught
give forth fruit a hundred fold.

St Ephraim the Syrian
A homily on the nativity

3rd Sunday of Lent

I am the guardian of a well. It is not my well, for the water was there long before I discovered it and it will remain long after I've been forgotten. The water flows deep down and I stand by the well, day after day, clanking away at the handle, to lower the bucket into the living water. It is God's water, life-giving and sweet, offered to anyone who thirsts, even to Samaritans. (John 4)

Strangers and travellers, tired and thirsty, come to the well in search of water. It is an oasis in their desert. Many are led to the water by their friends, sometimes by their teachers or guides. And when I see them coming, I call out like Isaiah:

'*Oh, come to the waters, all you who thirst!*
Though you have no money, come!
Listen, listen to me and you will have good things to eat and
*   rich food to enjoy.*
Pay attention, come to me, listen and your soul will live . . .
And you will draw water joyfully from the springs of
*   salvation.*' Isaiah 55 & 12

Sometimes the pilgrims come running and shouting, eager to drink and splash about. And they will share food together, joyfully singing songs and exchanging stories about the way. Their stories celebrate life and often carry warnings, encouragement and questions.

Not all the pilgrims are eager. There are travellers who drag themselves painfully, hesitantly, to the well. They have been misled in the past, or they have lost their way. Some have drunk bitter waters from poisoned wells or have been let down by old familiar wells which dried up unexpectedly. No wonder they are disillusioned and suspicious of what they may find here. But they are thirsty. Their wounds must be washed clean in the healing water, their tired feet rested, their spirits raised before they resume the journey across the desert. What can I do to look after them all? I invite them to minister to one another, wearing the apron of love. They do this gladly and effectively.

The time passes, and before they leave, sometimes with tears in their eyes, I tell them where other wells are to be found. They carry with them for the journey bottles filled with water. It will need to be replaced. Above all, it must be shared with other travellers. If it is not given away it evaporates. And the more you give away, the more you have and the thirstier you become.

Damian Lundy

3rd week of Lent

I was to live among the Chinese, Hakka people of Sandakan in North Borneo for many years. Their Buddhist religion has always meant a lot to me.

A Buddhist monk was once asked: 'What is sin?' Very often in the East, a question is answered by a question, it is part of their wisdom, a result of deep meditation. The monk asked the pupil to open his hands wide open. 'What can you do with your open hands?' The reply was: 'I can arrange flowers, embrace a loved one, work and in general do all manner of things.' All beautiful things he thought to himself. Then the monk went on: 'Now, close your hands slowly, starting with each finger. What have you now? What can you do?'

The pupil did as he was told and stared at his two fists. He realized the terrible things he could do and finally said: 'I can hurt, injure, even kill someone.' 'That,' said the Buddhist monk, 'is what sin is.'

When you think about this story, it's very much what Jesus said in the Gospels.

People who are like the open hands, open people who can only love, do beautiful things. They are people who are concerned and aware of the needs of others; they are helpful people. On the other hand, closed people cut themselves off from others. They are selfish, they can hate. They sulk, harbour grudges and are vindictive, like the closed hand, they can only hurt, even kill those near them, their family and friends.

The Chinese call the priest a *Sin-fu*, holy one, which labels a priest in people's expectation. It can be very demanding living up to these expectations because a priest is human too ... What a title to live up to and be faithful to. I often think to myself, where do people get so grandiose an idea of the priest?

I remember climbing a tortuous mountain road in the interior of Brazil, in my little 'Beetle', the Volkswagen. Hugging the mountain side, I was always conscious of a 200-foot drop on the other side, if I deviated too much. Then, horror of horrors, the one nightmare that cannot happen as you climb a dusty, narrow mountain road: a lorry approaching on its way down. Obviously we both stopped.

The first to descend was the lorry driver who approached and looked at me before asking: 'Are you Padre Pedro?' 'Yes,' thinking that there would be understanding and some sort of privilege being a priest. Perhaps the lorry driver would negotiate the difficult passage first and allow me the freedom of a safe upward journey. Unworthy of me, I know, but the reply took my breath away. 'Look, Padre,' he explained, 'if you fall over the precipice you will go to heaven. If I go over the top, I will go to hell, so you negotiate the manoeuvre first.' He helped me as, sweating profusely, I managed to pass his lorry and not fall 200 feet into oblivion.

Peter Windram
Priest

4th Sunday of Lent
(Mothering Sunday)

I sense a strong and all-prevailing spirit rising in me to replace this mother Church I have lost. I have been touched by the image of God as Mother. This morning I prayed that Mother God will show her face to me. God has planned a future full of hope. God waits for my response – God is my Mother who gives the gift of life freely.

But I must call, I must seek – then God will listen and I will find her. Much of the action comes from me. God waits, like a mother waiting for her child to be born, while the new life turns in the womb. I am excited. I experience joy because I am being called to give birth. I am called to be creative as God is creative. I, who have received, must now bring forth new life.

I remember, last week, rescuing a baby chipmunk from the cats. I held the tiny thing in my hand – it was all wet and trembling – its mouth was open in fear and its eyes were wide and beautiful . . .

I have thought of it often since then. I feel like the chipmunk. Maybe that is how God experiences me as she holds me in the palm of her hand. Her love is far deeper than I could have felt as I held the chipmunk. I am in her hands – longing to allow her to love me – but still kicking and biting.

Edwina Gateley

In the attic at home my mother had a big chest. Inside she kept all the little treasures that were so precious and meaningful to her: ribbons, a teapot, some china that was a wedding gift, a baptismal dress and so on. One day she called me upstairs. The chest was open and you could see she was looking for something. Finally, she handed me a little shoe. Then she found another and another, four in all. Each one was just a little bit bigger than the other. 'These were your first pair of shoes,' she said with an indescribable look of pleasure and joy on her face. It was almost as if she was reliving the moment when she gave them so many years before. She was now 82 years of age. I was completely overwhelmed . . . I looked down and held those little shoes in my hands. I was filled with a tremendous sense of mystery and wonder at the thought of my little feet and all the steps I had taken since then. The endless journeys to school each day and then round and round the playground, the entry and the block so blissfully unaware, just playing. Leaving home and growing up. Away from all those early classmates and friends in the same street with whom I had lived for so many years.

John Shevlin

For are you not my mother and more than my mother? The mother who bore me laboured in delivering me for one day or one night, but you, my sweet and lovely Lord, laboured for me for more than thirty years. Ah . . . with what love you laboured for me and bore me through your whole life. But when the time approached for you to be delivered, your labour pains were so great that your holy sweat was like great drops of blood that came out from your body and fell on the earth . . . When the hour of your delivery came, you were placed on the hard bed of the cross . . . and your nerves and all your veins were broken. And truly it is no surprise that your veins burst when in one day you gave birth to the whole world.

Marguerite d'Oingt

4th week of Lent

An Hymn to God the Father

Wilt thou forgive that sin where I begun,
   Which is my sin, though it were done before?
Wilt thou forgive those sins through which I run,
   And do them still, though still I do deplore?
When thou hast done, thou hast not done,
   For I have more.

Wilt thou forgive that sin by which I won
   Others to sin? And made my sin their door?
Wilt thou forgive that sin which I did shun
   A year or two, but wallowed in a score?
When thou hast done, thou hast not done,
   For I have more.

I have a sin of fear, that when I have spun
   My last thread, I shall perish on the shore;
Swear by thyself, that at my death thy Sun
   Shall shine as it shines now, and heretofore;
And, having done that, thou hast done,
   I have no more.

John Donne

Judgement would hold nothing but terror for us if we had
no sure hope of forgiveness. And the gift of forgiveness itself
is implicit in God's and people's love. Yet it is not enough to

be granted forgiveness, we must be prepared to receive it, to accept it.

We must consent to be forgiven by an act of daring faith and generous hope, welcome the gift humbly, as a miracle which love alone, love human and divine, can work, and forever be grateful for its gratuity, its restoring, healing, reintegrating power.

We must never confuse forgiving with forgetting, or imagine that these two things go together. Not only do they not belong together, but they are mutually exclusive. To wipe out the past has little to do with constructive, imaginative, fruitful forgiveness; the only thing that must go, be erased from the past, is its venom; the bitterness, the resentment, the estrangement; but not the memory.

Metropolitan Anthony of Sourozh
Creative Prayer

Martin Luther King,
4 April

We have a dream.

I say to you today, my friends, that in spite of the difficulties, frustrations and fears of this moment, we still have a dream. It is a dream deeply rooted in our faith.

We have a dream that one day this nation will live out its Christian creed that all people are created one and equal in the Lord.

We have a dream that one day on the green hills of Drumcree the children of Orange and the children of Green will be able to sit down together at the table of unity.

We have a dream that one day even the town of Portadown, sweltering in the heat of mistrust and division, will be transformed into an oasis of community and togetherness.

We have a dream where *all* our children will one day live in a nation where they will not be judged by the beliefs of their community but by the content of their character.

We have a dream today.

We have a dream today, that one day our country will be transformed into a land where little Catholic boys and Catholic girls will be able to join hands with little Protestant boys and Protestant girls and walk together as sisters and brothers.

We have a dream today.

We have a dream that every valley shall be exalted, every hill and mountain laid low, the rough places will be made plains, and the crooked places will be made straight, and the glory of the Lord shall be revealed, and all people shall see it together.

This is our hope. This is the faith with which we will return to our homes. With this faith we will be able to make out of the mountains of despair a stone of hope.

With this faith, we will be able to transform the jangling discords of our country into a beautiful symphony of to-getherness.

With this faith we will be able to work together, to pray together, to struggle together.

And if our nation is to be a great nation this dream must become true.

We have a dream.

Catholic community of Portadown
adapted from Martin Luther King

Martin Luther King was assassinated on 4 April 1968

5th Sunday of Lent

We're none of us ready for death, we thrust it out of our consciousness; one of the most tragic things about so many funerals is not just the sense of shock at the terrible intruder, reminding everyone of their own mortality, but also the sense of lost time, of missed opportunities. We live as if we were immortal, but time is not on our side; by the time the funeral comes, it's too late to say, 'If only . . .' But the real problem of death concerns not sadness or a sense of loss, not even our own mortality; it is to do with the question that mortality asks us – what, after all, is this whole rigmarole about? Are we born to die, and does that inevitable death make all our achievements, our dreams, hopes, loves and longings of as much worth as an empty cigarette packet? At the end of the game, says the Spanish proverb, king and pawn go back into the same box.

Richard MacKenna
God for Nothing

Anyone is capable of going to heaven. Heaven is our home. People ask me about death and whether I look forward to it and I answer, 'Of course, because I am going home. Dying is not the end, it is just the beginning. Death is a continuation of life. This is the meaning of eternal life; it is where our soul goes to God, to be in the presence of God, to see God, to speak to God, to continue loving him with greater love because in Heaven we shall be able to love him with our whole heart and our soul because we only surrender our body in death – our heart and our soul live forever.

When we die we are going to be with God, and with all those we have known who have gone before us: our family and our friends will be there waiting for us. Heaven must be a beautiful place. Every religion has an eternity, another life. People who fear death are the ones who believe this is the end. I have not known anyone die in fear if they have witnessed the love of God. They have to make their peace with God, as do we all. People die suddenly all the time so it could happen to us too at any moment. Yesterday is gone and tomorrow has not yet come, so we must live each day as if it were our last, so that when God calls us we are ready, and prepared, to die with a clean heart.

Mother Teresa of Calcutta
A Simple Path

5th week of Lent

What words can I say today? What words can I say, that would not be better spoken by others? What words could I say, today, that would be worth the remembering?

'Daddy, I love you!' were the only words that I remember from another tragedy spoken by a girl called Marie Wilson, just before she died in the bomb blast at the war memorial in Enniskillen that Sunday morning in 1987. 'Daddy, I love you!' And she died in her father's arms. Few of us were not moved as her father recalled it on TV that night, after that dreadful massacre.

There were those who tried to whip up a reaction by saying it was time for Protestants to take the law into their own hands, and take a stand. But all the dark verbiage of their bigotry and bitterness was scattered by the tiny flicker of love in those simple words of Marie Wilson and the words of her father, that he forgave his daughter's killers . . .

What words can I say today? What words can I say, that would not be better spoken by others? What words could I say, today, that would be worth the remembering? Anything I say or anyone else says at this time, to those bereaved yesterday, to the parents who lost children, to the children who lost parents, and to those who lost friends, and to those who are still waiting and don't know . . . seems so weak and inappropriate and shallow that one is tempted to be silent in the presence of such grief.

Those words that we read from the Old Testament come to mind (Ecclesiastes 3:7): 'There is a time to keep silent, and a time to speak.' And if one must speak, what comes in to my mind are the words of the writer in the letter to the Hebrews. Hold on to Christ 'as an anchor of the soul, sure and steadfast'. For where there's Christ, there's hope.

That hope is no kind of sedative. It doesn't leave us in a rocking chair vainly waiting for things somehow 'to work out'. It comes to us on the front line where the battle can be fierce and the suffering intense and life can be very sore but where we will be held safe and enabled to go on even in the dark! . . .

Let us pray . . . We can only lisp the longings of our hearts, and the prayers that go out in love for those in pain, and sorrow, and grief. We lift them up in our prayers to you, and ask you, in your tender mercy, to deal kindly and gently with them.

Their grief is so great, and the hurt so intense, that we can only leave them in silence in your care. As the One who bore his only Son through the sorrow of Calvary, and who has unfailingly carried his children in troubled times, we bestow all those in tears this day, into your arms, and ask you, in your tender mercy, to bear them through these days, and in time, bless the memories of loved ones, gone, and those who still survive, and take them by the hand, and lead them tenderly through this dark valley.

The Revd Jim Frazer

Dietrich Bonhoeffer,
9 April

I have never regretted my decision in the summer of 1939 to return to Germany, for I'm firmly convinced – however strange it may seem – that my life has followed a straight and unbroken course, at any rate in its outward conduct. It has been uninterrupted enrichment of experience, for which I can only be thankful. If I were to end my life here in these conditions, that would have a meaning that I think I could understand.

Dietrich Bonhoeffer
From his last writings in prison

Please don't ever get anxious or worried about me, but don't forget to pray for me – I'm sure you don't. I am so sure of God's guiding hand that I hope I shall be kept in that certainty. You must never doubt that I'm travelling with gratitude and cheerfulness along the road where I'm being led. My past life is brimful of God's goodness, and my sins are covered by the forgiving love of Christ crucified. Forgive my writing this. Don't let it grieve or upset you for a moment, but let it make you happy. But I did want to say it for once, and I could not think of anyone else who I could be sure would take it aright.

Bonhoeffer's last letter to his friend Eberhard Bethge

I have had the experience over and over again that the quieter it is around me, the clearer do I feel the connection to you. It is as though in solitude the soul develops senses which we hardly know in everyday life. Therefore I have not felt lonely or abandoned for one moment. You must not think that I am unhappy. What is happiness and unhappiness? It depends so little on the circumstances. It depends really on that which happens inside a person. I am grateful every day that I have you, and that makes me happy.

Bonhoeffer's last letter to his fiancée, Maria Von Wedemeyer,
Christmas 1944

Through the half-open door in one room of the huts I saw Pastor Bonhoeffer, before taking off his prison garb, kneeling on the floor praying fervently to his God. I was most deeply moved by the way this lovable man prayed, so devout and so certain that God heard his prayer. At the place of execution, he again said a short prayer and then climbed the steps to the gallows, brave and composed. His death ensued after a few seconds. In almost fifty years that I worked as a doctor, I have hardly ever seen a man die so entirely submissive to the will of God.

Testimony of the Flossenburg prison doctor
All taken from
A Third Testament by Malcolm Muggeridge

Dietrich Bonhoeffer was executed on 9 April 1945

Palm Sunday

Come then, let us run with him as he presses on to his passion. Let us imitate those who have gone out to meet him, not scattering olive branches or garments or palms in his path, but spreading ourselves before him as best we can, with humility of soul and upright purpose. So may we welcome the Word as he comes, so may God who cannot be contained within any bounds, be contained within us.

For he is pleased to have shown us this gentleness, he who is gentle and who 'rides upon the setting sun', which refers to our extreme lowliness. He is pleased to come and live with us and to raise us up or bring us back to him through his kinship with us.

As the first fruits of the whole batch of man he is said to 'ride upon the heaven of heavens to the rising of the sun', which I interpret as his own glory and divinity. But because of his love for man he will not cease until he has raised man's nature from the ground, from one degree of glory to another, and has manifested it with himself on high.

So it is ourselves that we must spread under Christ's feet, not coats or lifeless branches or shoots of trees, matter which wastes away and delights the eye only for a few brief hours. But we have clothed ourselves with Christ's grace, or with the whole Christ – 'for as many of you as were baptized into Christ have put on Christ' – so let us spread ourselves like coats under his feet.

As those who were formerly scarlet from sin but became white as wool through the purification of saving baptism, let us offer not palm branches but the prizes of victory to the conqueror of death.

Today let us too give voice with the children to that

sacred chant, as we wave the spiritual branches of our soul: 'Blessed is he who comes in the name of the Lord, the King of Israel.'

Andrew of Crete

L et the mountains and all the hills
Break out into great rejoicing at the mercy of God,
And let the trees of the forest clap their hands.
Give praise to Christ, all nations,
Magnify him, all peoples, crying:
Glory to thy power, O Lord.

Seated in heaven upon thy throne
And on earth upon a foal, O Christ our God,
Thou hast accepted the praise of the angels
And the songs of the children who cried out to thee:
Blessed art thou that comest to call back Adam.

Orthodox hymn for Palm Sunday

W e are candles that only have meaning if we are burning, for only then do we serve our purpose of being light. Free us from the cowardly prudence that makes us avoid sacrifice and look only for security. Losing one's life should not be accompanied by pompous or dramatic gestures. Life is to be given simply, without fanfare, like a waterfall, like a mother nursing her child, like the humble sweat of the sower of seed. Train us, Lord, and send us out to do the impossible, because behind the impossible is your grace and your presence; we cannot fall into the abyss. The future is an enigma; our journey leads us through the fog; but we want to go on giving ourselves because you are waiting there in the night, in a thousand human eyes brimming over with tears.

Luis Espinal
in *Base Communities: an introduction*

The whole Church in El Salvador was becoming a prophetic, priestly Church. How many times we relived, in our flesh and history, the passion of our elder brother Jesus!

January 22 1980. Despite so many differences, the popular organizations had joined forces and had set up the Revolutionary Co-ordinating Committee of the Masses. This new oneness was a sign of the liberation to come, and so it was celebrated in the streets in the most gigantic rally El Salvador had ever seen. Jesus, who died 'that they may be one', made his triumphal entry into Jerusalem on this day.

This is how we saw it and felt it. His entry was simple, poor, and humble. On a donkey, you might say. The only 'triumphal entries' we had ever seen had been the big, showy parades when the military flaunted all its war material – big 'rallies' celebrating violence and oppression, and all the people were expected to cheer the empty, foolish speeches.

But today was different. This was truly Hosanna Sunday in El Salvador. This was the advance celebration of the liberation. This new popular oneness could mean only one thing: we were going to win. And so the young and the poor – in other words, the ever-downtrodden – took over the streets. This was popular triumph. Triumph, yes, but triumphalism it was surely not. In our very joy, we found the Cross. Poison rained down from the sky. Bullets ricocheted in the corners. Many, many people were killed or wounded. And yet, in spite of all their suffering, the priestly people of El Salvador grasped that this was their Palm Sunday celebration.

Pablo Galdámez
Faith of a People

Monday of Holy Week

The secret of my ministry is in that crucifix you see opposite my bed. It's there so I can see it in my first waking moment and before going to sleep. It's there also so that I can talk to it during the long night hours. Look at it, see it as I see it. Those open arms have been the programme of my pontificate: they say that Christ died for all, for all. No one is excluded from his love, from his forgiveness . . .

For my part, I'm not aware of having offended anyone, but if I have, I beg their forgiveness; and if you know anyone who has not been edified by my attitudes or actions, ask them to have compassion on me and to forgive me. In this last hour I feel calm and sure that my Lord, in his mercy, will not reject me. Unworthy though I am, I wanted to serve him, and I've done my best to pay homage to truth, justice, charity, and the meek and humble heart of the gospel.

My time on earth is drawing to a close. But Christ lives on and the Church continues his work. Souls, souls. *Ut unum sint! Ut unum sint!*

Pope John XXIII
as he received the last anointing

Once only in the year, yet once, does the world which we see show forth its hidden powers, and in a manner manifest itself. Then the leaves come out; and the blossoms on the fruit trees and flowers; and the grass and corn spring up. There is a sudden rush and burst outwardly of that hidden life which God has lodged in the material world. Well, that shows you as by a sample, what it can do at God's command, when he gives the word. This earth, which now buds forth in leaves and blossoms, will one day burst forth into a new world of light and glory, in which we shall see saints and angels dwelling. Who would think, except from his experience of former springs all through his life, who could conceive two or three months before, that it was possible that the face of nature, which then seemed so lifeless, should become so splendid and varied?

So it is with the coming of that eternal Spring for which all Christians are waiting. Come it will, though it delay; yet though it tarry, let us wait for it, 'because it will surely come, it will not tarry'.

Shine forth, O Lord, as when on the nativity thy angels visited the shepherds; let thy glory blossom forth as bloom and foliage on the trees. Bright as is the sun, and the sky, and the clouds; green as are the leaves and the fields; sweet as is the singing of the birds; we know that they are not all, and we will not take up with a part for the whole. They proceed from a centre of love and goodness, which is God himself; but they are not his fullness; they speak of heaven, but they are not heaven; they are but as stray beams and dim reflections of his image; they are but the crumbs from the table.

John Henry Newman
Parochial and Plain Sermons

Tuesday of Holy Week

F ive years ago I came to believe in Christ's teaching, and my life suddenly changed: I ceased to desire what I had previously desired, and began to desire what I formerly did not want. What had previously seemed to me good seemed evil, and what had seemed evil seemed good. It happened to me as it happens to a man who goes out on some business and on the way suddenly decides that the business is unnecessary and returns home. All that was on his right is now on his left, and all that was on his left is now on his right; his former wish to get as far as possible from home has changed into a wish to be as near as possible to it. The direction of my life and my desires became different, and good and evil changed places . . .

I, like that thief on the cross, have believed Christ's teaching and been saved. And this is no far-fetched comparison, but the closest expression of the condition of spiritual despair and horror at the problem of life and death in which I lived formerly, and of the condition of peace and happiness in which I am now. I, like the thief, knew that I had lived and was living badly . . . I, like the thief, knew that I was unhappy and suffering . . . I, like the thief to the cross, was nailed by some force to that life of suffering and evil. And as, after the mean-ingless sufferings and evils of life, the thief awaited the terrible darkness of death, so did I await the same thing.

In all this I was exactly like the thief, but the difference was that the thief was already dying, while I was still living. The thief might believe that his salvation lay there beyond the grave, but I could not be satisfied with that, because besides a life beyond the grave life still awaited me here. But I did not under-stand that life. It seemed to me terrible. And suddenly I heard

the words of Christ and understood them, and life and death
ceased to seem to me evil, and instead of despair I experienced
happiness and the joy of life undisturbed by death.

Count Leo Tolstoy
What I Believe

Wednesday of Holy Week

I know you through and through – I know everything about you. The very hairs of your head I have numbered. Nothing in your life is unimportant to me, I have followed you through the years, and I have always loved you – even in your wanderings.

I know every one of your problems. I know your needs and your worries. And yes, I know all your sins. But I tell you again that I love you – not for what you have or haven't done – I love you for you, for the beauty and dignity my Father gave you by creating you in his own image.

It is a dignity you have often forgotten, a beauty you have tarnished by sin. But I love you as you are, and I have shed my blood to win you back. If you only ask me with faith, my grace will touch all that needs changing in your life; and I will give you the strength to free yourself from sin and all its destructive power.

I know what is in your heart – I know your loneliness and all your hurts – the rejections, the judgements, the humiliations. I carried it all before you. And I carried it all for you, so you might share my strength and victory. I know especially your need for love – how you are thirsting to be loved and cherished. But how often have you thirsted in vain, by seeking that love selfishly, striving to fill the emptiness inside you with passing pleasures – with the even greater emptiness of sin. Do you thirst for love? 'Come to me all you who thirst' (John 7:37). I will satisfy you and fill you. Do you thirst to be cherished? I cherish you more than you can imagine to the point of dying on a cross for you.

I thirst for you. Yes, that is the only way to even begin to describe my love for you: *I thirst for you*. I thirst to love and to be loved by you – that is how precious you are to me. *I thirst for you.* Come to me, and I will fill your heart and heal your wounds . . .

If you feel unimportant in the eyes of the world, that matters not at all. For me, there is no one any more important in the entire world than you. *I thirst for you.* Open to me, come to me, thirst for me, give me your life – and I will prove to you how important you are to my heart . . .

No matter how far you may wander, no matter how often you forget me, no matter how many crosses you may bear in this life; there is one thing I want you to remember always, one thing that will never change: *I thirst for you* – just as you are. You don't need to change to believe in my love, for it will be your belief in my love that will change you. You forget me, and yet I am seeking you every moment of the day – standing at the door of your heart, and knocking.

Do you find this hard to believe? Then look at the cross, look at my heart that was pierced for you. Have you not understood my cross? Then listen again to the words I spoke there – for they tell you clearly why I endured all this for you: *I thirst* (John 19:28). Yes, I thirst for you – as the rest of the psalm verse I was praying says of me: 'I looked for love, and I found none' (Psalm 69: 20).

All your life I have been looking for your love – I have never stopped seeking to love and be loved by you. You have tried many other things in your search for happiness; why not try opening your heart to me, right now, more than you ever have before.

Whenever you do open the door of your heart, whenever you come close enough, you will hear me say to you again and again, not in mere human words but in spirit: 'No matter what you have done, I love you for your own sake.'

Come to me with your misery and your sins, with your trouble and needs, and with all your longing to be loved. I stand at the door of your heart and knock . . . Open to me, for *I thirst for you.*

Mother Teresa of Calcutta

Maundy Thursday

How could he have loved our feet? Under some aspects, Lord, the stuff we're made of isn't at all unpleasant – we even have beautiful and lovable parts ... Feet are miles away from their possessors' smiles, feet are rough wild animals, and looking at a foot makes it harder to believe in man's soul and easier to think we're just transitory puppets whose destiny is dissolution. Perhaps that's why the dead are all feet, they stick them out in front of them without any shame at all. And perhaps that's why the living hide these protuberances with a kind of instinctive modesty. As Peter said: '*You'll never wash my feet!*' O fisherman, it wasn't your zealous determination not to be done a service that made you cry out in protest, it was deep-seated: our feet, even if they can give a caress, even if they can make history with their ever-hopeful forward march, are dirty and ridiculous. Only our mothers could handle our feet without disgust.

And yet ... it's precisely through surrendering all our pride to the hands of Christ-as-mother, through identifying him bent over the bowl with her when she scrubbed us clean, that our salvation must pass. '*If I don't wash you, you'll have no part with me.*'

Let's all become mothers, creatures with no feelings of revulsion; because in Christ there's the mother-figure (as well as the master) and it's only by taking her as our example – just as it's only by becoming children again – that the Kingdom can become a reality.

Luigi Santucci
Wrestling with Christ

The Lord crucifies my wisdom and my will every way. But I must be crucified as the thieves. All my bones must be broken, for there is still in me that impatience with wisdom which would stir when the tempter says, 'Come down from the cross.' It is not for us to know the times and seasons, the manner and mystical means of God's working, but only to hunger and thirst and lie passive before the great Potter. In short, I begin to be content to be a vessel of clay and of wood, so I may be emptied of self and filled with my God, my all.

John Fletcher
Letter to Henry Brooke

The primary significance of the Eucharist isn't mystical but physical, almost a clinging to the material being of his friends who would stay on and live. He said 'This is my body' with a tenderness that first and foremost exulted in itself. Not 'This is my spirit' or 'This is generalized goodness or well-being' – possibly they wouldn't have known what to do with such things. It was necessary to them that he should remain with the only thing we really know and attach our hearts and memories to – the body; and that it should be a desirable, acceptable and homely body. That's why he looked over that tablecloth for the easiest, most familiar and most concrete thing: bread. So as to quench hunger and give pleasure. Above all so as to stay. That evening Christ measured out for us all the millions of evenings before we'd see him face to face; he measured out the long separation. He knew that men forget things within a few days, that distance destroys things, that it's useless for lovers to insert a lock of hair in letters that are going far away across land and sea. If Peter himself, and John and Andrew and James would forget, then in order that their children and their grandchildren's children shouldn't forget he

had to throw between himself and me that never-ending bridge
of bread. 'Do *this in memory of me*.'

Luigi Santucci
Wrestling with Christ

L ove bade me welcome: yet my soul drew back,
    Guiltie of dust and sin.
But quick-ey'd Love, observing me grow slack
    From my first entrance in,
Drew nearer to me, sweetly questioning,
    If I lacked any thing.

A guest, I answered, worthy to be here:
    Love said: You shall be he.
I the unkinde, ungratefull? Ah my deare,
    I cannot look on thee.
Love took my hand, and smiling did reply,
    Who made the eyes but I?

Truth Lord, but I have marr'd them: let my shame
    Go where it doth deserve.
And know you not, says Love, who bore the blame?
    My deare, then I will serve.
You must sit down, says Love, and taste my meat:
    So I did sit and eat.

George Herbert

At Easter we are close to the agony of Good Friday.
To the terrible humiliation of Jesus.
Scourged and crucified;
mocked and driven out,
as your children are hurt and humiliated still.

Yet that same agony flowered in joy.
The flower grew in the dark of the tomb
and burst apart the rock.
In taking bread and wine,
touching, breaking, pouring, drinking,
we know that we enter the holiest mystery
and that by doing so our hearts will be changed.

Jesus, on the night of betrayal, took bread,
gave thanks and broke it
and gave it to his friends, saying:
'Take and eat. This is my own body which
I surrender because of you.
Do the same to remember me.'

Then, after supper, he picked up the cup of wine,
Gave thanks for that and passed it around,
saying, 'Everyone drink of this.
This is my blood witnessing to a new understanding;
I spill it for you and for many more to cure the wounds of
    the spirit and to take away ignorance.
When you eat together, drink like this,
and remember what I say.'

At Easter, as at every Eucharist, we recall the days of Jesus'
    Passion, with wonder and love.
We ask you, God creator, to enter this action so that our
    hearts are moved to loving.

We only partly understand what we do, and we ask you to fill out our intention, that all who partake of this Easter feast may be completed in grace.

Glory be to you, and may a glimpse of that glory be allowed to us.

St Hilda Community
The New Women Included: a book of services and prayers

Good Friday

L ord O Lord my God
  why have you left me?
I am a caricature of a man
People think I am dirt
  they mock me in all the papers.

I am encircled
  there are tanks all round me
Machine-gunners have me in their sights
  there is barbed wire about me
  electrified wire
I am on a list
I am called all day
They have tattooed me
  and marked me with a number
They have photographed me behind the barbed wire
All my bones can be counted
  as on an X-ray film
They have stripped me of my identity
They have led me naked to the gas-chamber
They have shared out my clothes and my shoes
I call for morphine
  and no one hears me
In my straitjacket I cry out
I scream all night in the mental home
  in the terminal ward
  in the fever hospital
  in the geriatric ward
  in an agony of sweat in the psychiatric clinic
In the oxygen tent I suffocate

I weep in the police cell
  in the torture chamber
  in the orphanage
I am contaminated with radioactivity
  no one comes near me
  for I am contagious
Yet
I shall tell my brothers and sisters
  about you
I shall praise you in our nation
and my hymns will be heard
  in a great generation
The poor will go to a banquet
and our people will give a great feast
  the new people
     yet to be born

Ernesto Cardenal

Tortured Till Dead
For the crucified victims of repression

Mocked king clown,
  stag thorn-crowned,
carpenter's nails impale wrists and feet.
Stripped peasant,
powerless slave sold
for thirty silver pesos.

Back bled, skin flayed,
failed prophet
forgotten for all time,
writhes displayed.
Man's creation
bitter fruit on tree of damnation.

Heat, sweat, thirst,
shroud of darkness curse.
Yeshoua screams,
lungs burst
in deep, sea-deep
despair.

Head bows,
heart tears,
corpse slumps limp
into night's silent vault.

Thomas Greenan
Give Sorrow Words: poems from
El Salvador

One day when we came back from work, we saw three gallows rearing up in the assembly place; three black crows. Roll call. SS all round us, machine guns trained: the traditional ceremony. Three victims in chains – one of them, the little servant, the sad-eyed angel ... All eyes were on the child. He was lividly pale, almost calm, biting his lips. The gallows threw its shadow over him ... The three mounted together on to the chairs. The three necks were placed at the same moment within the nooses.

'Long live liberty!' cried the two adults. But the child was silent.

'Where is God? Where is he?' someone asked behind me.

At the sign from the head of the camp, the three chairs tipped over. There was total silence throughout the camp. On the horizon the sun was setting. 'Bare your heads!' yelled the head of the camp. His voice was raucous. We were weeping.

'Cover your heads!' The march past began. The two adults were no longer alive. Their tongues hung, swollen, blue-tinged. But the third rope was still moving; being so light, the child was still alive ... For more than half an hour he stayed there, struggling between life and death, dying in slow agony under our eyes. And we had to look him full in the face. He was still alive when I passed in front of him. His tongue was still red, his eyes were not glazed. Behind me, I heard the same man asking:

'Where is God now?'

And I heard a voice within me answer him: 'Where is he? Here he is. He is hanging here on this gallows.'

Elie Wiesel
Night

L isten . . . can you hear it? . . . it's the sound of the hillsides and fields of Rwanda where in their hundreds of thousands the dead lie silent.

Listen . . . it's the sound of fear in neighbouring Burundi where people are praying that the killing machetes will not come their way.

Listen . . . it's the stored up, concentrated silence of prisoners locked away for years for a thing they once thought, or believed, or were.

Listen . . . it's the only message there will ever be from the disappeared, snatched by death squads, never to be seen or heard from by their families again.

Listen . . . it's the silence of the small room after the torturers have left.

Listen . . . it's the silence in the councils of great nations when these difficult subjects are left unmentioned.

Listen . . . it's the silence of ordinary, decent people who think these things have nothing to do with them, and that they can do nothing to help.

Listen . . . deep inside yourself. What do you hear?

Break the silence.

Amnesty International
(banned radio advertisement)

'Surely he hath borne our griefs and carried our sorrows.'
Jesus became one with tortured humanity in the
darkness of the pain and loneliness of the crucifixion.
His words were twisted to suit the religious authorities'
political designs.
He was accused of actions he did not do.
He was tried and judged at the kangaroo court of Pilate.
He lost his dignity through the scourging and the jeering of
the soldiers.
He was led to the slaughter like a lamb.
He opened not his mouth in condemnation of his destroyers.
He became the innocent victim.

And so Jesus stands, wounded hands outstretched, with all
who are tortured;
with those who are deliberately and systematically torn
apart mentally by the vicious manipulations of
interrogators;
with those who are physically damaged, their wounds
unseen, by anonymous torturers.
He stands, wounded hands outstretched, with those racked
by fearful imaginings in solitary confinement;
with the anguished relatives of missing persons, presumed
dead;
with all innocent victims of institutional repression and
cruelty.

Andrew Wadsworth
both from *Words are not enough:
a resource pack for Christian Worship on the theme of torture*

The Agonie

Philosophers have measur'd mountains,
　Fathom'd the depths of seas, of states, and kings,
Walk'd with a staff to heav'n and trac'd fountains:
　But there are two vast, spacious things,
The which to measure it doth more behove:
Yet few there are that sound them: Sinne and Love.

　Who would know Sinne, let him repair
Unto Mount Olivet: there shall he see
A man so wrung with pains, that all his hair,
　His skinne, his garments bloudie be.
Sinne is that presse and vice, which forceth pain
To hunt his cruell food through ev'ry vein.

　Who knows not Love, let him assay
And taste that juice, which on the crosse a pike
Did set again abroach; then let him say
　If ever he did taste the like.
Love is that liquor, sweet and most divine,
Which my God feels as bloud; but I, as wine.

George Herbert

Holy Saturday

S oul of Christ, sanctify me.
Body of Christ, heal me.
Blood of Christ, inebriate me.
Water from the side of Christ, wash me.
Passion of Christ, strengthen me.

Good Jesus, hear me.

In your wounds shelter me.
From turning away keep me.
From the evil one protect me.
At the hour of my death call me.
Into your presence lead me,
to praise you with all your saints
for ever and ever.

Fourteenth-century prayer used
by St Ignatius of Loyola

I nto your hands, Lord,
This solitude,
Into your hands, Lord,
This emptiness.
Into your hands, Lord,
This loneliness.
Into your hands –
This all.
Into your hands, O Lord,
This grief.

Into your hands,
This sleeping fear.
Into your hands, O Lord –
What is left,
What is left
Of me.

St Hilda Community
*The New Women Included: a book
of services and prayers*

M y kind earth,
They cut your tongue,
But you didn't become silent,
You sang louder than before.

They cut your feet,
You became a stronger walker.
You are a volcano.

One day winter will pass.
Birds and flowers,
When the darkness of the night is dying,
when the sun of truth kisses the dawn,
when the morning star is laughing,
let the warmth of your hands,
your kind hands,
be a medicine on my wounds.

When the chill of the lash is settling on my soul,
when my friend is screaming with the pain,
of the hands of cruelty,
let our hope be in your name.

When the enemy's bullet settles in my loving heart,
as my blood is dripped from heart,
in the warmth of your hands

They will come with the spring,
Your flowers along with all the mothers will laugh.
I know it for sure.
All friends know it.
You will know it.
We are fire
and we will be free.

A client of the Medical Foundation for the
Care of Victims of Torture

Canto Grande in Peru is a shanty town in which about a
half million people live in the desert of dust and stone
north-east of Lima. Their dwellings consist of reed mats, cardboard, and remnants of plastic; there is no electricity and, what
is worse, no water. Nor are there any trees or bushes. In front
of a few huts I discovered flowers, planted in the desert sand,
watered, protected from the merciless sun. I had not known
that a sickly flower could stand for so much happiness or
express so much resistance.

During Holy Week a group of Christians followed the way
of the cross of Jesus' passion; they presented the stations of
his sufferings in simple street theatre.

A woman who works with a human rights group explains
that the cross of Christ consists of the many small crosses of
the very poor. The participants inscribe the crosses they have
to bear on small cardboard crosses: crosses of destitution, of
injustice, of egoism, of indifference. All these small crosses are
stuck on to the large wooden cross, which is now carried
jointly. Only when we carry the cross together and entrust it
to God can the many crosses be overcome . . .

Latin American Christians of our century have added to the
fourteen traditional stations of the cross, which came from
Spain, a fifteenth, which they call the resurrection. In Canto
Grande the many cardboard crosses are taken back down from

the wooden cross and replaced by white carnations as signs of the resurrection. The cross of hunger is replaced by the flower of sharing which takes place in the *comedores populares*, the kitchens for the poor, where mothers come together to prepare in common economical and nutritious meals for their children. The cross of injustice is replaced by the justice that the people demand on their protest marches, so that the officials will finally meet their obligations toward the families by providing water, light, health care, and schools. The cross of disease becomes the flower of health, for which voluntary health workers speak up by carrying out education and organizing campaigns for hygiene. The cross of poverty becomes the flower of solidarity. The cross of thirst becomes the flower of water, reflected in the water project: all residents of the communities have agreed to communal work Sunday after Sunday to construct a drinking-water tank for Motupe and Montenegro.

The cross of death is replaced by the flower of life. In this symbolic action the cross of dark wood appears whiter and whiter, covered by the flowers of resurrection. Then the people also kiss this new cross.

Dorothee Soelle
Celebrating Resistance: the way of the
Cross in Latin America

It is therefore Death alone that can suddenly make man to know himself. He tells the proud and insolent, that they are but abjects, and humbles them at the instant, makes them cry, complain, and repent, yea, even to hate their forepast happiness. He takes the account of the rich, and proves him a beggar, a naked beggar, which hath interest in nothing but in the gravel that fills his mouth. He holds a glass before the eyes of the most beautiful, and makes them see therein their deformity and rottenness, and they acknowledge it.

O eloquent, just and mighty Death! whom none could

advise, thou hast persuaded; what none hath dared, thou hast done; and whom all the world hath flattered, thou only hast cast out of the world and despised.

Sir Walter Raleigh

I am no longer afraid of death,
    I know well
its dark and cold corridors
leading to life.

I am afraid rather of that life
which does not come out of death
which cramps our hands
and retards our march.

I am afraid of my fear
and even more of the fear of others,
who do not know where they are going,
who continue clinging
to what they consider to be life
which we know to be death!

I live each day to kill death:
I die each day to beget life,
and in this dying unto death,
I die a thousand times and
am reborn another thousand
through that love
from my people,
which nourishes hope!

Julia Esquivel
Threatened with Resurrection

G ive us peace, Lord God, for you have given us all else; give us the peace that is repose, the peace of the Sabbath, and the peace that knows no evening. This whole order of exceedingly good things, intensely beautiful as it is, will pass away when it has served its purpose: these things too will have their morning and their evening.

But the seventh day has no evening and sinks toward no sunset, for you sanctified it that it might abide for ever. After completing your exceedingly good works you rested on the seventh day, though you achieved them in repose; and you willed your book to tell us this as a promise that when our works are finished (works exceedingly good inasmuch as they are your gift to us) we too may rest in you, in the Sabbath of eternal life.

And then you will rest in us, as now you work in us, and your rest will be rest through us as now those works of yours are wrought through us.

St Augustine
Confessions

Easter Sunday

I rose early and went out into the fresh, brilliant morning, between six and seven o'clock. The sun had already risen some time, but the grass was still white with the hoar frost. I walked across the common in the bright sunny quiet empty morning, listening to the rising of the lark as he went up in an ecstasy of song into the blue unclouded sky and gave in his Easter morning hymn at Heaven's Gate. Then came the echo and answer of earth as the Easter bells rang out their joy peals from the church towers all round. It was very sweet and lovely, the bright silent sunny morning, and the lark rising and singing alone in the blue sky, and then suddenly the morning air all alive with music of sweet bells ringing for the joy of the resurrection. 'The Lord is risen' smiled the sun, 'The Lord is risen' sang the lark. And the church bells in their joyous pealing answered from tower to tower, 'He is risen indeed'.

Francis Kilvert
Diary

Ask the loveliness of the earth, ask the loveliness of the sea, ask the loveliness of the wide airy spaces, ask the loveliness of the sky; ask the order of the stars, ask the sun making the daylight with its beams, ask the moon tempering the darkness of the night that follows; ask the living things which move in the waters, which tarry on the land, which fly in the air; ask the souls that are hidden, the bodies that are perceptive, the visible things which must be governed, the invisible things which govern – ask all these things, and they will all answer

you, 'Look, see, we are lovely.' Their loveliness is their confession. And these lovely but mutable things, who has made
them, save beauty immutable?

St Augustine
Sermons

L ast night did Christ the Sun rise from the dark,
    The mystic harvest of the fields of God,
And now the little wandering tribes of bees
    Are brawling in the scarlet flowers abroad.
The winds are soft with birdsong; all night long
    Darkling the nightingale her descant told,
And now inside church doors the happy folk
    The Alleluia chant a hundredfold.
O father of thy folk, be thine by right
The Easter joy, the threshold of the light.

Sedulius Scottus
'Easter Sunday'

N ew daytime dawning, breaking like the Spring.
    New voices singing, and new songs to sing!
Christ has come back, alleluia! He is risen, like the
    spring-time! Say, what does he bring?

Death in the tree tops! Jesus cried with pain,
hanging in the branches. Now he lives again!
For the tree of death has flowered, life has filled the furthest
    branches! Sunlight follows rain.

The man of sorrows, sleeping in his tomb,
the man of sorrows, he is coming home.

He is coming like the spring-time. Suddenly you'll hear him
   talking, you will see him come.

Say, are you hungry? Come and eat today!
Come to the table, nothing to pay!
Take your place, the meal is waiting. Come and share the
   birthday party, and the holiday.

Look where the garden door is open wide!
Come to the garden there's no need to hide.
God has broken down the fences and he stands with arms
   wide open. Come along inside!

Damian Lundy

Thou who sendest forth the light, createst the morning,
makest the sun to rise on the good and the evil, enlighten
the blindness of our minds with the knowledge of the truth:
lift thou up the light of thy countenance upon us, that in thy
light we may see light, and, at the last, the light of grace, the
light of glory.

Lancelot Andrewes

O Lord God, our Father. You are the light that can never
be put out; and now you give us a light that shall drive
away all darkness. You are love without coldness, and you
have given us such warmth in our hearts that we can love all
when we meet. You are the life that defies death, and you have
opened for us the way that leads to eternal life. None of us is
a great Christian; we are all humble and ordinary. But your
grace is enough for us. Arouse in us that small degree of joy
and thankfulness of which we are capable, the timid faith
which we can muster, the cautious obedience which we cannot
refuse, and thus the wholeness of life which you have prepared
for all of us through the death and resurrection of your Son.

Do not allow any of us to remain apathetic or indifferent to the wondrous glory of Easter, but let the light of our risen Lord reach every corner of our dull hearts.

Karl Barth

The people say that the sun dances on this day in joy for a risen Saviour.

Old Barbara Macphie at Dreimsdale saw this once, but only once, during her long life. And the good woman, of high natural intelligence, described in poetic language and with religious fervour what she saw or believed she saw from the summit of Benmore:

'The glorious gold-bright sun was after rising on the crests of the great hills, and it was changing colour – green, purple, red, blood-red, white, intense-white, and gold-white, like the glory of the God of the elements to the children of men. It was dancing up and down in exultation at the joyous resurrection of the beloved Saviour of victory.

'To be thus privileged, a person must ascend to the top of the highest hill before sunrise, and believe that the God who makes the small blade of grass to grow is the same God who makes the large, massive sun to move.'

Alexander Carmichael

Jesus Christ, inner Light, you came not to judge the world but so that, through you, the Risen Lord, every human being might be saved, reconciled. And when the love that forgives becomes a fire within us, then the heart, even when afflicted, can begin to love anew.

Brother Roger Schutz

Easter

Rise, heart; thy Lord is risen. Sing his praise
Without delayes,
Who takes thee by the hand, that thou likewise
With him mayst rise:
That, as his death calcined thee to dust,
His life may make thee gold, and much more just.

Awake, my lute, and struggle for thy part
With all thy art.
The crosse taught all wood to resound his name,
Who bore the same.
His streched sinews taught all strings, what key
Is best to celebrate this most high day.

Consort both heart and lute, and twist a song
Pleasant and long:
Or since all musick is but three parts vied
And multiplied;
O let thy blessed Spirit bear a part,
And make up our defects with his sweet art.

                                        George Herbert

Easter Monday

'Now, woman, let your tongue proclaim these things
and explain them to the sons of the Kingdom,
to those who await the rising of me, the Living.
Hurry, Mary, and assemble my disciples.
I am using you as a loud-sounding trumpet.
Sound peace to the terrified ears of my friends in hiding.
Rouse them all as if from sleep,
that they may come to meet me and light torches.
Say, "The Bridegroom has been raised from the tomb
and has left nothing within the tomb.
Apostles, banish deadness, for he has been raised,

who grants resurrection to the fallen."'

When therefore she had understood all the words of the
  Word,
the maiden returned and said to her companions,
'Wondrous, O women, the things I have seen and now tell.
Let no one consider my words to be ravings,
I did not see mere phantoms, but I was inspired.
I have been filled with the sight and words of Christ. Learn
  both how and when.
When Peter and his companion left me,
I stood weeping near the sepulchre,
for I imagined that the divine body
of the Immortal had been taken from the tomb.
But at once, taking pity on my tears, he appeared to me, the
  One

who grants resurrection to the fallen.

'Instantly my grief was changed to joy,
and everything became for me gladness and happiness.
I do not hesitate to say, "I was glorified like Moses."
For I saw, I saw, not on a mountain, but in the grave,
not veiled by a cloud, but by a body
the Master of the bodiless ones and of the clouds, he who
   was, is now and for ever,
saying, "Mary, hurry and say
to those who love me that I have been raised.
Taking me on your tongue like a sprig of olive
bring the good tidings to Noë's descendants
signifying that death has ceased and that he has been raised,
   the One

    who grants resurrection to the fallen."'

St Romanos the Melodist
On the Resurrection

Trade with the gifts God has given you.
Bend your minds to holy learning that you
may escape the fretting moth of littleness of
mind that would wear out your souls.
Brace your wills to action that they may
not be the spoil of weak desires.
Train your hearts and lips to song which
gives courage to the soul.
Being buffeted by trials, learn to laugh.
Being reproved, give thanks.
Having failed, determine to succeed.

St Hilda

Easter Tuesday

Today you will be baptized a Christian. All those great ancient words of the Christian proclamation will be spoken over you, and the command of Jesus Christ to baptize will be carried out on you, without your knowing anything about it. But we are once again being driven right back to the beginnings of our understanding. Reconciliation and redemption, regeneration and the Holy Spirit, love of our enemies, cross and resurrection, life in Christ and Christian discipleship – all these things are so difficult and so remote that we hardly venture any more to speak of them. In the traditional words and acts we suspect that there may be something quite new and revolutionary, though we cannot as yet grasp or express it . . .

Our earlier words are therefore bound to lose their force and cease, and our being Christians today will be limited to two things: prayer and action by the just person on behalf of people . . .

It is not for us to prophesy the day (though the day will come) when men will once more be called so to utter the word of God that the world will be changed and renewed by it. It will be a new language, perhaps quite nonreligious, but liberating and redeeming – as was Jesus' language; it will shock people and yet overcome them by its power; it will be the language of a new righteousness and truth, proclaiming God's peace with people and the coming of his Kingdom . . .

Dietrich Bonhoeffer
A Testament of Hope

O Son of the living God, old eternal King, I desire a hidden hut in the wilderness that it may be my home.

A narrow little blue stream beside it and a clear pool for the washing away of sin through the grace of the Holy Ghost.

A lovely wood close about it on every side, to nurse birds with all sorts of voices and to hide them with its shelter.

Looking south for heat, and a stream through its land, and good fertile soil suitable for all plants.

A beautiful draped church, a home for God from Heaven, and bright lights above the clean white Gospels.

Enough of clothing and food from the King of fair fame, and to be sitting for a while and praying to God in every place.

attrib. St Manchan
Tenth-century hermit's prayer

Easter Wednesday

D eep in the forest
  I found my God
leaping through the trees,
spinning with the glancing sunlight,
caressing with the breeze.
There where the grasses
rose and fell
fanning the perfumed air,
I smelt her beauty,
elusive, free,
dancing everywhere.

Edwina Gateley

I feel in myself the future life. I am like a forest once cut
down; the new shoots are stronger and livelier than ever.
The sunshine is on my head. The earth gives me its generous
sap, but heaven lights me with the reflection of unknown
worlds. You say that the soul is nothing but the resultant of
the bodily powers. Why, then, is my soul more luminous when
my bodily powers begin to fail? Winter is on my head, but
eternal spring is in my heart. I breathe at this hour the fragrance
of the lilies, the violets and the roses, as at twenty. The nearer
I approach the end, the plainer I hear around me the immortal
symphonies of the worlds which invite me. It is marvellous,
yet simple. It is a fairy tale and it is history.

  For half a century I have been writing my thoughts in prose
and in verse; history, philosophy, drama, romance, tradition,

satire, ode and song; I have tried all. But I feel I have not said the thousandth part of what is in me.

When I go down to the grave I can say like many others 'I have finished my day's work'. But I cannot say, 'I have finished my life'. My day's work will begin the next morning. The tomb is not a blind alley; it is a thoroughfare. It closes on the twilight; it opens on the dawn.

Victor Hugo

We cannot live without joy, and that is why I consider life, the universe, and the planet earth, all as a single, multiform, celebratory event. Throughout the vast extent of space and time, it is a single, multiform, celebratory event. This capacity for celebration is of ultimate importance . . . That is one of the things religion can give: the gift of delight in existence. Such delight is a source of immense energy.

Thomas Berry

Concern for beauty is not a moral cop-out. It leads us firmly into the midst of all that is going on in our world. Where there is beauty apparent, we are to enjoy it; where there is beauty hidden, we are to unveil it; where there is beauty defaced, we are to restore it; where there is no beauty, we are to create it. All of which places us, too, in the arena where oppression occurs, where the oppressed congregate, and where we are called to be.

Robert McAffee Brown

Easter Thursday

Heaven and earth and all creation cry out to me
That I must love.
Everything tells me: with all your heart
Love the love that loves you;
Love the love which desires you,
Which has created you to draw you
Wholly to itself.
Therefore I desire never to stop drawing
On this holy light
And this ineffable goodness.

St Francis of Assisi

In a truly loving mind there is always a song of glory and an inner flame of love. They surge up out of a clear conscience, out of an abundant spiritual joy, out of inward gladness. Small wonder if a love like this wins through to a perfect love. Love of this sort is immense in its fervour, its whole direction Godwards, totally unrestrained in its love for him . . .

There is no tension in the fervour, but there is vigour in this love; there is sweetness in this song, and a warmth about this radiance; delight in God is irresistible; contemplation rises with unimpeded ascent. Everything the lover conquers; everything he overcomes; nothing seems impossible to him. For while a man is striving to love Christ with all his might, he knows it to be true that within him is eternal life, abundant and sweet . . .

The nature of love is that it is diffusive, unifying, and transforming. It is diffusive when it flows out and sheds the rays of its goodness not merely on friends and neighbours, but on enemies and strangers as well. It unites because it makes lovers one in deed and will and draws into one Christ and every holy soul. He who holds on to God is one in spirit with him, not by nature, but by grace and identity of will. Love has also the power of transforming, for it transforms the lover into his beloved and makes him dwell in him. Thus it happens that when the fire of the Holy Spirit really gets hold of the heart, it sets it wholly on fire and, so to speak, turns it into flame, leading it into that state in which it is most like God. Otherwise it would not have been said, 'I have said, "You are gods; all of you are children of the Most High."'

Richard Rolle
The Fire of Love

Easter Friday

Nothing is sweeter than love, nothing stronger, nothing higher, nothing broader; nothing is more lovely, nothing richer, nothing better in heaven or in earth. Love is born of God and it cannot rest anywhere but in God, beyond all created things. One who loves is borne on wings; he runs, and is filled with joy; he is free and unrestricted. He gives all to receive all, and he has all in all; for beyond all things he rests in the one highest thing, from whom streams all that is good. He does not consider the gift, but beyond all good things he turns himself to the giver.

Love often knows no measure, but burns white-hot beyond all measure. Love feels no burden, and counts up no toil; it aspires to do more than its strength allows; it does not plead impossibility, but considers it may do and can do all things. So it finds strength for anything; it completes and carries through great tasks where one who does not love would fail and fall. Love is vigilant, it sleeps without losing control; it is wearied without exhaustion, cramped without being crushed, alarmed without being destroyed. Like a living flame or a burning torch, it leaps up and safely passes through all. When a man loves, he knows the meaning of that cry that sounds in the ears of God from the burning love of the soul: My God, it cries, my love! You are wholly mine, and I am wholly yours!

Expand my heart with love, so that the lips of my soul may taste how sweet it is to love, to melt in love and float upon a sea of love. Let me be gripped by love as I rise in adoration and wonder beyond the limits of my being. Let the song of love be on my lips as I follow my love to the heights; let my soul, triumphant with love, faint in intensity of worship. May

I love you more than myself, and myself only because of you; and in you let me love all those who truly love you. The law of love that shines from you gives us this command.

St Thomas à Kempis
The Imitation of Christ

Easter Saturday

I was learning the far more secret doctrine that pleasures are shafts of the glory as it strikes our sensibility. As it impinges on our wills or our understanding, we give it different names – goodness or truth or the like. But its flash upon our senses is pleasure.

C. S. Lewis
Letters to Malcolm

How do I see Jesus glorified in my interior? This happens in a very different way from when I see him next to me, before me, above me as somehow elevated like between heaven and earth . . . For instance, when Jesus of late manifested himself on my right side and seemed to embrace me . . . then I felt that I was different from him and not one with him, receiving that embrace as if from someone outside me, although not in as sensuous and rough a manner as it may sound . . . it seemed to take place on the outside, but it penetrated the interior, and thus it was spiritually sensuous and sensuously spiritual . . .

But it is something quite different when Jesus shows himself in my interior. I do see him with the same glorified body, but in such a way that I am more united with him. My interior is then so broadened and expanded in him, and he in me, that my interior seems to be swallowed up and one with him. And yet, I do not sense myself nor my body in such a way as to imagine that I am enclosing that huge Christ in my narrow body. But my spiritual interior appears to be broadened and

expanded so that the whole world and all that is contained in
it, even the whole of the sky, could appear therein and be seen.

Maria Petyt
Seventeenth-century Flemish mystic

F or I have learned
    To look on nature, not as in the hour
Of thoughtless youth; but hearing often-times
The still, sad music of humanity,
Nor harsh nor grating, though of ample power
To chasten and subdue. And I have felt
A presence that disturbs me with the joy
Of elevated thoughts; a sense sublime
Of something far more deeply interfused,
Whose dwelling is the light of setting suns,
And the round ocean and the living air,
And the blue sky, and in the mind of man:
A motion and a spirit, that impels
All thinking things, all objects of all thought,
And rolls through all things.

William Wordsworth
Tintern Abbey

St Catherine of Siena,
29 April

I wish therefore that you lock yourself up in the open side of the Son of God, which is an open storehouse, so full of fragrance that there sin becomes perfumed. There the sweet Bride rests on the bed of fire and of blood. There is seen and manifested the secret of the heart of the Son of God. He is a winecask which, when it is broached, gives drink and inebriates every enamoured desire, and gives mirth and illumines every intelligence and refills every memory, that struggles so hard to comprehend, so much so that it cannot retain, nor mean, nor love anything else, except this good and sweet Jesus . . .

I went to visit him whom you know, from which he received such strengthening and consolation that he made his confession and prepared himself very well. He made me promise by the love of God that when the moment of justice came, I would be there with him. And thus I promised and did. Then in the morning, before the church bells, I went to him and he received great consolation. I led him to hear Mass, and he received Holy Communion, which he had never before received. His will was accorded and submitted to the will of God, and there only remained a fear of not being strong enough when the time came . . .

So I waited for him at the place of justice, and I waited there with continual prayer and in the presence of Mary and of St Catherine, virgin and martyr. But before I attained that, I prostrated myself and stretched out my neck on the block, but it did not happen, but I had my desire full of myself . . .

Then he arrived, like a gentle lamb, and seeing me he began to smile, and wanted me to make the sign of the cross. And when he had received the sign, I said, 'Down! To the wedding, my sweet brother! Soon you shall be in the enduring life.' He prostrated himself with great meekness, and I stretched out his neck, and bent myself down, and reminded him of the blood of the Lamb. His mouth said nothing except 'Jesus' and 'Catherine'. And while he was speaking, I received his head in my hands, closing my eyes in the divine goodness, and saying, 'I will' . . .

I remain on earth with the greatest envy. And it seems to me that the first new stone has already been put in place. And therefore do not wonder if I impose on you nothing except to see you drowned in the blood and fire that the side of the Son of God pours out. Now then, no more negligence, my sweetest sons, because the blood is beginning to pour, and to receive the life. Sweet Jesus, Jesus love.

St Catherine of Siena
Letter to Br Raymond of Capua OP

2nd Sunday of Easter

It is a matter of great significance to Christians that on the very day that the earliest disciples realized that Jesus was still alive and active, in his new order of being, he sent them out on his mission to the world. John in his thinking and interpretation brings Pentecost forward to Easter.

God's love and Jesus' own have been shown to the uttermost in the Cross: 'Greater love has no man than this, that a man lay down his life for his friends.' Jesus has done this not only for them but also for those who would call themselves his enemies. He practises his command, 'Love your enemies.' The circle of divine love includes within its circumference every sort and condition of men, everyone living at the present time, everyone who has lived in the past, everyone to be born in the countless generations of the future.

In addition to all-inclusive love, the Cross of Jesus shows us God's and his own unlimited forgiveness, however cruel and tragic and however often repeated sins may be. Christ's gospel has been enacted on the Cross, and it is now to be lovingly proclaimed to the world. So his mission can begin at once: 'As the Father sent me, so I send you.'

The Good Friday-Easter-Pentecost good news is not only for individuals – it is for nations and groups, however hostile and embittered. The original disciples, the women at the tomb, and all who will later experience the risen Christ, are not only to be a community of love and forgiveness, they are to undertake a ministry of reconciliation, they are to be gatherers, bridge-builders, witnesses and messengers to humanity.

In death and resurrection, Jesus is released from bodily presence, space and time, to become a personal cosmic force, the spearhead of divine evolution towards the kind of world that God originally planned and is still creating, a kingdom that will be perfected at the great consummation.

We have a gospel, a mission of love, an embassy of reconciliation – and a cosmic leader!

George Appleton

2nd week of Easter

When they were all gathered together in the palace, they saw a woman in a strange dress in the middle of the hall. Then she sang these verses to Bran while the company listened to them, and they all saw the woman.

She sang: 'Here is a branch from the apple tree of paradise, like those that are familiar; twigs of white silver on it, and crystal fringes with flowers.

'There is an island far away, around which the sea-horses glisten, flowing on their white course against its shining shore; four pillars support it.

'It is a delight to the eye, the plain which the hosts frequent in triumphant ranks; coracle races against chariot in the plain and the sea.

'Pillars of white bronze are under it, shining through aeons of beauty, a lovely land through the ages of the world, on which many flowers rain down.

'There is a huge tree there with blossom, on which the birds call at the hours; it is their custom that they all call together in concert every hour.

'Weeping and treachery are unknown in the pleasant familiar land; there is no fierce harsh sound there, but sweet music striking the ear.

'Without sorrow, without grief, without death, without any sickness, without weakness, that is the character of Paradise.

'There comes a host across the clear sea, to the land they display their rowing; then they row to the bright stone from which a hundred songs arise.

'Throughout the long ages it sings to the host a melody which is not sad; the music swells up in choruses of hundreds, they do not expect decay nor death.

'Freedom and health come to the land around which laughter echoes. With its purity come immortality and joy.

'My words are not all for you, though their great wonders have been told; from among the throng of the world let Bran listen to the wisdom expounded to him . . .'

Then the woman went from them, and they did not know where she went, and she took her branch with her . . .

Anon. Irish, seventh to eighth century
A Celtic Miscellany

St Joseph the Worker,
1 May

To me the greatest inspiration for the spirituality of the laity is in the life of Jesus, Mary and Joseph . . .

The workman is a priest in his work; the father of a family is a priest for his wife and children; the head of a community is a priest before its members; the peasant is a priest for his farm, animals, fields and flowers.

The royal priesthood of which Peter spoke and the meaning of the 'offering of spiritual sacrifices which Jesus Christ has made acceptable to God' have been emphasized too little. This has created the dryness apparent in so much discussion on the apostolate of the laity, and, what is more, of the position of the layman in the Church.

How can we speak of the spirituality of the laity if we omit this fundamental prerogative of the priest of created things, voice of nature, consecrator of the goods of the earth, saint of the earthly city?

Carlo Carretto
Letters from the Desert

God, most vitally active and most incarnate, is not remote from us, wholly apart from the sphere of the tangible: on the contrary, at every moment God awaits us in the activity, the work to be done, which every moment brings. God is, in a sense, at the point of my pen, my pick, my paint brush, my needle – and my heart and my thought. It is by carrying to completion the stroke, the line, the stitch I am working on that I shall lay hold on that ultimate end towards which my will at its deepest levels tends.

Pierre Teilhard de Chardin
Hymn of the Universe

I began in the autumn of 1940 to work as a labourer in a stone quarry attached to the Solvay chemical plant. This was at Zakrowek, about half an hour from my home in Debniki, and every day I would walk there. I later wrote a poem about that quarry. Re-reading it after so many years, I still find that it expresses very well that extraordinary experience:

> Listen: the even knocking of hammers,
>   so much their own,
> I project on to the people
>   to test the strength of each blow.
> Listen now, electric current
>   cuts through a river of rock.
> And a thought grows in me day after day:
>   the greatness of work is inside man.

Pope John Paul II
Gift and Mystery

Donald Nicholl,
3 May

In '41 Mama took me back to Moscow. There I saw our enemies for the first time. If my memory is right, nearly 20,000 German war prisoners were to be marched in a single column through the streets of Moscow. The pavements swarmed with onlookers, cordoned off by soldiers and police. The crowd was mostly women – Russian women with hands roughened by hard work, lips untouched by lipstick, and thin hunched shoulders which had borne half the burden of the war. Every one of them must have a father or a husband, a brother or a son killed by the Germans. They gazed with hatred in the direction from which the column was to appear. At last we saw it. The generals marched at the head, massive chins stuck out, lips folded disdainfully, their whole demeanour meant to show superiority over their plebeian victors.

'They smell of eau de Cologne, the bastards,' someone in the crowd said with hatred. The women were clenching their fists. The soldiers and policemen had all they could do to hold them back. All at once something happened to them. They saw German soldiers, thin, unshaven, wearing dirty blood-stained bandages, hobbling on crutches or leaning on the shoulder of their comrades: the soldiers walked with their heads down. The street became dead silent – the only sound was the shuffling of boots and the thumping of crutches.

Then I saw an elderly woman in broken-down boots push herself forward and touch a policeman's shoulder, saying, 'Let me through'. There must have been something about her that made him step aside. She went up to the column, took from inside her coat something wrapped in a coloured handkerchief and unfolded it. It was a crust of black bread. She pushed it awkwardly into the pocket of the soldier, so exhausted that he was tottering on his feet. And then suddenly from every side women were running towards the soldiers, pushing into their hands bread, cigarettes, whatever they had. The soldiers were no longer enemies. They were people.

Yevgeny Yevtushenko
in Donald Nicholl
Triumphs of the Spirit in Russia

This incident, one of the late Donald Nicholl's favourite passages, was read at his memorial service.

Donald Nicholl died on 3 May 1997.

3rd Sunday of Easter

There is a gap between the probable and the proved. How was I to cross it? If I were to stake my whole life on the risen Christ, I wanted proof. I wanted certainty. I wanted to see him eat a bit of fish. I wanted letters of fire across the sky. I got none of these . . . It was a question of whether I was to accept him – *or reject*. My God! There was a gap *behind* me as well! Perhaps the leap to acceptance was a horrifying gamble – but what of the leap to rejection? There might be no certainty that Christ was God – but, by God, there was no certainty that he was not. This was not to be borne. I could not reject Jesus. There was only one thing to do once I had seen the gap behind me. I turned away from it, and flung myself over the gap towards Jesus.

Sheldon Vanauken
A Severe Mercy

Praise the Lord in his cosmos
    Praise him in his sanctuary
Praise him with a radio-signal
       100,000 million light-years away
Praise him in the stars
    in inter-stellar space
Praise him in the galaxies
    in inter-galactic space
Praise him in atoms
    in inter-atomic space
Praise him on violin and flute
    on the saxophone

Praise him with clarinet and horn
　　with cornet and trombone
　　　on alto-sax and trumpet
Praise him with viola and cello
　　on piano and harpsichord
Praise him with blues and jazz
　　with an orchestra
Praise him with spirituals
　　with soul-music and Beethoven's fifth
　　with marimbas and guitars
Praise him with discs and cassettes
　　with hi-fi systems
　　and quadraphonic sound
Let everything that draws breath praise him
　　Alleluia!
Let all living cells praise the Lord
　　Alleluia!
　　　　Praise the Lord!

Ernesto Cardenal
Psalms

3rd week of Easter

It was the sight of the Mill, when I was walking alone, aged about seventeen, and when I came out of Green Street Gorse and saw her suddenly (though not unexpectedly) below me, with Chanctonbury and the Downs beyond, that caught me up in the first of my ecstasies, a glory beyond words or anything I had previously experienced. I was inebriated, exalted, totally free of all limitation or restraint, at one with the whole incredible adventure of living. It came without any warning, as suddenly as a gap in the clouds when one is walking in the hills; it took me outside time, outside the ordinary joys of sense or intellect, it came as a gift, and I thanked God as the giver. I did not talk about it to anyone at the time, and it was only much later that I came across accounts of similar experiences, notably in my grandfather's *Path to Rome*, where he describes his 'Vision of the Alps' . . . These have been the most important experiences of my life, for I believe them to be the nearest we can get on earth to the reality of heaven – what Bishop Bossuet called 'an eternal gasp of wonder'.

In 1967 I was told that my dear friend, Siegfried Sassoon, was dying of cancer in a hospital in Warminster, and the next day I rode the 25 miles on a bicycle to see him. When I went into the room the disease had got so fierce a grip on him that I thought for a moment he was already dead: his neck seemed no thicker than my arm, his cheeks and eyes sunk into great hollows. But then he opened his eyes, and gave that great smile of his and said that he knew I would come to see him before he went. We talked of Belloc and of his influence in bringing Siegfried into the Church, of how Kent was doing in the county

cricket, of his own cricket with the Downside Ravens and of
our very different boyhoods in the Weald.

Then he said, 'I am sorry not to be in better form,' and I
replied that I thought him in fine form, and he said, 'Yes,
underneath this little heap of a body I am at the very top of
my form, and is it wrong to be looking forward to being in
Paradise this week?' I said he must do just that thing, and then
urged him to go home to Heytesbury to die in his own bed
and not be bullied by all the medical people. And so I left him,
and he went to heaven two days later.

Philip Jebb
in *A Touch of God: eight monastic journeys*

Julian of Norwich,
13 May

Our Mother in nature, our Mother in grace, because he wanted altogether to become our Mother in all things, made the foundation of his work most humbly and most mildly in the maiden's womb. And he revealed that in the first revelation, when he brought that meek maiden before the eye of my understanding in the simple stature which she had when she conceived; that is to say that our great God, the supreme wisdom of all things, arrayed and prepared himself in this humble place, all ready in our poor flesh, himself to do the service and the office of motherhood in everything. The mother's service is nearest, readiest and surest: nearest because it is most natural, readiest because it is most loving, and surest because it is truest. No one ever might or could perform this office fully, except only him. We know that all our mothers bear us for pain and for death. O, what is that? But our true Mother Jesus, he alone bears us for joy and for endless life, blessed may he be. So he carries us within him in love and travail, until the full time when he wanted to suffer the sharpest thorns and cruel pains that ever were or will be, and at the last he died. And when he had finished, and had borne us so for bliss, still all this could not satisfy his wonderful love. And he revealed this in these great surpassing words of love: 'If I could suffer more, I would suffer more.' He could not die any more, but he did not want to cease working; therefore he must needs nourish us, for the precious love of motherhood has made him our debtor.

The mother can give her child to suck of her milk, but our precious Mother Jesus can feed us with himself, and does, most courteously and most tenderly, with the blessed sacrament, which is the precious food of true life; and with all the sweet sacraments he sustains us most mercifully and graciously, and so he meant in these blessed words, where he said: 'I am he whom Holy Church preaches and teaches to you.' That is to say: All the health and the life of the sacraments, all the power and the grace of my word, all the goodness which is ordained in Holy Church for you, I am he.

The mother can lay her child tenderly to her breast, but our tender Mother Jesus can lead us easily into his blessed breast through his sweet open side, and show us there a part of the godhead and of the joys of heaven, with inner certainty of endless bliss. And that he revealed in the tenth revelation, giving us the same understanding in these sweet words which he says: 'See, how I love you,' looking into his blessed side, rejoicing.

This fair lovely word 'mother' is so sweet and so kind in itself that it cannot truly be said of anyone or to anyone except of him and to him who is the true Mother of life and of all things.

Julian of Norwich
Showings

4th Sunday of Easter
(World Day of Prayer for Vocations)

Ever since this burden, for which I must render a difficult accounting, has been placed on my shoulders the concern of my position [as bishop] has disturbed me. Nevertheless, I am all the more concerned by thoughts of this nature when the anniversary of my ordination renews the memory of that day.

Although I am terrified by what I am for you, I am consoled by what I am with you. For you, I am a bishop; with you, I am a Christian. The former is a title of an office which has been undertaken, the latter is a title of grace. The first is a danger, the second salvation. Furthermore, we are tossed about as though in a great ocean by the tempest of our responsibilities. However, when we recall by whose blood we have been redeemed, it is as though we enter into a safe harbour by the tranquillity of this recollection. Precisely as we struggle in this office we find rest in our common good.

It consoles me more that I have been redeemed with you than that I have been placed over you. I will seek to make my service to you all the more bountiful, as the Lord has commanded . . .

I must indeed love the Redeemer. I am aware of what he said to Peter, 'Peter, do you love me? Tend my sheep' (John 21:17). He asked this once, again, and a third time. Love was first asked for, then the burden imposed, since, where love is greater, the burden is lesser. Aid us by your prayers and your obedience that we may rejoice not so much in being set over you as in serving you.

St Augustine
Sermon on the anniversary of his
episcopal ordination

Curb for wild horses,
    Wing for bird-courses
Never yet flown!
Helm, safe for weak ones,
Shepherd, bespeak once,
The young lambs Thine own.
Rouse up the youth,
Shepherd and Feeder,
So let them bless Thee
Praise and confess Thee –
Pure words on pure mouth –
Christ, the child-leader!
Oh, the saints' Lord,
All-dominant Word!
Holding, by Christdom,
God's highest wisdom!
Column in place
When sorrows seize us –
Endless in grace
Unto man's race,
Saving one, Jesus!
Pastor and ploughman,
Helm, curb, together –
Pinion that now can
(Heavenly of feather)
Raise and release us!

St Clement of Alexandria
transl. Elizabeth Barrett Browning

I know, Lord, that as a priest of your true Church, I should not let the sense of my vocation, and the courage to preach your gospel in season and out of season, depend on the consciousness of my own personal worth. Your priest does not approach people as a revivalist or an enthusiast, not as a purveyor of mystic wisdom or gnostic or pentecostal prophet, or whatever else such persons may call themselves. These can communicate to others no more of you than they have themselves. But as a priest, I come as your legate, as a messenger sent by your Son, Our Lord. And that is at the same time less and more, a thousand times more than anything else.

But, O God of my calling, it would be so much easier if I could just deliver your message and then, when your work is done, go back to living my own life. Then the burden of being your messenger would be no heavier than that of any other messenger or administrator who does his job and is done with it . . .

It's unavoidable: your official business and my private life cannot be separated. And that is precisely the burden of my life. For look, Lord: even when I announce your pure truth, I'm still preaching my own narrowness and mediocrity along with it. I'm still presenting myself, the 'average man'. How can I bring my hearers to distinguish between you and me in the frightful mixture of you and me that I call my sermons? How can I teach them to take your word to their hearts, and forget me, the preacher? . . .

O God of my vocation, when I consider these things, I must confess that I don't at all feel like taking my place in the proud ranks of your confident and conquering apostles. I rather feel that I should be on my way, simply and humbly, walking in fear and trembling. I don't mean to criticize those among my brethren who can be so happily sure of themselves, those of your servants who so unmistakably reflect the inner confidence that they are coming in the name of the Lord God of Hosts, and who are quite amazed if anyone does not immediately recognize in them the ambassadors of the Almighty.

I cannot belong to that fortunate group, O Lord. Grant me rather the grace to belong to the number of your lowly servants who are rather amazed when they are received by their fellow human beings. Let my heart tremble again and again in grateful surprise at the miracles of your grace, which is mighty in the midst of weakness. Let me continue to marvel that I meet so many persons who allow me, poor sinner that I am, to enter into the secret chamber of their hearts, because they have been able to recognize you hidden in me.

Karl Rahner
Prayers for a Lifetime

4th week of Easter

Revelation comes in two volumes: that of the Bible and that of Nature.

Thomas Aquinas

You never enjoy the world aright, till you see how a sand exhibiteth the wisdom and power of God: and prize in everything the service which they do you, by manifesting his glory and goodness to your soul, far more than the visible beauty on their surface, or the material services they can do your body. Wine by its moisture quencheth my thirst, whether I consider it or no: but to see it flowing from his love who gave it unto man, quencheth the thirst even of the Holy Angels. To consider it, is to drink it spiritually. To rejoice in its diffusion is to be of a public mind. And to take pleasure in all the benefits it doth to all is heavenly, for so they do in Heaven. To do so is to be divine and good, and to imitate our infinite and eternal Father.

Your enjoyment of the world is never right, till every morning you awake in Heaven; see yourself in your Father's palace; and look upon the skies, the earth, and the air as celestial joys: having such a reverend esteem of all, as if you were among the angels. The bride of a monarch, in her husband's chamber, hath no such causes of delight as you.

You never enjoy the world aright, till the sea itself floweth in your veins, till you are clothed with the heavens, and crowned with the stars: and perceive yourself to be the sole heir of the whole world, and more than so, because men are

in it who are every one sole heirs as well as you. Till you can
sing and rejoice and delight in God, as misers do in gold, and
kings in sceptres, you never enjoy the world.

Yet further, you never enjoy the world aright, till you so
love the beauty of enjoying it, that you are covetous and earnest
to persuade others to enjoy it.

                                                    Thomas Traherne

E verything in the universe is uniformly true and valuable:
so much so that the fusion of the individual must be affected with all, *without distinction and without qualification.*
Everything that is active, that moves or breathes, every physical, astral or animate energy, every fragment of force, every
spark of life, is equally sacred; for, in the humblest atom and
the most brilliant star, in the lowest insect and the finest intelligence, there is the radiant smile and thrill of the *same Absolute.*

                                              Pierre Teilhard de Chardin

5th Sunday of Easter

Glory in all my seeing
Glory in all my being
Glory in all my speaking
Glory in all my seeking
Glory in all my hearing
Glory in every appearing
Glory in all my feeling
Glory in God's revealing
Glory of the mighty Three
Glory entwining round me
Glory in the opening day
Glory in the rocky way
Glory in the morning light
Glory in the darkest night
Glory there for beholding
Glory ever me enfolding.

Glory of God
Hand above
Glory of Christ
Heart of love
Glory of Spirit
Covering dove.

May the God who dances in creation,
who embraces us with human love,
who shakes our lives like thunder,
bless us and drive us out with power
to fill the world with her justice. Amen.

When people turn
     from the table
where bread is broken
and candles glow,
be sure you have invited them
not to your house
but to their own,
and offered not your wisdom
but your love.

May the power and the mystery go before us, to show us
the way,
shine above us to lighten our world,
lie beneath us to bear us up,
walk with us and give us companionship,
and glow and flow within us to bring us joy. Amen.

The blessing of the God of Sarah and Hagar, as of Abraham.
The blessing of Jesus born of the woman Mary.
The blessing of the Holy Spirit who broods over us
as a mother over her children.
Be with us now and forever. Amen.

St Hilda Community
The New Women Included:
a book of services and prayers

5th week of Easter

The end I seek is thy glory, O God, and my own
    happiness.
Not the happiness of the body, but of the mind,
which is incapable of true happiness
till renewed and sanctified,
till restored to its native liberty,
till recovered from its lapse, and in all things
made conformable to Thy will and laws.

O Lord,
    I understand now that to know you only as a
   philosopher;
to have the most sublime and conscious speculations
concerning your essence, your attributes, your providence;
to be able to demonstrate your Being from all,
or any of the works of nature;
and to discourse with the greatest elegancy
and propriety of words of your existence or operations,
will avail us nothing unless at the same time we know you
experimentally, unless the heart perceives and knows you to
   be her supreme good, her only happiness!

I know too,
that unless the soul feels and acknowledges
that she can find no repose, no peace, no joy,
but in loving and being beloved by you;
and does accordingly rest in you as the centre of her being,
the fountain of her pleasures, the origin of all virtue and

goodness, her light, her life, her strength, her all,
everything she wants or wisheth in this world and for ever
   in a word, her Lord, her God!

Susanna Wesley
both from *Devotional Journal*

6th Sunday of Easter

So until Ascensiontide he worked with his pupils to conclude his translation of St John's Gospel into the English tongue: but the Tuesday before Ascensiontide his sickness increased upon him. Nevertheless, he taught and bade his scholars work, saying cheerfully, 'Write with speed now, for I cannot tell how long I may last.'

The day broke (that is, Wednesday), and about the third hour the scribe said, 'There is yet a chapter wanting: it is hard for thee to continue vexing thyself.' 'This is easily done,' said Bede. 'Take thy pen again and write quickly.' And joyfully he dictated until the evening at the ninth hour.

'Dear Master,' said the boy, 'there is yet one sentence to be written.' He answered, 'Write it quickly.' Soon after, the boy said, 'It is finished now.'

Bede answered, 'Thou hast well said, It is finished. Raise my head in thy arms, and turn my face towards the holy spot where I was wont to pray, for I desire to sit facing it and call upon my Father.'

So they held him up on the pavement, and he chanted, 'Glory be to the Father, and to the Son, and to the Holy Spirit.' Then, as he named the Holy Spirit, his spirit took leave, and departed to the heavenly Kingdom.

St Cuthbert
(a pupil of Bede)

I place before my inward eyes myself with all that I am –
my body, soul, and all my powers – and I gather round me
all the creatures which God ever created in heaven, on earth,
and in all the elements, each one severally with its name,
whether birds of the air, beasts of the forest, fishes of the
waters, leaves and grass of the earth, or the innumerable sand
of the sea, and to these I add all the little specks of dust which
glance in the sunbeams, with all the little drops of water which
ever fell or are falling from dew, snow, or rain, and I wish
that each of these had a sweetly sounding stringed instrument,
fashioned from my heart's inmost blood, striking on which
they might each send up to our dear and gentle God a new
and lofty strain of praise for ever and ever. And then the loving
arms of my soul stretch out and extend themselves towards
the innumerable multitude of all creatures, and my intention
is, just as a free and blithesome leader of a choir stirs up the
singers of his company, even so to turn them all to good
account by inciting them to sing joyously, and to offer up their
hearts to God – '*Sursum corda*'.

Henry Suso
Meditations

6th week of Easter

There are two loves only

Tonight I ask you to help me to love.

Grant me, Lord, to spread true love in the world.
Grant that it may penetrate into offices, factories, apartment
   buildings, cinemas, dance-halls;
Grant that it may penetrate the hearts of men and that I
   may never forget that the battle for a better world is a
   battle of love.

For man and the world are hungry for an infinite love,
And God alone can love with a boundless love,
But if you want, son, I give you my life,
Draw it within you.
I give you my heart, I give it to my sons.
Love with my heart, son,
And all together you will feed the world, and you will
   save it.

Michel Quoist
Prayers of Life

May the power of your love, Lord Christ, fiery
and sweet as honey, so absorb our hearts as to
withdraw them from all that is under heaven.
Grant that we may be ready to die for love of
your love, as you died for love of our love.

St Francis of Assisi

I love you, O God,
my Love,
my Warmth,
my Solace,
my Fulfilment.
All that I am,
all that I do
finds meaning and purpose in you.
Fill me with the full force
of your Love
and its passionate splendour,
so that I might hold
and heal all those who are crying out for love.
Love through me
all the unreconciled
whose homes and hearts
are broken,
and let them know
I am able to love
because you have first loved me.

Miriam Therese Winter
Woman Wisdom

St Joan of Arc,
30 May

I thought God would have friends everywhere, because he is the friend of everyone; and in my innocence I believed that you who now cast me out would be like strong towers to keep harm from me. But I am wiser now; and nobody is any the worse for being wiser. Do not think you can frighten me by telling me that I am alone. France is alone; and God is alone; and what is my loneliness before the loneliness of my country and my God? I see now that the loneliness of God is his strength: what would he be if he listened to your jealous little counsels? Well, my loneliness shall be my strength too; it is better to be alone with God: his friendship will not fail me, nor his counsel, nor his love. In his strength I will dare, and dare, and dare, until I die.

Bernard Shaw
Saint Joan

She said that, from the age of thirteen, she received revelation from Our Lord by a voice which taught her how to behave. And the first time she was greatly afraid. And she said that the voice came that time at noon, on a summer's day, a fast day, when she was in her father's garden, and that the voice came on her right side, in the direction of the church. And she said that the voice was hardly ever without a light, which was always in the direction of the voice.

She said further that, after she had heard it three times, she knew that it was the voice of an angel.

She said also that this voice had always taken good care of her.

Questioned as to what teaching this voice gave her as to the salvation of her soul, she answered that it taught her how to behave. And it said to her that she ought to go often to church. And later it said to her that it was necessary that she should go into France.

The Trial of Joan of Arc

With the name of Jesus ever on her lips, she died the precious death of the just, distinguished, as the story runs, by signs from Heaven ... Men then began to repent of the deed, and in the very place of execution to venerate the sanctity of the Maid; so that, to prevent the people from possessing themselves of her relics, her heart, uninjured by the flames and running with blood, was thrown together with her ashes, into the river.

Papal decree 1894
introducing cause of Joan's canonization

Visitation, 31 May

S ing out, my soul,
  sing of the holiness of God:
who has delighted in a woman,
lifted up the poor,
satisfied the hungry,
given voice to the silent,
grounded the oppressor,
blessed the full-bellied with emptiness,
and with the gift of tears
those who have never wept;
who has desired the darkness of the womb,
and inhabited our flesh.
Sing of the longing of God,
sing out, my soul.

Janet Morley
All Desires Known

M y heart is bubbling over with joy;
  with God it is good to be woman.
From now on let all peoples proclaim:
it is a wonderful gift to be.
The one in whom power truly rests
has lifted us up to praise;
God's goodness shall fall like a shower
on the trusting of every age.
The disregarded have been raised up:
the pompous and powerful shall fall.

God has feasted the empty-bellied,
and the rich have discovered their void.
God has made good the word
given at the dawn of time.

Phoebe Willetts
from
Celebrating Women: the new edition

I am special. I am not special.
Because everyone is special.
My body, my soul, the Divine Inner-dwelling
glories you, O God.
I have joy because of this.
You have blessed me with the greatest gift
that was yours to give . . . your very Life, your Be-ing.
When all the blocks and prejudices and hang-ups are shattered
And I can forget myself and let you BE
Then I need not plan or devise or calculate
I can only let you BE yourself in me.
As long as I do not try to take over
I am free with your freedom, and strong with your strength
so there is nothing that can't be done
if it is appropriate.
You are the power-filled ONENESS
and I glorify you for giving me this happening.
Help me to keep that balance
You the DO-ER
I the instrument
And when this proceeds to enactment
then your Kingdom is Be-coming
Thank you. Amen.

Elaine MacInnes
talk to Alister Hardy Institute

Ascension Day
(Thursday after
6th Sunday of Easter)

G od of holy dreaming, Great Creator Spirit, from the dawn of creation you have given your children the good things of Mother Earth.

You spoke and the gum tree grew. In the vast desert and dense forest, and in cities at the water's edge, creation sings praise.

Your presence endures as the rock at the heart of the earth.

When Jesus hung on the tree you heard the cries of all your people and became one with your wounded ones: the convicts, the hunted, and the dispossessed. The sunrise of your Son coloured the earth anew, and bathed it in glorious hope.

In Jesus we have been reconciled to you, to each other and to your whole creation.

Lead us on, Great Spirit, as we gather from the four corners of the earth; enable us to walk together in trust, from the hurt and shame of the past, into the full day which has dawned in Jesus Christ. Amen.

Aboriginal prayer

T he ascension of Christ is his liberation from all restrictions of time and space. It does not represent his removal from the earth, but his constant presence everywhere on earth.

During his earthly ministry he could only be in one place at a time. If he was in Jerusalem he was not in Capernaum; if he was in Capernaum he was not in Jerusalem. But now he is united with God, he is present wherever God is present; and that is everywhere. Because he is in heaven, he is everywhere on earth; because he is ascended, he is here now. In the person of the Holy Spirit he dwells in his Church, and issues forth from the deepest depths of the souls of his disciples, to bear witness to his sovereignty.

William Temple

You are not only risen and alive, you are Lord.
   This is your ascension, your ascendancy over the whole
universe.
You stand over and above all that is best in life as its
   source.
You stand above all that is worst as ultimate victor.
You stand above all powers and authorities as judge.
You stand above all failure and weakness and sin
   as forgiveness and love.
You alone are worthy of total allegiance, total commitment.
You are Lord,
'My Lord and my God.'

Rex Chapman

Today Jesus Christ Our Lord went up to heaven: let our
   hearts go up with him.
   Listen to the words of Saint Paul: 'If you have been raised with Christ, seek the things that are above, where Christ is, seated at the right hand of God. Set your minds on things that are above, not on things that are on earth.' Just as he ascended without leaving us, so too we are already with him in heaven,

although his promises have not yet been fulfilled in our bodies.

Christ is now raised above the heavens; but he still experiences on earth whatever sufferings we his members feel. He showed that this is true when he called out from heaven: 'Saul, Saul, why do you persecute me?' And: 'I was thirsty and you gave me drink.'

Why then do we not exert ourselves on earth so as to be happy with him already in heaven through the faith, hope and charity which unite us with him? Christ, while in heaven, is also with us; and we, while on earth, are also with him. He is with us in his godhead and his power and his love; and we, though we cannot be with him in godhead as he is with us, can be with him in our love, our love for him.

He did not leave heaven when he came down to us from heaven; and he did not leave us when he ascended to heaven again. His own words show that he was in heaven while he was here: 'No one has ascended into heaven but he who descended from heaven, the Son of man who is in heaven.'

He came down from heaven, then, in mercy; and it is he alone who has ascended, since we are in him through grace. This is why no one has descended but Christ, and no one but Christ has ascended: not that the dignity of the head is fused with the body but that the body in its unity is not separated from its head.

St Augustine
Sermon on the Ascension

Who shall speak of thy power, O Lord, and who shall be able to tell the tale of all thy praises? Thou didst descend to human things, not leaving behind heavenly things. Thou art returned to things above, not abandoning things below. Everywhere thou art thy whole self, everywhere wonderful. In the flesh, thou hast yet thy being in the Father; in thine Ascension thou art not torn away from thy being in man. Look upon the prayer of thy people, holy Lord, merciful God; that in this day of thy holy Ascension, even as glory is given to thee on high, so grace may be vouchsafed to us below.

Mozarabic Sacramentary

T his is my day
    A day of rest
A day of hope
A day of peace and happiness.
This is the day the Lord has made
A day to sing
A day to praise
A day to become one in the Spirit.
This is the day the Lord has made
This is my day
This is your day
This is our day.

Doreen Alexander
Guyana

The Ohlone (Native Americans) practise the 'Prayer in Six Directions'.

I n an unhurried fashion, one greets the six directions in prayer.
We turn to the *east* and face the rising sun. God is praised for the gift of new life, of new days, of youth, of beginnings.
Turning towards the *south*, thanks are given for those people, events and things which warm our lives and help us to grow and develop.

The sun sets in the *west*, and so we praise God for sunsets,
    nights, for the endings in our lives.
As we face the *north*, we remember the challenges and
    difficulties in life.
Bending down to touch mother *earth*, we praise the Creator
    for the things which sustain our lives.
Finally, as we gaze into the *sky*, we thank God for our
    hopes and dreams.
Centred in the Creator's universe, we remember God's
    mighty deeds in our lives and can thus move into the
    future.

Michael Galvin
USA

T he Light has returned as it came once before,
    the Song of the Lord is our own song once more;
so let us sing with one heart and one voice
the Song of the Singer in whom we rejoice.

To you, God the Singer, our voices we raise,
to you, Song Incarnate, we give all our praise,
to you, Holy Spirit, our life and our breath,
be glory for ever, through life and through death.

Peter W. A. Davison
Canada
all from *Dare to Dream: a prayer and worship anthology
from around the world*

7th Sunday of Easter
(World Communications Day)

About thirty years ago I underwent what spiritual writers would describe as a fairly typical religious experience. I was 21 years old, and had had a conventional Catholic schooling followed by two years' national service in the army and twelve months' hard slogging as a first-year student in the seminary, which I found tough, especially prayer. One day during prayer I all of a sudden underwent the prolonged experience of being unified, simple, collected, at ease before God. The experience, which took place in church – I can name the precise place and time to this day – brought me to birth spiritually.

From then on I learnt to pray easily, simply, contemplatively and found that where before it had been hard labour it was now extremely relaxed . . . Not only my prayer but the whole of my life began to be changed. The presence of God became 'real' to me in a way that had not happened before. I started to read the Bible and found that passages glowed on the pages as if addressed personally to me by God. I realized, as if for the first time, that he loved me.

In the communal life I was leading I found myself undertaking hard tasks which previously I had slid away from or thought myself incapable of. I felt the power of God within me, again as if for the first time. It is not exaggerating to say that my life was filled with an inward ardour, from waking in the morning to going to bed at night, an ardour which lasted at least a year. I can remember that the most important discovery was to know that my mediocrity and sins were no obstacle, but even an advantage, to receiving the gracious mercy of God, that pursuing perfection and pleasing God were two quite different aims and that I could do the latter without achieving the former. This so thrilled me that I became somewhat of a prig and a bore explaining this, unsolicited, to my friends . . .

I am grateful for that first experience of exuberant joy which set me alight. I am more grateful for the subsequent modifications of that first joy which have made me dip beneath mere 'experience' to reality itself. These modifications have taken different forms. Some have been deeper versions of the initial experience of oneness with God in prayer. Others have been experiences in life of public failure or painful humiliations, which have helped me to be less sentimental and more real in my dealings with God. They have all helped me to learn the lesson that the gifts given by our divine Lover are as nothing compared to the Giver himself.

John Dalrymple
*Longest Journey: notes on Christian
maturity*

7th week of Easter

The two children of the party, although one was fifty years older than the other, went down on their knees at once, assuming the humble attitude which comes naturally to children before their toys, as it comes to men before their God. It is in this attitude that we shall always remember him, crouching eagerly in front of the diminutive stage, while the small electric bulbs which brightened it rose like so many suns over the barren yellow mountains and the vivid green valleys. He had seen these landscapes and crossed these streams, but this was better than Spain, it was better than the world. It was the world made miraculously small so that it stood comfortably on a table; a reality brought nearer to the eye and made dearer to the soul; a thing infinitely big and infinitely little. As I was watching him, some words of his came back into my mind, something about immortality and the next world, and I felt a pang of pain. I found these words, the same evening, in *Tremendous Trifles*: 'If I am ever in any other and better world, I hope that I shall have enough time to play with nothing but toy theatres . . .'

Chesterton has told us, in his *Autobiography*, that his earliest memory of life was brightened by a scene painted by his own father: a medieval castle in which a wonderful princess is imprisoned by a wicked king and towards which a young prince is approaching boldly, holding a golden key (no doubt the same key which fits the lock of knowledge). There is nothing wonderful in the fact that a man of sixty should remember the toys with which he played when he was six; it is more remarkable that he should still play with them in his house at that advanced age. But what is even more surprising is to discover that the same man should confess such a child-like fondness for toys at the age of thirty, and Innocence, or at least Chesterton's conception of this virtue, may be considered as a kind of spiritual chastity. A soul untainted by sin will instinctively restrain its passions, or rather exercise them in the right direction. Innocence may be fierce in its indignation, violent in its love, but must remain a kind of instinctive and unconscious form of restraint.

Emile Cammaerts
The Laughing Prophet:
the seven virtues and G. K. Chesterton

Pentecost

The gift and the presence of the Holy Spirit is the most magnificent and wonderful thing that can happen to us, the human community, all living beings and this earth. For present in the Holy Spirit is not one of the many good or evil spirits lurking about; rather it is God himself, the God who creates and gives life, who redeems and blesses. In the presence of the Holy Spirit the end of the history of guilt, suffering and death has begun . . .

'And it shall come to pass afterward . . .' says God, we read in Joel 2:28. And what the first Christians experienced at the first 'Pentecost' according to Acts 2 took place during the first days of the new creation of the world: the pouring out of God's creative power and spirit that gives life eternally, a stormy wind and tongues of fire with divine breath.

'Pentecost,' as Christians call this event, is thus not an appendix and also not an addition to 'Good Friday' and 'Easter'. 'Pentecost' is the goal of Jesus' death on the cross and his resurrection by God into the glory to come. Where the Holy Spirit is, God is present in a special way and we experience God in our lives that are thus quickened by a source out of the depths of our being. We experience life, healed and redeemed, complete and in its entirety, with all of our senses. We feel and taste, we touch and see our life in God and God in our life. There are many names for God the Holy Spirit. The most beautiful among them for me are the names 'Comforter' (*Paraclete*) and 'source of life' (*fons vitae*).

In praying for the coming of the Spirit, those who pray open themselves for the expectation and let the energy of the Spirit flow into their lives. Even when humans can still only groan for salvation and in their groaning become silent, God's Spirit is already groaning in them and interceding for them (Rom 8:26).

Praying and groaning for God's Spirit to come into this life of imprisonment and this devastated world come itself from the Holy Spirit and are its first signs of life.

The response to the prayer for the Holy Spirit is his coming and staying, his being poured out and indwelling in us. Whoever prays for the Holy Spirit to come to us, into our hearts, into our community and to our earth does not want to flee to heaven or be removed to the great beyond. He or she has hope for his or her heart, his or her community and this earth. We do not pray, 'Let us come into your kingdom . . .' We pray, 'Your kingdom come . . . *on earth* as it is in heaven.' Magnificent, unbroken affirmation of life lies behind this prayer for the divine Spirit to come to us fragile and earthly human beings.

Jürgen Moltmann
'Pentecost and Theology of Life'

It is done.
Once again the Fire has penetrated the earth.

Not with sudden crash of thunderbolt, riving the mountain tops: does the Master break down doors to enter his own home? Without earthquake, or thunderclap: the flame has lit up the whole world from within. All things individually and collectively are penetrated and flooded by it, from the inmost core of the tiniest atom to the mighty sweep of the most universal laws of being: so naturally has it flooded every element, every energy, every connecting link in the unity of our cosmos; that one might suppose the cosmos to have burst spontaneously into flame . . .

At this moment when your life has just poured with superabundant vigour into the sacrament of the world, I shall savour with heightened consciousness the intense yet tranquil rapture of a vision whose coherence and harmonies I can never exhaust.

Pierre Teilhard de Chardin
Hymn of the Universe

I n this storm of love two spirits strive together: the Spirit of
God and our own spirit. God, through the Holy Ghost,
inclines himself towards us; and, thereby, we are touched in
love. And our spirit, by God's working and by the power of
love, presses and inclines itself into God: and, thereby, God is
touched. From these two contacts there arises the strife of love,
at the very deeps of this meeting; and in that most inward and
ardent encounter, each spirit is deeply wounded by love.

These two spirits, that is, our own spirit and the Spirit of
God, sparkle and shine one into the other, and each shows to
the other its face. This makes each of the spirits yearn for the
other in love. Each demands of the other all that it is: and each
offers to the other all that it is and invites it to all that it is.

This makes the lovers melt into each other. God's touch and
his gifts, our loving craving and our giving back: these fulfil
love. This flux and reflux causes the fountain of love to brim
over; and thus the touch of God and our loving craving become
one simple love.

Jan van Ruysbroeck
The Adornment of the Spiritual Marriage

E nter my heart, O Holy Spirit,
come in blessed mercy and set me free.
Throw open, O Lord, the locked doors of my mind;
cleanse the chambers of my thought for thy dwelling:
light there the fires of thine own holy brightness in new
    understandings of truth,
O Holy Spirit, very God, whose presence is liberty,
grant me the perfect freedom to be thy servant
today, tomorrow, evermore.

Eric Milner-White

The soul of man is a flame, a bird of fire that leaps from bough to bough, from head to head, and that shouts: 'I cannot stand still, I cannot be consumed, no one can quench me!'

Nikos Kazantzakis

People hardly know the Holy Spirit as a person, and then only in an incomplete, dim and confused fashion. It cannot be otherwise. For a full knowledge of the Holy Spirit would make all created being entirely spirit-bearing, entirely deified, and would confer a completely realized illumination. Then history would be ended; then the fullness of time would be at hand, and all waiting would be over; then there would indeed be no more time.

But as long as history continues, only instants of illumination by the Spirit are possible; only certain individuals at certain moments know the Paraclete, when they are raised above time into eternity.

Certainly, the Holy Spirit is indeed at work in the Church. But knowledge of the Spirit has always been a pledge or reward – at special moments and with exceptional people; and this is how it will be until 'all is fulfilled'. That is why, when reading the Church's writings, we cannot fail to be struck by something that seems strange at first but that later, in the light of what precedes, manifests its inner necessity. It is this: that all the holy fathers and mystical philosophers speak of the importance of the idea of the Spirit in the Christian world-view, but hardly any of them explains himself precisely and exactly. It is evident that the holy fathers know *something*; but what is even clearer is that this knowledge is so intimate, so hidden, without echo, ineffable, that they lack the power to express it in precise language . . .

But the closer we draw to the End of History, the more do new, hitherto invisible roseate rays of the coming Day without evening appear on the domes of the holy Church.

Our characteristic attitude towards the Holy Spirit, it seems to me, is precisely one of expectation, of hope; a gentle and reconciling hope.

Paul Florensky

Holy spirit,
mighty wind of God,
inhabit our darkness,
brood over our abyss
and speak to our chaos
that we may breathe with your life
and share your creation
in the power of Jesus Christ.
Amen.

Janet Morley
All Desires Known

Cardinal Basil Hume,
17 June

First thoughts about death are normally ones of fear and dread. It is partly having to face the unknown, partly the recoiling from the final agony, as we lie helpless and perhaps wired up to all those machines competing for access to our body. On a bad day there is that common fear which tells us that there is no future, only a blank, nothing. We are no more. And then another thought comes to trouble us, and it is how quickly we are forgotten . . .

Then in a very bad moment I think about the relief my demise will bring to some people. I do worry about the insensitive and clumsy ways I have handled some people, about my selfishness . . . no, I won't go on listing my faults here. It is a bit embarrassing. 'Don't forget' – I once heard a great abbot say – 'when you die somebody will be relieved . . .'

But there is another voice that speaks within us. It is not the voice that brings news that depresses and frightens. It has another message. 'You have loved so many persons in your life; are you to be frustrated and denied that which you have sought throughout your life?' It is not so . . .

Some instinct, a positive and optimistic one, speaks of hope leading to life after death. In the animal world the instinct for survival is strong. It is so with humans as well. We want to go on, unless overwhelmed by depression or weariness. Our fear is that we may not. That instinct beckons us. Our mind says, 'It may be; it must be.' Then faith finally takes over, and with triumph declares, 'It is so.' Yes, there is life after death. The instinct for survival is a true one; it does not deceive. How could it be otherwise since it is God-given? Faith brings the reassurance which instinct was seeking.

The vision of God is that for which we were made. To see him as he is, face to face, that is the moment of ecstasy, the ever-present 'now' of total happiness. . . .

I now have no fear of death. I look forward to this friend leading me to a world where my parents, my brother and other relatives are, and my friends. I shall see those who fashioned me in my monastic life. I shall see Abbot Byrne, Anthony, Kenneth, David, Barnabas, Hubert, James, Denis, Robert, Peter, Walter, John and many others. I look forward to that.

Cardinal Basil Hume
Basil in Blunderland

Trinity Sunday

Ah, now I have found what I was looking for! In symbolic form a Trinity now dawns clear for me, the Trinity which is yourself, my God. You, Father, made heaven and earth in that Beginning who originates our wisdom, that is to say in the Wisdom who is your Son, coequal and coeternal with yourself. And already we have spoken at length of heaven's heaven, and of the invisible and unorganized earth, and spoken too of the abyss, dark with the unstable flux of spiritual formlessness and destined so to remain until it should be converted to him from whom it drew such life as it had. But once illuminated by him it was transformed into a life so beautiful that it became the heaven overarching that other heavenly vault to be established later between upper and lower waters. I understood already that the name 'God' signified the Father who made these things, and the name 'Beginning' the Son in whom he made them; and believing as I did that my God is a Trinity, I sought for a Trinity among his holy utterances. And there was your Spirit poised above the waters! Here, then, is the Trinity who is my God; Father, Son and Holy Spirit, creator of the whole created universe . . .

To whom should I speak, and how express myself, about the passion that drags us headlong into the deep, and the charity that uplifts us through your Spirit, who hovered over the waters? To whom should I say this, and in what terms? These are not literally places, into which we plunge and from which we emerge: what could seem more place-like than they, yet what is in reality more different? They are movements of the heart, they are two loves. One is the uncleanness of our own spirit, which like a flood-tide sweeps us down, in love with restless cares; the other is the holiness of your Spirit, which bears us upward in a love for peace beyond all care, that our hearts may be lifted up to you, to where your Spirit is poised above the waters, so that once our soul has crossed over those waters on which there is no reliance we may reach all-surpassing rest . . .

Can anyone comprehend the almighty Trinity? Everyone talks about it – but is it really the Trinity of which they talk? Rare indeed is the person who understands the subject of his discourse, when he speaks of that. People argue and wrangle over it, yet no one sees that vision unless he is at peace.

St Augustine
The Confessions

One the love that did unite them,
One the Lover in all Three:
Lover that is the Belovèd,
In whom each dwelt equally.

For the Being of three Persons
They possess'd the same each one,
Each one loving both the others
Since they had it as their own . . .

Infinite and everlasting
Was the love that bound them so.
One alone this love that bound them
Which as Essence we may know,
And the more this love had oneness,
More the love that thence did grow.

As belovèd dwells in lover
Each in other did reside,
And that same love that unites them
Did in both of them abide;
Each was equal to the other
And in worth ranked equally.
Thus there were in that tri-union
One Belovèd, Persons three.

St John of the Cross
Poems

Almighty God, most blessed and most holy, before the brightness of whose presence the angels veil their faces: with lowly reverence and adoring love we acknowledge thine infinite glory, and worship thee, Father, Son, and Holy Spirit, eternal Trinity. Blessing, and honour, and glory, and power be unto our God, for ever and ever.

Church of Scotland, *Book of Common Order*

Tender Trinity and true,
    Lie with me this night.
        Enfold my thoughts. Bless:
Those whose passions have no homecoming;
Those whose touch is fierce, without grace;
Those whose kisses stand at death's wall.

Dread and friendly Trinity,
    Lie with me this night.
        Encircle my mind. Bless:
Those afraid, hurt in fierce desire;
Those taken in love with numb hearts;
Those haunted by limbs from memory's
    store.

Hard and smiling Trinity,
    Lie with me this night.
        Enclose my spirit. Bless:
Those whose hate chokes purity;
Those whose flesh surges past giving;
Those whose lives sink in yearning.

Derek Webster
Our Time Now

I arise today:
in the might of Heaven;
brightness of Sun;
whiteness of Snow;
splendour of Fire;
speed of Lightning;
swiftness of Wind;
depth of Sea;
stability of Earth;
firmness of Rock.

I arise today:
in the might of God for my piloting;
Power of God
for my upholding;
Wisdom of God
for my guidance;
Eye of God
for my foresight;
Ear of God
for my hearing;
Word of God
for my utterance;
Hand of God
for my guardianship;
Path of God
for my precedence;
Shield of God
for my protection;
Host of God
for my salvation;

Christ for my guardianship today:
against poison, against burning,
against drowning, against wounding,
that there may come to me a multitude of rewards;
Christ with me, Christ before me,
Christ behind me, Christ in me,

Christ under me, Christ over me,
Christ to right of me, Christ to left of me,
Christ in lying down, Christ in sitting,
Christ in rising up,
Christ in the heart of every person who may think of me!
Christ in the mouth of everyone who may speak to me!
Christ in every eye which may look on me!
Christ in every ear which may hear me!

I arise today:
in vast might, invocation of the Trinity
belief in a Threeness;
confession of Oneness;
meeting in the Creator;
Domini est salus, Domini est salus,
Christi est salus;
Salus tua, Domine, sit semper
nobiscum.

St Patrick from *The Lorica (Breastplate)*

11th week of the year

W hat makes a landscape or a person or an idea come to life for me and become a presence towards which I surrender myself? I recognize, I respond, I fall in love, I worship – yet it was not I who took the first step. In every such encounter there has been an anonymous third party who makes the introduction, acts as a go-between, makes two beings aware of each other, sets up a current of communication between them. What is more, this invisible go-between does not simply stand between us but is activating each of us from inside. Moses approaching the burning bush is no scientific observer; the same fiery essence burns in his own heart also. He and the thorn-bush are caught and held, as it were, in the same magnetic field.

I have already started to talk about this force of influence in very personal terms. I am bound to do so because the effect of this power is always to bring a mere object into a personal relationship with me, to turn an *It* into a *Thou*.

So Christians find it quite natural to give a personal name to this current of communication, this invisible go-between. They call him the Holy Spirit, the Spirit of God.

Walking down the long gallery of the Academy of Fine Arts in Florence one meets three of Michelangelo's supreme statements in marble which seem to present a progression of insight. First comes the group of four slaves, unfinished giants struggling to emerge from the raw stone that still imprisons them. Next one's attention is caught and held by the gigantic David which, as one studies the face from different angles, presents all the conflicting emotions of a moment of decision, doubt, resolution and terror. And the third, also unfinished, is the

Palestrina Pieta, which some find theatrical; but the monumental grief of the Virgin and the peace of total abandonment in the dead Christ combine to speak the ultimate word about sacrifice. These are the three aspects of the creative activity of the Holy Spirit, the Lord, the Giver of Life . . .

From within the depths of its being he urges every creature again and again to take one more tiny step in the direction of higher consciousness and personhood; again and again he creates for every creature the occasion for spontaneity and the necessity for choice, and at every turn he opposes self-interest with a contrary principle of sacrifice, of existence for the other.

And, in the fulness of time, all of this was perfectly disclosed in Jesus Christ, who was conceived by the Holy Spirit and to whom the Holy Spirit has been directing men's attention ever since. It is not difficult to see how this must affect our understanding of that mission which is the continuing Christ-centred activity of that same Holy Spirit.

John V. Taylor
The Go-Between God

Corpus Christi
(Thursday after Trinity Sunday)

I once heard a Zen Master lecture on Buddhist and Christian symbolism. He spoke of the Buddha on the lotus as the central Buddhist symbol and of Jesus nailed to the cross as the central Christian symbol. Afterwards, having occasion to speak with him, I said that while the cross is undoubtedly a great Christian symbol, Christianity has a more important symbol, namely, the Eucharist. For while the cross speaks of the death of Jesus, the Eucharist speaks not only of his death but also of his resurrection and second coming: *Christ has died; Christ has risen; Christ will come again.*

The point is important. Every student of religion knows that symbols are of the very essence of religion and of mysticism. Symbols, and symbols alone, can carry us to mystical levels of awareness and to states of consciousness which are completely unknown to dry, discursive theology. I used to think naïvely that Zen Buddhism was without symbols because of its stress on emptiness and nothingness and 'no dependence on words and letters'. Now I realize that the very emptiness and nothingness are symbols, as also are the lotus posture and the rhythmic breathing. Now I know that Zen is full of symbols.

One of the characteristics of the Judeo-Christian tradition is that the most important symbols are also historical events or historical persons. The Eucharist is a symbol and it is also the reality: the body of Christ. It is the true bread, the true manna which came down from heaven and gives life to the world.

Bread is indeed a powerful symbol. Alas, those who live in

the first world do not appreciate bread because they have it in abundance and have never experienced hunger. Let them go to the Third World. Let them see people undernourished, people starving, people desperate because they have no bread for their children, then they will realize that every scrap of bread is precious. Then they will appreciate the delicate command of Jesus: 'Gather up the fragments left over, that nothing may be lost' (John 6:12). The children of Israel, starving in Sinai, appreciated the gift of bread; and the gospel tells us that what they, and we, really desire is the true bread which gives eternal life. This is Jesus who makes the extraordinary claim that 'he who comes to me shall not hunger, and he who believes in me shall never thirst' (John 6:35).

William Johnston
Christian Mysticism Today

The body has been prepared for the burial; the body is not a piece of outworn clothing, as some seemingly devout people like to say, which has been cast off for the soul to be free. A body is much more than this for a Christian; there is nothing that befalls the soul in which the body does not take part. We receive impressions of this world, but also of the divine world partly through the body.

Every sacrament is a gift of God, conferred on the soul by means of physical actions; the waters of baptism, the oil of chrism, the bread and wine of communion are all taken from the material world. We can never do either good or evil otherwise than in conjunction with our body.

The body is not there only, as it were, for the soul to be born, mature and then to go, abandoning it; the body, from the very first day to the last, has been the co-worker of the soul in all things and is, together with the soul, the total man. It remains marked for ever, as it were, by the imprint of the soul and the common life they had together. Linked with the soul, the body is also linked through the sacraments to Jesus Christ himself. We commune to his Blood and Body, and the body is thus united in its own right with the divine world with which it comes into contact.

Metropolitan Anthony of Sourozh
Creative Prayer

As outcasts of society
locked up in prisons bare,
the Eucharist, Lord, is the gift to us
in which we all can share.

In communion, Lord, we are made as one by you,
    our God and gracious king;
by your sacrifice you give us life,
    and we in joy your praises sing.

No longer are we outcasts
for in you we realize
that to love and trust in your sweet word
will lead to paradise.

We are a community of sorrow;
    now hope sets our heart aflame:
by the Eucharist you have changed us, Lord,
    to a community of your name.

Richard McIlkenny
One of the 'Birmingham Six'

 We went for walks in the Tuscan fields, and visited a villa called La Petraia. There we sat watching dragonflies skimming over a pond at evening time. The trees were reflected in the water and I was conscious again of thinking that probably I preferred the mystery of reflections to the clearness of reality. This had always puzzled me since Plato maintained that our world was but the reflection of reality and I seemed to prefer unreality, and surely that was wrong? But somehow that did not seem to matter: it was good to be alive.

All the while I attended daily Mass and prayed for the gift of faith. But I seemed no nearer belief, despite my intellectual acceptance of Christianity. Then one day Madre Geltrude and I knelt alone in church. She quietly turned to me and, pointing to the tabernacle, asked: '*Ist Er da?*' ('Is he there?'). Did I believe in the Real Presence of Christ? Poised between the answers 'No' and 'Yes', neither of which I wanted to give, I suddenly heard myself saying 'Yes'. In that moment I received the gift of faith, which has ever remained with me.

After I had received the gift of faith I was silently inebriated for many days. On one of these days I made a trip to San Cresci in the Mugello. There among the terraced slopes and deserted farmhouses Madre Geltrude and I walked and talked, often laughing for sheer joy.

I was very happy. Towards evening we sat down on a small hill. Cattle were moving slowly in the deep valley and birds were swooping low beneath us. We now sat in silence, the sun still pleasantly warm on our backs. I became powerfully aware of God's presence. It was absolutely overwhelming. I had to close my eyes and could hardly breathe; his presence was almost tangible. He was all around me, enfolding me in the warm evening air.

This experience has never been repeated, but the happiness of it comes back whenever I feel the sun warm on my back. Sometimes when I am gardening this gladness comes upon me. I understand the value of memory and appreciate the psalms in which the Israelites recalled God's saving help.

The remembrance gives one confidence in the present moment and allows one to hope in the future. Simple awareness has sometimes come to me when I have heard people talking about God or something beautiful. I would feel my heart glowing within me for the moment, in affirmation of the recognized truth. Perhaps this is how the disciples on the road to Emmaus responded to the sensed but unrecognized presence of the Lord.

Paula Fairlie
in *A Touch of God: eight monastic journeys*

St Thomas More and St John Fisher, 22 June

Think how Thomas More lived in this place,
think of that bookish, that sand-blasted face:
that life so heaven-loving, so death-fated,
the example too strong to be imitated,
the simplest and greatest of Englishmen.
Wisdom is justified in its children.
Truth is scribbled on water, it breaks like bone,
what Thomas suffered is written in stone.
His wisdom was not in earthquake and fire,
it was like the persistent, whistling air.
Thomas loved truth, not dragged it by the hair,
he said variety of opinion
would be of one mind in the world to come . . .

Thomas More in his words and his living
was a man obedient to the king,
and his whole family in his presence
showed gentle manners and obedience:
his reason was free, God was his confidence.
He was Cato: he would not compromise;
terrible honesty sat in his eyes.
God's spirit descended on his prison
like a dark pentecost to his reason.
Heavenly wisdom the last thirst of Christ
human sorrow's acid and analyst
gave him knowledge of God, freedom of mind,
true lover and true brother of mankind.

Wisdom is a city and the spirit

of Christ in his last hour is building it,
the tower of his last breath still soars up
over the broken bread, the given cup,
and to recall it, to speak it again
is new life and religion of all men.
The river of wisdom in this city
runs from a rock the people cannot see:
London has lived with unwisdom so long,
we are all fugitives from that chain gang,
unreason, avarice, lack of delight,
unbrotherhood, unliberty, unlight.
Christ in his death spoke the first words of life,
there is no other bedrock of belief,
we believe and enact his death and love,
this is a reasoning nothing can move,
this is the city of heaven's graces
where the children are as tall as the trees:
nothing can live in it but what is pure
and what is without fear, and will endure;
what we look for is what we started from.
God is the city, love is the wisdom.

Peter Levi
from Sermon on St Thomas More

Birth of St John the Baptist, 24 June

Elisabeth was married to a priest call Zacharias and they had grown old together serving God. They must have been happy people, for the servants of God are always happy, but they had one grief; they had no child. They had prayed long and earnestly to God to give them one, but the years had passed and they had grown old and still there was no child. So then after the foolish fashion of men and women they had imagined that God had not heard them. They had learned a good deal in a long life but not yet that God never fails to answer prayer. But he answers it in the way and at the moment that is best for everybody, and man who does not know all about everybody, and cannot see the wonderful pattern that God is weaving with the lives of us all, gets discouraged if the way is not to his liking and the moment delayed.

Elisabeth's baby had to be delayed because God had chosen her child to do a particular piece of work for him at a special time.

Elizabeth Goudge
God So Loved the World

The disciple John, who we are quite sure went to Jesus at the behest of the Baptist (John 1:35–37), dared to put the spontaneous remark about the 'friend of the bridegroom' (John 3:29) on the lips of the Baptist, which none of the Twelve would have dared claim for themselves, since the greeting 'friend' is first found in the mouth of Jesus at the hour of the Eucharist (John 15:14–15). Thus it is theologically correct that medieval pictures of the judgement place beside the judging Lord, as the two great intercessory mediators, not Mary and Peter, but Mary and the Baptist, because he embodies in his person the fullness of the Old Covenant, of the already-begun saving action of the Father, and because in the interconnection of their missions and in personal intimacy he is the closest to Jesus after his mother, Mary. And just as Mary, the beginning of the New Covenant, is, on the occasion of the visit from Jesus' relatives (Mark 3:31–33), placed back together with the 'brothers' in the abandoned Old Covenant, which is now to be superseded, so John, who himself remains standing at the border of the Old Covenant, is lifted over this border into the New as the 'Elias who is come,' as 'more than a prophet,' as the 'greatest to be born of woman' (Matthew 11:15, 9, 11), as the one who in his own 'being-as-self-giving' (Mark 1:14) gives the signal for the entrance of Jesus into his own self-giving. Such a person will not be left behind and forgotten in the work which Jesus will found; as the earthly starter of the mission of Jesus, he enters into it along with him. His feast day, up to now still with vigil, is celebrated shortly before Peter and Paul. In the theology of the Church, however, he is forgotten.

Hans Urs von Balthasar
The von Balthasar Reader

12th week of the year

I like shadows on the road, Lord.
It was a quiet and warm evening,
and the sun put long shadows on the road.

I thought of the shadows of life,
times when the light seems dim,
like when I fail an exam,
or I seem to mess up the family with my temper,
or I think of the fights at home,
or when I don't know what I'll do in the future.

In the shadow of failure,
let me know the light of hope,
and in the shadow of quarrels,
let me know the light of forgiveness.
For there's no shadow without some light,
like the shadows on the road
are caused by the sun or the moon.

In the shadows of a fall-out in friendship,
let me know the light of love,
that there can always be a making-up or new friends
round the corner.

In the shadows of rows at home,
let me know the light of compassion,
and let me know I can find security in many people,
and in your love and care for me, Lord.
When I don't know what to do in the future,
give me patience and guidance;
I believe you have hopes for my life,
that I can do something really worthwhile for you.

Help me believe, find meaning
in all the darkness of life;
help me see darkness
as the beginning of new light,
like your cross was the beginning of resurrection.
May I always believe in the light within all the shadows.

Donal Neary
*Lighting the Shadows: reflections and
prayers for young people*

D o not look forward to what might happen tomorrow; the
same everlasting Father who cares for you today will take
care of you tomorrow and every day. Either he will shield you
from suffering or he will give you unfailing strength to bear
it. Be at peace, then, and put aside all anxious thoughts and
imaginings.

St Francis de Sales

St Peter and St Paul,
29 June

You know, brethren, that of all Our Lord's apostles and martyrs the two whose feast we celebrate today seem to possess a special grandeur. Nor is this surprising, since to these two men the Lord entrusted his Church in a special way. For when St Peter proclaimed that the Lord was the Son of God, the Lord told him: 'You are Peter, and on this rock I will build my Church. And I will give you the keys of the kingdom of heaven.' But in a way the Lord put St Paul on the same level, as Paul himself said: 'He who worked through Peter in the apostolate also worked through me among the Gentiles . . .'

These are the pillars that support the Church by their teaching, their prayers, their example of patience. Our Lord strengthened these pillars. In the beginning they were very weak and could not support either themselves or others. This had been wonderfully arranged by Our Lord, for if they had always been strong, one might have thought their strength was their own. Our Lord wished to show first what they were of themselves and only afterwards to strengthen them, so that all would know that their strength was entirely from God. Again, these men were to be fathers of the Church and physicians who would heal the weak. But they would be unable to pity the weaknesses of others unless they had first experienced their own weakness.

And so Our Lord strengthened these pillars of the world, that is, of the Church. One pillar, St Peter, was very weak indeed, to be overthrown by the words of a single maidservant. Afterwards the Lord strengthened this pillar. He did so first when he asked him three times: 'Peter, do you love me?' and

Peter three times answered, 'I love you'. For when he had three times denied the Lord, his love for him was to some extent lessened and this pillar became weak and broke, but by three times confessing his love for him it was strengthened. This strengthening was followed by another when the Holy Spirit was sent. Then this pillar became so strong that he could not be moved by being flogged, stoned, threatened, and at last even by being put to death.

Again, that other pillar, Paul, was undoubtedly weak at first, but hear how strong he became afterwards. 'I am certain,' he said, 'that neither death nor life, nor angels nor anything else in all creation will be able to separate me from the love of God.'

St Aelred

Sacred Heart
(2nd Friday after Trinity Sunday)

I often wonder why people are so anxious about their future, as though they did not believe in the omnipotent love of God for us. If they claim to be atheists or agnostics, I can understand. But if they say they are believers, and then doubt how things will work out – why so-and-so still has no job, why his brother-in-law is not yet able to marry, and so on – it makes one wonder how firm one's faith really is.

One of the gifts of God I am most grateful for is having met, at the age of sixteen, a Franciscan priest. I was not yet a Catholic, but a Zoroastrian who was gradually falling in love with Jesus. This Franciscan came into my life at a crucial moment and taught me one solid doctrine – to trust in God by living one day at a time. Thus when I asked him what would I do if I were thrown out of my house for becoming a Catholic – I had no profession yet (I was eighteen on my baptism day) – he taught me that God would tell me what I should do when that day came.

I was truly blest to be taught and brought up by him for the next few years on this wonderful principle of Jesus: to live one day at a time. 'Be not solicitous for the morrow, for the morrow will be solicitous for itself.' What other way of life can bring one more peace and certitude of God's love for us? This way of believing in his love, and truly trying to live one day at a time, has brought me nothing but blessings and peace. Anxiety about the morrow has never been a headache for me. I have also tried to help others to live like that: sure of God's love for one and one day at a time. If you've never tried this, please do! You'll find it a great blessing and a peaceful way of living.

It simply means telling God as often as one can, 'Lord, I believe in your love for me,' or the triple invocation I learned in my college days, which brought total assurance and peace:

> Sacred Heart of Jesus, I trust in thee.
> Sacred Heart of Jesus, I believe in thy love for me.
> Sacred Heart of Jesus, may thy kingdom come.

Try it and you'll find life ever so much easier and calmer to live.

Sr Vandana
Written in Rishikesh, India, for *The Tablet*

Immaculate Heart of Mary
(2nd Saturday after Trinity Sunday)

Mary,
by love's sacrifice
your heart is pierced.
Mary,
by love's generosity
you are emptied.
Mary,
in temptation
may we imitate your obedience.
Mary,
in the hour of trial
may we know
the love you gazed upon
at Calvary.

Frank Topping
An Impossible God (adapted)

Much of what [Léon Bloy] writes about Our Lady in his La Salette book is very fine and often goes straight to one's heart: for instance that Mary, weeping, suffering for her people, 'is' the Heart of Jesus – wounded, open. This is so clear, for me, that it seems like 'something one ought always to have known'. Scheeben already spoke of Mary as 'the Heart of the Church' – and if the Church 'is' the 'form of a slave', the torn, wounded Body of Our Lord, then this is perfectly obvious!

Or, again, that because the children saw Our Lady with a 'living Crucifix' on her breast, she is the bride of the Song of Songs: 'A bundle of myrrh is my beloved to me: he shall abide between my breasts' – things overpowering in their simplicity, yet, as far as I know, no one ever saw them before or at least thought of expressing them. You could also call her the Mourning Lady: the Shekhinah.

Ida Friederike Görres

R ejoicing with you,
grieving with you,
Mary, graced by God –
Love's Mystery did come to you –
of our race we deem you most the blessed,
save but the Blessed One,
the Child who came to birth in you.

Woman holy,
trembling at the Presence of the Angel,
willing the rare and marvellous exchange,
in the darkness holding the Unseen,
bearing forth the Word made flesh for
    Earth's redeeming,
hold to your heart our world,
and pray for humankind,
that we with you be bearers of the Christ,
through this and all our days,
and at the last.

Jim Cotter
Prayer at Night's Approaching

13th week of the year

But how hard it is, sometimes, to love! How often it seems you turn the other cheek, you give your cloak and your trousers and your shoes, and then when you are left naked, you are beaten and reviled besides. There are two women at this moment, as there have been many more through the years, who accept for months our ministrations, our help and loving kindness, only to turn and rend us. Lies, scandal, accusations roll from their lips in a torrent and a flood of poison.

Failures. It is these things that overwhelm one. Physical sickness like epilepsy, senility, insanity, drug cases, alcoholics; and just the plain, ordinary poor who can't get along, can't find a place to live, who need clothes, shelter, food, jobs, care, and most of all love; these are our daily encounters.

So it is wonderful that this retreat comes in the middle of summer, when one can stop and think in one's heart about these things. I have made this retreat eight times, and always there is something new, always there is something to learn about how to progress in the love of God and one's neighbour.

I am speaking of heavenly things, but heaven and earth are linked together as truly as body and soul. We begin to live again each morning, we rise from the dead, the sun rises, spring comes around, and then resurrection. And the great study of how truly to become the children of God, to be made like God, to participate in the life of God, this is the study of the retreat. It is a painful study. It is breathing rarefied air; one must get used to this air of the mountains, so clear, cold, sharp, and fresh. It is like wine, and we have prayed to Mary and said, 'We have no wine', and she has given us wine, the body and blood of her Son, the life of her Son, the love of her Son.

Dorothy Day
Selected Writings

B y being attentive, by learning to listen (or recovering the natural capacity to listen which cannot be learned any more than breathing), we can find ourself engulfed in such happiness that it cannot be explained: the happiness of being at one with everything in that hidden ground of Love for which there can be no explanations.

Thomas Merton

Sea Sunday
(2nd Sunday in July)

Though our mouths were full of song as the sea, and our tongues of exultation as the multitude of its waves, and our lips of praise as the wide-extended firmament; though our eyes shone with light like the sun and the moon, and our hands were spread forth like the eagles of heaven, and our feet were swift as hinds, we should still be unable to thank thee and to bless thy name, O Lord our God and God of our fathers, for one thousandth or one ten-thousandth part of the bounties which thou hast bestowed upon our fathers and upon us.

The Hebrew Morning Service

Come down, O Christ, and help me! reach thy hand,
　For I am drowning in a stormier sea
　Than Simon on thy Lake of Galilee:
The wine of life is spilled upon the sand,
My heart is as some famine-murdered land
　Whence all good things have perished utterly,
　And well I know my soul in Hell must lie
If I this night before God's throne should stand.

Oscar Wilde

E ternal and most glorious God, suffer me not so to under-value myself as to give away my soul, thy soul, thy dear and precious soul, for nothing; and all the world is nothing, if the soul must be given for it. Preserve therefore my soul, O Lord, because it belongs to thee, and preserve my body because it belongs to my soul. Thou alone dost steer my boat through all its voyage, but hast a more special care of it, when it comes to a narrow current, or to a dangerous fall of waters. Thou hast a care of the preservation of my body in all the ways of my life; but, in the straits of death, open thine eyes wider, and enlarge thy providence towards me so far that no illness or agony may shake and benumb the soul. Do thou so make my bed in all my sickness that, being used to thy hand, I may be content with any bed of thy making. Amen.

John Donne (adapted)

O Christ, who art the way and the truth, send now thy guardian Angel to go with thy servants, as once thou didst send him to Tobias, and for thy glory keep them safe and sound from all harm and evil by the prayers of the Mother of God, O thou who alone lovest mankind.

Eastern Church

P rotect me, O Lord;
   My boat is so small,
And your sea is so big.

Old Breton fishermen's prayer
All from *God of a Hundred Names*
ed. Barbara Greene and Victor Gollancz

14th week of the year

Great are you, O Lord, and exceedingly worthy of praise; your power is immense, and your wisdom beyond reckoning. And so we humans, who are a due part of your creation, long to praise you – we who carry our mortality about with us, carry the evidence of our sin and with it the proof that you thwart the proud. Yet these humans, due part of your creation as they are, still do long to praise you. You arouse us so that praising you may bring us joy, because you have made us and drawn us to yourself, and our heart is unquiet until it rests in you.

I love you, Lord, with no doubtful mind but with absolute certainty. You pierced my heart with your word, and I fell in love with you. But the sky and the earth too, and everything in them – all these things around me are telling me that I should love you; and since they never cease to proclaim this to everyone, those who do not hear are left without excuse. But you, far above, will show mercy to anyone with whom you have already determined to deal mercifully, and will grant pity on whomsoever you choose. Were this not so, the sky and the earth would be proclaiming your praises to the deaf.

But what am I loving when I love you? Not beauty of body nor transient grace, not this fair light which is now so friendly to my eyes, not melodious song in all its lovely harmonies, not the sweet fragrance of flowers or ointments or spices, not manna or honey, not limbs that draw me to carnal embrace: none of these do I love my God.

And yet I do love a kind of light, a kind of voice, a certain fragrance, a food and an embrace, when I love my God: a light, voice, fragrance, food and embrace for my mind, where

something limited to no place shines into my mind, where
something not snatched away by passing time sings for me,
where something no breath blows away yields to me its scent,
where there is savour undiminished by famished eating, and
where I am clasped in a union from which no satiety can tear
me away. This is what I love, when I love my God.

St Augustine
Confessions

St Benedict,
11 July

I believe profoundly in academic excellence, and the pursuit of it as important just for its own sake. It will be a sad day if we fall into the trap of assessing the importance of things such as higher education solely in terms of their usefulness. We need men and women to explore the secrets of the universe and to work relentlessly to discover truth.

There is, however, another knowledge, a different wisdom. It comes to those who have glimpsed something of God in prayer. It is a knowledge of him as the ultimate truth; it is a wisdom which gives proper perspective to the created universe. St Benedict once had a vision as he looked out from the tower at the monastery at Monte Cassino. He saw 'the whole world as if gathered into one sunbeam'. St Gregory commented 'Animae videnti creatorem, angusta est omnis creatura – To the soul which sees the creator, all creation seems small.' If we catch a glimpse of the glory of God, we see the world, its peoples and events in their true perspective. We see them as they really are. Alone in his cave, Benedict learned that the prayerful study of God leads to a partial understanding of who and what he is. It is no more than a small shaft of light breaking through the cloud of unknowing. It is an exploration of that Reality which gives meaning to all else.

The call to be a hermit is a rare one; it requires a balanced mind, a tough constitution, an ability to stick at it in moments of darkness. None the less, there is something which we can learn from it. It is that each of us needs an opportunity to be alone and silent, or even, indeed, to find space in the day or in the week, just to reflect and to listen to the voice of God that speaks deep within us. Ours is a noisy and hectic world. There is too much clamour, too many preoccupations and distractions. So much so that God is squeezed out of our lives, if indeed he had ever been admitted into them. Of course, people want to know whether there is a God before they seek to admit him into their lives, where he can be found, what he is like. Oddly enough, it does not always work that way. Very often the starting point is a constant and prayerful search for God. We search precisely because we have not yet discovered the object of our seeking. In fact, our search for God is only our response to his search for us. He knocks at our door, but for many people, their lives are too preoccupied for them to be able to hear.

Cardinal Basil Hume
Address to the Parliamentary
Christian Fellowship

15th week of the year

I hope these few hours will be a time for you to relax from your busy lives and just be and rejoice in this wonderful world God has given us to live in . . . to listen to the song of creation and to the messages created things convey just by being themselves . . . They are in great simplicity what they are intended to be – a tree, a sheep, a flower – and this wonderful presentness gives the natural world a transparency to God which can catch us by surprise and delight. Mungo Park, the great explorer, so the story goes, had been journeying for days and miles in the bleak wilderness of China when quite suddenly he saw at his feet a little blue flower – and he said gently, 'God has been here'.

This transparency can also be found in a young child before he or she has become too complex and grown-up. Jesus indicated that this was the way into his kingdom . . . 'unless you become as little children' . . . almost an affront to sophisticated, achieving, modern men and women, but something the created world is telling us if we would listen. For creation is all of a piece and human beings are not on a solitary pedestal but very much part of the blood and sweat and the glory of the universe: biologically and spiritually the place where all life meets and is lifted up in praise of the Creator in the conscious awareness of men and women.

There is something else too, which was brought home in the dedication of our chapel. When God became flesh he as it were assumed and sanctified the whole of creation, bringing it to that glory which is its true end, as Paul says in his letter to the Romans. Our wooden chapel was burnt down six years ago in an electric storm, and a few months later the hurricane took down three of our 600-year-old yew trees – for some of us an even greater disaster. We wanted somehow to incorporate the wood from these trees into our new chapel and, after a few tussles with our architect, brought in part of the trunk as the base of the altar. The branches support the lectern and the candlesticks have been carved out of the yew. In the north window the evergreen stoneoak takes the place of stained glass and we feel that in some way the chapel has grown out of the soil of Minster.

During the dedication the bishop, using the basic elements of water and fire and oil, hallowed the chapel and gave it the promise of the new creation – when all things will be made one in Christ – a true place of reconciliation.

Ancilla Dent
'Ecology, faith, stewardship'

St Mary Magdalene,
22 July

W ell, when she comes to his brethren, what then? *Et dic eis*, 'and say to them', or tell them. By which words he gives her a commission. *Vade* is her mission, *dic eis* her commission. A commission, to publish the first news of his rising, and as it falls out, of his ascending too.

The Fathers say that by this word she was by Christ made an Apostle, nay *Apostolorum Apostola*, 'an Apostle to the Apostles themselves'.

An Apostle; for what lacks she? 1. Sent first, immediately from the Christ himself; and what is an Apostle but so? 2. Secondly, sent to declare and make known; and what difference between *Ite praedicate*, and *Vade et dic*, but only the number? the thing is the same. 3. And last, what was she to make known? Christ's rising and ascending. And what are they but *Evangelium*, 'the gospel', yea the very gospel of the gospel?

This day, with Christ's rising, begins the gospel; not before. Crucified, dead and buried, no good news, no gospel they in themselves. And them the Jews believe as well as we. The first gospel of all is the gospel of this day, and the gospel of this day is this Mary Magdalene's gospel . . . 'the prime Gospel' of all, before any of the other four. That Christ is risen and upon his ascending, and she the first that ever brought these glad tidings. At her hands the Apostles themselves received it first, and from them we all . . .

And by this, lo, the amends we spake of is made her for her *Noli me tangere* – full amends. For to be thus sent, to be the messenger of these so blessed tidings, is a higher honour, a more special favour done here, a better good turn, every way better than if she had been let alone, had her desire, touched Christ, which she so longed for, and so eagerly reached at. Better sure, for I reason thus. Christ we may be sure, would never have enjoined her to leave the better, to take the worse; to leave to touch him, to go to tell them, if to go to tell them had not been the better.

So that hence we infer, that to go and carry comfort to them that need it, to tell them of Christ's rising that do not know it, is better than to tarry and do nothing but stand touching Christ. Touching Christ gives place to teaching Christ. *Vade et dic* better than *mane et tange*. Christ we see is for *vade et dic*. That if we were in case where we might touch Christ, we were to leave Christ untouched, and even to give ourselves a *noli me tangere*, to go and do this; and to think ourselves better employed in telling them, than in touching him.

Will you observe withal how well this agrees with her offer a little before of *Ego tollam eum*? She must needs know of the gardener, 'Tell me where you have laid him', et *ego tollam*, and she 'would take him and carry him', that she would. Why, you that would so fain take and carry me being dead, go take and carry me now alive; that is, carry news that I am alive, and you shall better please me with this *ego tollam* a great deal; it shall be a better carrying, *ego tollam* in a better sense than ever was that. Stand not here then touching me, go and touch them; and with the very touch of this report you shall work in them a kind of that you see in me, a kind of resurrection from a doleful and dead, to a cheerful and lively estate.

Lancelot Andrewes
Sermon to King James I and his court

16th week of the year

When you meditate, be like a mountain
immovably set in silence.
Its thoughts are rooted in eternity.
Do not do anything, just sit, be
    and you will reap the fruit flowing from your prayer.

When you meditate, be like a flower
always directed towards the sun.
Its stalk, like a spine, is always straight.
Be open, ready to accept everything without fear
    and you will not lack light on your way.

When you meditate, be like an ocean
always immovable in its depth.
Its waves come and go.
Be calm in your heart
    and evil thoughts will go away by themselves.

When you meditate, remember your breath:
thanks to it man has come alive.
It comes from God and it returns to God.
Unite the word of prayer with the stream of life
    and nothing will separate you from the Giver of life.

When you meditate, be like a bird
singing without a rest in front of the Creator.
Its song rises like the smoke of incense.
Let your prayer be like the coo of a dove,
    and you will never succumb to discouragement.

When you meditate, be like Abraham
giving his son as an offering.

It was a sign that he was ready to sacrifice everything.
You, too, leave everything
 and in your loneliness God will be with you.

When you meditate, it is Jesus
praying to you to the Father in the Spirit.
You are carried by the flame of his love.
Be like a river, serving to all,
 and the time will come, you will change into Love.

Every mountain teaches us the sense of eternity,
every flower, when it fades, teaches us the sense of
 fleetingness.
The ocean teaches us, how to retain peace among adversities,
 and love always teaches us Love.

Fr Seraphion of Mount Athos
(adapted by Fr Jan Bereza OSB)

17th week of the year

Tonight, Lord, I am alone.
Little by little the sounds died down in the church,
The people went away.
And I came home,
Alone.

I passed people who were returning from a walk.
I went by the cinema that was disgorging its crowd.
I skirted café terraces where tired strollers were trying to
    prolong the pleasure of a Sunday holiday.
I bumped into youngsters playing on the footpath,
Youngsters, Lord,
Other people's youngsters who will never be my own.

Here I am, Lord,
Alone.
The silence troubles me,
The solitude oppresses me.

Lord, I'm 35 years old,
A body made like others, ready for work,
A heart meant for love,
But I've given you all.
It's true, of course, that you needed it.
I've given you all, but it's hard, Lord.
It's hard to give one's body; it would like to give itself to others.
It's hard to love everyone and to claim no one.
It's hard to shake a hand and not want to retain it.
It's hard to inspire affection, to give it to you.
It's hard to be nothing to oneself in order to be everything
    to others.

It's hard to be like others, among others, and to be of them.
It's hard always to give without trying to receive.
It's hard to seek out others and to be unsought oneself.
It's hard to suffer from the sins of others, and yet be obliged
    to hear and bear them.
It's hard to be told secrets, and be unable to share them.
It's hard to carry others and never, even for a moment, be
    carried.
It's hard to sustain the feeble and never be able to lean on
    one who is strong.
It's hard to be alone,
Alone before everyone,
Alone before the world,
Alone before suffering,
    death,
    sin . . .

Lord tonight, while all is still and I feel sharply the sting of
    solitude,
While men devour my soul and I feel incapable of satisfying
    their hunger,
While the whole world presses on my shoulders with all its
    weight of misery and sin,
I repeat to you my 'yes' – not in a burst of laughter, but
    slowly, clearly, humbly,
Alone, Lord, before you,
In the peace of the evening.

                              Michel Quoist
                    'The Priest: a prayer on Sunday night'

St Ignatius of Loyola,
31 July

So great are the poor in the sight of God that Jesus Christ was sent on earth especially for them: 'Because the poor are despoiled, because the needy groan, I will now arise,' says the Lord, and in another place, 'He has sent me to preach good news to the poor.' This recalls the words of Jesus Christ when he sent an answer to St John, 'The poor have good news preached to them.' They are preferred to the rich to the extent that Jesus Christ wished to choose the most holy college of the apostles from among the poor, and to live and have dealings with them, and to leave them as princes of his Church, and to appoint them as judges 'over the twelve tribes of Israel,' that is, of all the un-believers, whose assessors will be the poor. So exalted is their standing!

Friendship with the poor makes us friends of the eternal king. Love of that poverty establishes kings, even on this earth, and kings not of earth but of heaven. This is evident because while the future heavenly kingdom may be promised to others, it is promised here and now to the poor and those who suffer tribulation; it is the abiding Truth who says, 'Blessed are the poor in spirit, for theirs is the kingdom of heaven' – 'even now they have a right to the kingdom'.

Not only are they kings, but they make others sharers in the kingdom, as Christ teaches us in St Luke when he says, 'Make friends for yourselves by means of unrighteous mammon, so that when it fails they may receive you into the eternal habita-tions.' These 'friends' are the poor, thanks to whose merits those whom they help enter into dwellings of glory, especially if they are poor of their own free will. According to St Augustine these are the little ones of whom Christ says, 'Anything you did for one of the least of these, you did for me.'

To members of the society
(7 August 1547)

To make the sign of the cross we put a hand to the head to indicate God the Father, who proceeds from no one.

When we put our hand to the middle it indicates his Son, Our Lord, who proceeds from the Father and who came right down to the womb of the most holy Virgin Mary.

When we put our hand to one side and then to the other it indicates the Holy Spirit, who proceeds from the Father and the Son.

When we join our hands, this indicates that the Three Persons are one true essence.

Catechizing the sign of the Cross

Any meditation that puts a strain on the understanding will fatigue the body. However, there are other types of meditation that have an order to them and are relaxed. These leave the understanding in peace and do not put a strain on the mind's inner workings. They can be performed without any forcing, internal or external. These do not tire the body, but rather allow it to rest.

To Teresa Rejadell
(11 September 1536)

All extracts by St Ignatius of Loyola
Iñigo: letters personal and spiritual

18th week of the year

When our heart gets its first direct, dark glimpse of God, it feels like a glimpse into emptiness and blankness. People who get to this stage frequently complain that they are doing nothing at prayer, that they are wasting their time, that they are idle, that nothing seems to happen, that they are in total darkness. To escape from this uncomfortable state they, unfortunately, have recourse once again to their thinking faculty, they take the bandage off their minds and begin to *think* and to *speak* with God – just the one thing they need *not* do.

If God is gracious to them, and he very frequently is, he will make it impossible for them to use their mind in prayer. They will find all thinking distasteful: vocal prayer will be unbearable to them because the words seem meaningless; they will just go *dry* every time they attempt to communicate with God in any way except the way of silence. And initially even this silence is painful and dry. They might then slip into the biggest evil of all: they may abandon prayer altogether because they find themselves forced, in prayer, to choose between the frustration of not being able to use their minds and the hollow feeling of wasting their time and doing nothing in the darkness that meets them when they silence their minds.

If they avoid this evil and persevere in the exercise of prayer and expose themselves, in blind faith, to the emptiness, the darkness, the idleness, the nothingness, they will gradually discover, at first in small flashes, later in a more permanent fashion, that there is a glow in the darkness, that the emptiness mysteriously fills their heart, that the idleness is full of God's activity, that in the nothingness their being is recreated and shaped anew ... and all of this in a way they just cannot describe either to themselves or to others. They will just know after each such session of prayer or contemplation, call it what you will, that something mysterious has been working within them, bringing refreshment and nourishment and well-being with it. They will notice they have a yearning hunger to return to this dark contemplation that seems to make no sense and yet fills them with life, even with a mild intoxication that they can hardly perceive with their mind, they can hardly feel with their emotions and yet is unmistakably there, and so real and satisfying that they would not exchange it for all the intoxication that comes from the delights that the world of the senses and the emotions and the mind has to offer. Funny that at the beginning it should have seemed so dry and dark and tasteless!

Anthony de Mello
Sadhana: a way to God

Transfiguration, 6 August

There are two icons of the transfiguration which struck me very deeply when I saw them in the original in the Tretiakov Gallery in Moscow. One is by Rublev and the other by his master, Theophan the Greek . . .

The Rublev icon shows Christ in the brilliancy of his dazzling white robes which cast light on everything around. This light falls on the disciples, on the mountain and the stones, on every blade of grass. Within this light, which is the divine splendour – the divine glory, the divine light itself inseparable from God – all things acquire an intensity of being which they could not have otherwise; in it they attain to a fullness of reality which they can have only in God.

The other icon is more difficult to perceive in a reproduction. The background is silvery and appears grey. The robes of Christ are silvery, with blue shades, and the rays of light falling around are also white, silvery and blue. Everything gives an impression of much less intensity. Then we discover that all these rays of light falling from the divine presence and touching the things which surround the transfigured Christ do not give relief but give transparency to things. One has the impression that these rays of divine light touch things and sink into them, penetrate them, touch something within them so that from the core of these things, of all things created, the same light reflects and shines back, as though the divine life quickens the capabilities, the potentialities of all things, and makes all reach out towards itself. At that moment the eschatological situation is realized, and in the words of St Paul, 'God is all and in all'.

Metropolitan Anthony of Sourozh
in *Sacrament and Image: Essays in the
Christian Understanding of Man*

Too often we think of the Transfiguration as a feast of light only, one that dazzles like the sun reflected off the mothering sea. Too often we seek to fix our feet in light alone, unrealistically or pridefully thinking that our transformation has reached a point where we will not be burned by uncreated light . . .

The story of the Transfiguration is surrounded by darkness: it is no mere ecstatic vision. It is surrounded by losing one's life to gain it, by denial of prophets, by being tossed between fire and water by the fits of our sins writing under the light of God, and in the end by the glory of crucifixion.

Mere ecstatic vision is vain and ephemeral, and if like Peter we wish to fix our feet in that light, we will perish.

Maggie Ross
The Fountain and the Furnace

St Dominic,
8 August

Except when he was moved to pity and compassion, Dominic always displayed great firmness of mind. A joyous heart is reflected in the countenance, and Dominic revealed his tranquillity of soul by the joyful kindliness of his look. Everywhere, in word and in deed, he showed himself to be a herald of the gospel. By day no one was more affable, more friendly than he with his brethren and companions: at night, no one more fervent than he in vigils and prayer. His conversation was always either with God or about God.

Jordan of Saxony

He always carried around with him the Gospel of Matthew and the letters of Paul, and he read them so often, that he knew them by heart.

From the canonization process of 1233

Sometimes he raised his hands to his shoulders, in the manner of a priest saying Mass, as if he wanted to fix his ears more attentively on something that was being said to him by someone else. If you had seen his devotion as he stood there, erect in prayer, you would have thought you were looking at a prophet conversing with an angel or with God, now talking, now listening, now thinking quietly about what had been said to him. When he was travelling, he would steal sudden moments of prayer, unobtrusively, and would stand with his whole mind instantaneously concentrating on heaven, and soon you would have heard him pronouncing, with the utmost enjoyment and relish, some lovely text from the heart of sacred Scripture, which he would seem to have drawn fresh from the Saviour's wells.

From the *Nine Ways of Prayer*

Another reason why preaching should have first preference for those who have the grace for it is that there is an exceptionally good precedent for so doing. When Christ was in the world, he celebrated Mass only once, on Maundy Thursday; we do not read of him ever hearing confessions, he administered few sacraments and those infrequently, he did not very often assist at any canonical divine worship; the same is true of all practices except prayer and preaching. And once he started preaching, we find in the Gospels that he is presented as having devoted his whole life to preaching, even more than to prayer.

Humbert of Romans
Early Dominican Treatise on the
Formation of Preachers

O wondrous hope which you gave to those who wept at the hour of your death! You promised you would come to the aid of your brethren: fulfil your promise.

Prayer to St Dominic in the
Dominican Liturgy

St Edith Stein,
9 August

Edith Stein adjured the sisters not to give their votes to Hitler, whatever the consequences, for he was the enemy of God and would pull Germany down to perdition with him. Two years passed, and Edith Stein, then in Holland, was summoned to the office of the Gestapo in Maastricht. Her whole future was at stake; still, she entered the office with the greeting: '*Gelobt sei Jesus Christus*', 'Praised be Jesus Christ'. For the Nazis, it was as if a bomb had fallen in their midst. On returning to the convent, she admitted to her prioress that, humanly speaking, her profession of faith was indeed imprudent, but that she had had to make it, for here was no battle of politics but the age-old war between Jesus and Lucifer.

It was at five in the afternoon of that bitter and bright 2 August that Edith Stein was taken prisoner. The community was assembled in choir and she was reading aloud what they would meditate on the next morning, when two SS men rang the bell. 'In ten minutes Sr Stein has to leave the house,' was their command. While the prioress protested, to no avail, Sr Benedicta returned to the choir, prayed for some moments and then went to her cell, where several Sisters helped her pack her few belongings – a blanket, cup, spoon, and food for three days, were all the SS men thought she needed. First she begged the Sisters to pray for her, then that they notify the Swiss consul; and for the rest, she was silent, the Sisters from Echt recall, as if her spirit was not in the cell but elsewhere.

There are about 1,200 Catholic Jews at Westerbork, of whom about 15 were religious. 'The distress in the camp and the confusion among the newcomers cannot be described. But Sr Benedicta stood out by her calm and composure, going among the women, comforting, helping, bringing peace, like an angel,' a Jewish prisoner who escaped deportation, and so survived, remembers.

'I am content with everything,' reads one of the little notes she was able to write to her prioress from the camp. 'A "science of the Cross" can be gained only if one is made to feel the Cross to the depths of one's being. Of this I was convinced from the first moment, and I have said, "*Ave crux, spes unica*", "Hail, cross, thou only hope".' Yet even as she was ready to die, she was ready to live.

Three times on their way across Germany she was able to send a short message, through a former pupil, through a station master, through a stranger: 'Greetings. I am on the journey to Poland. Sister Teresia Benedicta.'

No other last words than these were ever heard from her. But there is a great deal to indicate, though not with absolute certainty, that she was gassed in Auschwitz on 9 August, the vigil of St Lawrence, when the Church repeatedly remembers the words of Christ: 'If any man has a mind to come my way, let him renounce self, and take up his cross, and follow me.'

John M. Oesterreicher
Walls are Crumbling

St Clare,
11 August

B etween Francis and Clare there was an unusually tender relationship. On the rare occasions of his visits she entertained him with feminine attentiveness: flowers on the table during their scanty meals were but a small indication of this. The 'radiant one' – which is the meaning of the name Clare – outlived Francis by many years, yet she had only one ambition – to live as St Francis had lived. There are many beautiful legends about the mystical relationship between St Francis and St Clare which illuminate the essence of this association.

It was only to be expected that people began to whisper about the relationship between Francis and Clare, at all events Francis heard of more than one improper insinuation. St Francis then said to St Clare: 'Sister, do you know what people are saying about us?'

St Clare did not reply. Her heart failed her, and she felt that if she were to speak she would burst into tears.

At length St Francis said: 'It is time for us to part. You must be in the convent by nightfall. I shall go alone and follow at a distance as God guides me.' St Clare fell on her knees in the middle of the road, pulled herself together after a while, stood up and went on with bowed head without a backward look. The road led through a wood. But she did not have the strength to go on, without comfort and hope, without a word of fare-well from him. She waited. 'Father,' she said, 'when shall we see each other again?'

'When summer returns, when the roses are in bloom,' he replied. Then something wonderful happened. Suddenly it seemed to him as if a mass of roses sprang into bloom on the juniper bushes and thickly covered hedges. After her initial astonishment St Clare hurried forward, plucked a bunch of roses and put it in St Francis' hands. From that day onward St Francis and St Clare were never separated. . . .

St Francis was once deeply concerned about how St Clare was faring since she had such a heavy burden to bear through her love of poverty. Worried and tired he stumbled on until his feet almost sank into the ground. He dragged himself to a fountain which bubbled with fresh water and formed a clear surface in the trough into which the jet from the fountain outlet fell. For a long time the man of God stood bowed over the fountain. Then he raised his head and said happily to Brother Leo: 'Brother Leo, little lamb of God, what do you think I have seen in the water of the fountain?' 'The moon, Father, which is reflected in it,' replied the brother.

'No, Brother Leo, it is not our brother Moon that I have seen in the water of the fountain, but by the merciful grace of God I have seen the very face of our Sister Clare, and it was so pure and radiant with holy joy, that all my misgivings were suddenly banished, and I received an assurance that our sister at this very moment is enjoying that deep joy which God keeps for his favourites, in that he heaps upon them the treasures of poverty.'

Walter Nigg
Francis of Assisi

Florence Nightingale,
13 August

Where shall I find God? In myself. That is the true mystical doctrine. But then I myself must be in a state for him to come and dwell in me. This is the whole aim of the mystical life. That the soul herself should be in heaven, that our Father which is in heaven should dwell in her, that there's something within us infinitely more estimable than often comes out, that God enlarges this 'palace of our soul' by degrees so as to enable her to receive himself, that he gives her liberty but that the soul must give herself up absolutely to him for him to do this, the incalculable benefit of this occasional, but frequent intercourse with the perfect; this is the conclusion and sum of the whole matter, put into beautiful language by the mystics . . .

I believe in God the Father almighty, maker of heaven and earth. And in Jesus Christ, his best Son, our master, who was born to show us the way through suffering to be also his sons and his daughters, his handmen and his handmaidens, who lived in the same spirit with the Father, that we may also live in that Holy Spirit whose meat was to do his Father's will and to finish his work, who suffered and died saying, 'That the world may love the Father'. And I believe in the Father almighty's love and friendship, in the service of man being the service of God, the growing into a likeness with him by love, the being one with him in will at last, which is heaven. I believe in the plan of almighty perfection to make us all perfect. And thus I believe in the life everlasting.

My imagination is so filled with the misery of this world that the only thing in which to labour brings any return, seems to me helping and sympathizing there; and all that poets sing of the glories of this world appears to me untrue: all the people I see are eaten up with care or poverty or disease . . .

Life is no holiday game, nor is it a clever book, nor is it a school of instruction, nor a valley of tears; but it is a hard fight, a struggle, a wrestling with the Principle of Evil, hand to hand, foot to foot. Every inch of the way must be disputed. The night is given us to take breath, to pray, to drink deep at the fountain of power. The day, to use the strength which has been given us, to go forth to work with it till the evening. The Kingdom of God is coming; and 'Thy Kingdom Come' does not mean only 'My salvation come'.

Nursing is an art; and if it is to be made an art, requires an exclusive devotion, as hard a preparation, as any painter's or sculptor's work; for what is the having to do with dead canvas or cold marble compared with having to do with the living body – the temple of God's spirit. It is one of the arts; I had almost said, the finest of the Fine Arts.

Florence Nightingale

Florence Nightingale died on 13 August 1910

Assumption, 15 August

On the feast day of Mary the fragrant,
    Mother of the Shepherd of the flocks,
I cut me a handful of the new corn,
I tried it gently in the sun,
I rubbed it sharply from the husk
    With mine own palms.

I ground it in a quern on Friday,
I baked it on a fan of sheep-skin,
I toasted it to a fire of rowan,
And I shared it round my people.

I went sunways round my dwelling,
In name of the Mary Mother,
Who promised to preserve me,
Who did preserve me,
And who will preserve me,
In peace, in flocks,
In righteousness of heart.

Gaelic prayer
from *The Sun Dances*

The End of the Age

The woman went up in a whirlwind into heaven,
    Caught by the Son of God and to his throne
Whither the saints wheel, each in his order,
While we in this world watch and wonder
Seeing the present age, and the age to come
Under the wings of archangels in wisdom;

While Japan is lifted high into heaven
Light on the burning air of an explosion:
An emperor in compassion for his people
Slips to the microphone, and ends the struggle.
After an instant, the dust settles again.
Will the world forget the horrible pain?

Everything we know by a single example,
A beautiful image, a bitter taste, a sample
Of silk from a weaver's loom, far in the past.
So shall men come to understand at last
How all the science that has gone before
Has led them, step by step, to modern war.

Only Omnipotence has infinite power.
Teach us, dear Lady, even in this hour
When we are afraid of the small
Electron that no engine can control.
Planets and atoms the same law obey,
And when they swerve, explode, and die away.

George Every
(Written on or about 15 August 1945)

On 15 August 1990, one of the strange, wonderful stories of hope of the Latin American world begins: representatives of the indigenous tribes of the Bolivian lowlands set out on the long march from Trinidad to La Paz to stand before the government and demand their rights against the firms which are cutting down the ancient forests.

They march 650 kilometres; one-third of the 874 participants are women, children, and old people. They are natives from the ancient forests of Beni in north-east Bolivia . . . They stand up for their territorial rights and their dignity; on their placards is nothing more than *territorio y dignidad*.

Caroline, one of my daughters, who works as a doctor in

Bolivia, reports: 'Never before was the sensitive element of the middle and upper classes so deeply moved and ashamed: these people come, chronically undernourished, toothless, tubercular, lacking shoes – to say nothing of socks, sweaters or jackets – many of them illiterate, many who can barely speak Spanish, the poorest of the downtrodden, and they go on foot from the tropical forest up to a height of almost 5,000 metres over the pass, then descend in hail and rain to La Paz – all that with pregnant women, small children, and old people for over a month . . . all that for their dignity!

'A human chain of hundreds of women leads the march down to the capital. The bells of the cathedral ring; the Church stands on the side of the poor people in this matter. The standing bishops' conference refers to the speech by John Paul II in Ecuador in 1985 to the Indian peoples. The bishops demand respect for the Indians: a law to regulate ownership of land is necessary, and capitalistic economics must at least not take place at the cost of the indigenous population.

'Masses of people line the street . . . Many were moved to tears of respect, and many gave them hot coffee or candy, which in a poor country is a lot. Everyone clapped and hoped to see one or another adorned with feathers. And the chiefs did not stop making it known everywhere that they were not tourists and that they would not leave until they received land rights from the government, which were usually not granted to the nomadic peoples.'

An agreement was signed between the government and the lowland peoples guaranteeing their territorial rights. It is judged to be a historic event . . . This march, like the famous bus boycott in Alabama led by the young Baptist pastor Martin Luther King Jr, will go into the history of non-violence. And that is the secret history of freedom.

Dorothee Soelle
Celebrating Resistance: the way of the Cross
in Latin America

20th week of the year

We are deeply conscious of how often and how grievously we ourselves have sinned against the gospel; yet it remains our ambition to proclaim it worthily: that is in love, in poverty and in humility.

In love: a personal love for the person of Jesus Christ, for an ever more inward knowledge of whom we daily ask, that we may the better love him and follow him; Jesus, Son of God, sent to serve, sent to set free, put to death and risen from the dead. This love is the deepest well-spring of our action and our life. It was this personal love that engendered in Ignatius that divine discontent which kept urging him to the *magis* – the ever more and more giving – the ever greater glory of God.

In poverty: relying more on God's providence than on human resources; safeguarding the freedom of the apostle by detachment from avarice and the bondage imposed by it; following in the footsteps of Christ, who preached good news to the poor by being poor himself.

In humility: realizing that there are many enterprises of great worth and moment in the Church and in the world which we, as priests and religious inspired by one particular charism, are not in a position to undertake. And even in these enterprises which we can and should undertake, we realize that we must be willing to work with others: with Christians, people of other religious faiths, and all people of good will; willing to play a subordinate, supporting, anonymous role; and willing to learn how to serve from those we seek to serve.

General Congregation 32
of the Society of Jesus

At the end a big fellow, whose fearful looks could have inspired fear, told me: 'Come to my house, I have something to honour you.' I remained uncertain, not knowing whether I should accept or not, but the priest who was accompanying me said: 'Go with him, father, the people are very good.' I went to his house, which was a half-falling shack. He made me sit. From where I was seated the sun could be seen as it was setting. The fellow said to me: 'Señor, you see how beautiful it is!' And we remained silent for some minutes. The sun disappeared. The man added: 'I did not know how to thank you for all that you have done for us. I have nothing to give you, but I thought you would like to see this sunset. It pleased you, didn't it? Good evening.' He then gave me his hand. As I was leaving, I thought: 'I have met very few hearts that are so kind.'

Pedro Arrupe
in Jean-Claude Dietsch, *Pedro Arrupe:*
itinéraire d'un jésuite

St Bernard,
20 August

What are the four degrees of love? First, we love ourselves for our own sake; since we are unspiritual and of the flesh we cannot have an interest in anything that does not relate to ourselves. When we begin to see that we cannot subsist by ourselves, we begin to seek God for our own sakes. This is the second degree of love; we love God, but only for our own interests. But if we begin to worship and come to God again and again by meditating, by reading, by prayer, and by obedience, little by little God becomes known to us through experience. We enter into a sweet familiarity with God, and by tasting how sweet the Lord is we pass into the third degree of love so that now we love God, not for our own sake, but for himself. It should be noted that in this third degree we will stand still for a very long time . . .

Blessed are we who experience the fourth degree of love wherein we love ourselves for God's sake. Such experiences are rare and come only for a moment. In a manner of speaking, we lose ourselves as though we did not exist, utterly unconscious of ourselves and emptied of ourselves.

If for even a moment we experience this kind of love, we will then know the pain of having to return to this world and its obligations as we are recalled from the state of contemplation. In turning back to ourselves we will feel as if we are suffering as we return into the mortal state in which we were called to live.

But during those moments we will be of one mind with God, and our wills in one accord with God. The prayer, 'Thy will be done', will be our prayer and our delight. Just as a little drop of water mixed with a lot of wine seems to entirely lose its own identity as it takes on the taste and colour of wine; just as iron, heated and glowing, looks very much like fire, having lost its original appearance; just as air flooded with the light of the sun is transformed into the same splendour of the light so that it appears to be light itself, so it is like for those who melt away from themselves and are entirely transfused into the will of God.

This perfect love of God with our heart, soul, mind, and strength will not happen until we are no longer compelled to think about ourselves and attend to the body's immediate needs. Only then can the soul attend to God completely. This is why in the present body we inhabit this is difficult to maintain. But it is within God's power to give such an experience to whom he wills, and it is not attained by our own efforts.

St Bernard of Clairvaux
On the Love of God

21st week of the year

On the day when
the weight deadens
on your shoulders
and you stumble,
may the clay dance
to balance you.

And when your eyes
freeze behind
the grey window
and the ghost of loss
gets in to you,
may a flock of colours,
indigo, red, green
and azure blue
come to awaken in you
a meadow of delight.

When the canvas frays
in the curach of thought
and a stain of ocean
blackens beneath you,
may there come across the waters
a path of yellow moonlight
to bring you safely home.

May the nourishment of the earth be yours,
may the clarity of light be yours,
may the fluency of the ocean be yours,
may the protection of the ancestors be yours.

And so may a slow
wind work these words
of love around you,
an invisible cloak
to mind your life.

In summertime nature is bedecked with colour. There is great lushness everywhere, a richness and depth of texture. Summertime is a time of light, growth and arrival. You feel that the secret life of the year, hidden in the winter and coming out in the spring, has really blossomed in the summertime. Thus, when it is summertime in your soul, it is a time of great balance. You are in the flow of your own nature. You can take as many risks as you like, and you will always land on your feet. There is enough shelter and depth of texture around you to completely ground, balance and mind you.

Summertime grows into autumn. Autumn is one of my favourite times of the year; seeds sown in the spring, nurtured by the summer, now yield their fruit in autumn. It is harvest, the homecoming of the seeds' long and lonely journey through darkness and silence under the earth's surface. Harvest is one of the great feasts of the year. It was a very important time in Celtic culture. The fertility of the earth yielded its fruitfulness. Correspondingly, when it is autumn in your life, the things that happened in the past, or the experiences that were sown in the clay of your heart, almost unknown to you, now yield their fruit. Autumntime in a person's life can be a time of great gathering. It is a time for harvesting the fruits of your experiences.

John O'Donohue
*Anam Cara: spiritual
wisdom from the Celtic world*

St Monica,
27 August

Because the day when she was to quit this life was drawing near – a day known to you, though we were ignorant of it – she and I happened to be alone, through the mysterious workings of your will, as I believe. We stood leaning against a window which looked out on a garden within the house where we were staying at Ostia on the Tiber, for there, far from the crowds, we were recruiting our strength after the long journey, in preparation for our voyage overseas. We were alone, conferring very intimately. Forgetting what lay in the past, and stretching out to what was ahead, we inquired between ourselves in the light of present truth, the Truth which is yourself, what the eternal life of the saints would be like . . .

Our colloquy led us to the point where the pleasures of the body's senses, however intense and in however brilliant a material light enjoyed, seemed unworthy not merely of comparison but even of remembrance beside the joy of that life, and we lifted ourselves in longing yet more ardent toward *That Which Is*, and step by step traversed all bodily creatures and heaven itself, whence sun and moon and stars shed their light upon the earth. Higher still we mounted by inward thought and wondering discourse on your works, and we arrived at the summit of our own minds; and this too we transcended, to touch that land of never-failing plenty where you pasture Israel for ever with the food of truth. Life there is the Wisdom through whom all these things are made . . .

And as we talked and panted for it, we just touched the edge of it by the utmost leap of our hearts; then, sighing and unsatisfied, we left the first-fruits of our spirit captive there, and returned to the noise of articulate speech, where a word has beginning and end. How different from your Word, our Lord, who abides in himself, and grows not old, but renews all things.

You know, O Lord, how on that very day amid this talk of ours that seemed to make the world with all its charms grow cheap, she said, 'For my part, my son, I find pleasure no longer in anything this life holds. What I am doing here still, or why I tarry, I do not know, for all wordly hope has withered away for me. One thing only there was for which I desired to linger awhile in this life: to see you a Catholic Christian before I died. And this my God has granted to me more lavishly than I could have hoped, letting me see you even spurning earthly happiness to be his servant. What now keeps me here?'

St Augustine
Confessions

St Augustine,
28 August

Sixteen hundred years ago in a garden in Milan a young man from North Africa became a Christian believer. He had been searching for *something* for many years and had tried quite a few of the spiritual disciplines and therapies on offer. He had a girlfriend he'd abandoned – and a little son. He also had a ferocious mother who got at him for his fecklessness.

He managed to find a good job in a university, but his underlying depression weighed him down. As he sat in the garden with tears in his eyes he heard the sing-song voice of a child next door, chanting the Latin words: *'Tolle, lege . . . tolle, lege . . .'* ('Take, read'). In the end he took hold of a copy of the Scriptures and read: 'Arm yourself with the Lord Jesus Christ, and spend no more thought on nature's appetites.'

That conversion was a turning point in history, for the young man was Augustine, who became one of the greatest philosophers of the Western world.

I am thinking of summer gardens because this time of year reminds me of the weeks I spent in the garden years ago trying to revise for exams. Bird song, cherry and magnolia blossom bring back a *frisson* of fear. Yet they also bring a sense of grace. Gardens in May were the places I learned to learn. You see, I wasn't very attentive in class, but on my own, with a text, I would suddenly get the point – and my mind sang.

Without books, without reading, our understanding is uninformed, our judgements narrow . . . I sometimes think God would rather we were literate than that we were indiscriminately caring. Augustine found his true self through a child's cry and a challenging text. He met the living God on the page of a book, and it broke his heart and set him free.

Angela Tilby
'Thought for the Day'
BBC Radio 4

L ate have I loved you, O beauty so ancient and so new; late have I loved you. For behold you were within me, and I outside; and I sought you outside and in my ugliness fell upon those lovely things that you have made. You were with me and I was not with you. I was kept from you by those things, yet had they not been in you, they would not have been at all. You called and cried to me and broke upon my deafness; and you sent forth your light and shone upon me, and chased away my blindness; you breathed fragrance upon me, and I drew in my breath and do now pant for you; I tasted you and I now hunger and thirst for you; you touched me, and I have burned for your peace.

St Augustine
Confessions

St Aidan,
31 August

Oswin, King of Northumberland, had bestowed a very good horse upon Bishop Aidan, although, good man, he used commonly to perform his journeys on foot; yet, notwithstanding, for the easier passage of rivers and other such like occasions, he had accepted of the king's gift, and one day as he made use of it by riding, a poor man encountering him, begged for alms. The good bishop being full of pity, a special observer of the poor, and a father of the afflicted, instantly dismounting, wills that his horse, with all the royal harness, should be given to the poor man.

The king had speedy notice thereof; whereupon, going in to dinner with Aidan, he said, 'What is this that thou hast done, my Lord Bishop, in giving to the poor man the royal horse which thou shouldst have kept for thine own use? Were there not meaner horses, or other kinds of things good enough to have given to the poor man, so that thou didst not part with that horse, which I gave thee for thine own personal service?'

The bishop cutting him short made answer, 'What is this that thou sayest, oh king? Is that son of a mare which I have given away of more esteem with thee than that son of God for whose sake I have given it, and that son of God to whom I have given it?' Aidan having thus spoken sat down in his place, and the king and his servants that had been hunting go to the fire.

As they stand warming themselves the king takes the matter and the bishop's words into better consideration, and thereupon ungirding his sword and giving it to an officer to lay aside, he comes hastily to the bishop, and casting himself down at his feet, desired him that he would be at peace with him, 'for never hereafter will I speak any more of this business,' said he, 'nor from this day forward set any limit touching what or how much of my money and goods thou shouldst bestow and give amongst the sons of God.'

'I know,' answered Aidan, 'that this king cannot live long; for such a king as this I never saw. I perceive plainly that he will be shortly snatched out of this world, for this people are in no way worthy of such a governor as he is.' And in very truth the sad prophecy of this holy man was not long after accomplished. This blessed king was traitorously made away, and Aidan himself lived only twelve days after the other's death – death in the world's reckoning and the eyes of flesh and blood, but in truth the entrance of life and everlasting happiness.

The Story Books of Little Gidding (1631–32)

Diana, Princess of Wales, 31 August

You can't comfort the afflicted without afflicting the comfortable.

Note seen on desk of Diana, Princess of Wales,
in her own hand.

Faith admits us into death's secrets.
Death is not the end of the road, but a gateway to a
better place.
It is in this place that our noblest aspirations will be realized.
It is here that we will understand how our experiences of
goodness, love, beauty and joy are realities which exist
perfectly in God.
It is in heaven that we shall rest in him and our hearts will
be restless until they rest in God.
We, left to continue our pilgrimage through life, weep and
mourn.
You, Diana, and your companions too, are on your way to
union with him who loves you so. He knows the love
which you, Diana, had for others.
God speaks now of his love for you.
Our tears will not be bitter ones now but a gentle weeping
to rob our sadness of its agony and lead at last to peace,
peace with God.

Cardinal Basil Hume
From a meditation broadcast after the death
of Diana, Princess of Wales

Mortality brings its own understanding to us, for death lies in the interstices of our routine living. It circumscribes all of this day's prospects. Our very lives grow from the deaths of others. We are given to the world in places they left to us. We walk in ways they built for us. The tasks others bequeathed are the possibilities of our lives. Each of us leaves music for another to play after our own time.

Yet can death, unpostponable and always impending, have meaning? Why is it a journey which is unaccompanied? Why can time continue no longer? Why are comfort and consolation for the dead stayed?

Faith's understanding of death is of a homecoming and a great banquet; of lovers meeting and walking together; of a joyous exploration of the infinite mystery of love. Faith reminds its children that in death they are renewed. So is all creation. Each petal from every rose that ever blossomed; each leaf from every larch that ever grew; each feather from every wren that ever nested, is renewed in heaven. Each smile from every child that ever played; each kiss from every mother who ever conceived: each tear from every man who ever cried, is renewed in Heaven.

Through the redemption won by Christ in the unlimited love of God may we, who are of no consequence, hope for a like glory.

Derek Webster
Our Time Now

Whom the gods love dies young.

Menander (*c.* 342–292 BC)

22nd week of the year

When we try to pray, we must have some idea of God in our minds, and this idea will influence how we pray and whether we pray. As a university chaplain I used to spend much time listening to people who had either given up their Catholic faith, or were thinking of doing so, or they were worried about their own honesty in continuing as Catholics when they felt that they no longer really believed in the teachings of the Catholic Church. Having listened to them, I always tried to encourage them to speak about their own understanding of God. After many conversations, an identikit image of God formed in my imagination.

God was a family relative, much admired by Mum and Dad, who described him as very loving, a great friend of the family, very powerful and interested in all of us. Eventually we are taken to visit 'Good Old Uncle George'. He lives in a formidable mansion, is bearded, gruff and threatening. We cannot share our parents' professed admiration for this jewel in the family. At the end of the visit, Uncle George turns to address us. 'Now listen, dear,' he begins, looking very severe, 'I want to see you here once a week, and if you fail to come, let me just show you what will happen to you.' He then leads us down to the mansion's basement. It is dark, becomes hotter and hotter as we descend, and we begin to hear unearthly screams. In the basement there are steel doors. Uncle George opens one. 'Now look in there, dear,' he says. We see a nightmare vision, an array of blazing furnaces with little demons in attendance, who hurl into the blaze those men, women and children who failed to visit Uncle George or to act in a way he approved. 'And if you don't visit me, dear, that is where you will most certainly go,' says Uncle George. He then takes us upstairs again to meet Mum and Dad. As we go home, tightly clutching Dad with one hand and Mum with the other, Mum leans over us and says, 'And now don't you love Uncle George with all your heart and soul, mind and strength?' And we, loathing the monster, say, 'Yes I do,' because to say anything else would be to join the queue at the furnace. At a tender age religious schizophrenia has set in and we keep telling Uncle George how much we love him and how good he is and that we want to do only what pleases him. We observe what we are told are his wishes and dare not admit, even to ourselves, that we loathe him.

Gerard W. Hughes
God of Surprises

Mother Teresa of Calcutta, 5 September

M ake us worthy, Lord, to serve our fellow men throughout the world who live and die in poverty and hunger.
Give them, through our hands, this day their daily bread, and
by our understanding love, give peace and joy.

In a place in Melbourne I visited an old man whom nobody
seemed to know existed. I saw his room; it was in a terrible
state, I wanted to clean it, but he kept on saying: 'I'm all right.'
I didn't say a word, yet in the end he allowed me to clean his
room.

There was in that room a beautiful lamp, covered for many
years with dirt. I asked him: 'Why do you not light the lamp?'
'For whom?' he said. 'No one comes to me; I do not need the
lamp.' I asked him: 'Will you light the lamp if a Sister comes
to see you?' He said: 'Yes, if I hear a human voice, I will do
it.' The other day he sent me a word: 'Tell my friend that the
light she has lighted in my life is still burning.'

Jesus Christ has said that we are much more important to his
Father than the grass, the birds, the flowers of the earth; and
so, if he takes such care of these things, how much more would
he take care of his life in us. He cannot deceive us; because
life is God's greatest gift to human beings. Since it is created
in the image of God, it belongs to him; and we have no right
to destroy it.

You ask how I should see the task of the Missionaries of
Charity if I were a religious sister or priest in Surrey or Sussex.

Well, the task of the Church in such places is much more difficult than what we face in Calcutta, Yemen or anywhere else, where all the people need is dressing for their wounds, a bowl of rice and a cuddle – with someone telling them they are loved and wanted. In Surrey and Sussex the problems of your people are deep down, at the bottom of their hearts. They have to come to know you and trust you, to see you as a person with Christ's compassion and love, before their problems will emerge and you can help them. This takes a lot of time! Time for you to be people of prayer and time to give of yourself to each one of your people.

The Mass is the spiritual food which sustains me, without which I could not get through one single day or hour in my life; in the Mass we have Jesus in the appearance of bread, while in the slums we see Christ and touch him in the broken bodies, in the abandoned children.

Mother Teresa of Calcutta
A Gift for God

Birth of the Virgin,
8 September

In my view, Mary is, for women and men alike in the poorer areas, more than an individual person, even if a relationship with her is established in a personal way. She is the expression of a desire for fulfilment, which expresses itself as a response to the various needs of daily life. She is the one who is able to understand my difficulties with my husband or with my wife, or with my children, my problems at work, or with my health, my difficulties in relationships, and in all the other things that make up the innumerable sufferings of human life.

Mary is wife and mother. In Latin America she is above all mother: a mother who cares for her children, who feeds and protects them. She transcends all historical images of a mother. For in these images lies a fundamental human need to find symbolic expression, which is what happens in the different forms of devotion to Mary.

The devotions reveal the power which is accorded Mary by the believing people. She has the power to intervene in our history, to change certain events and difficult situations. In this way she is a powerful woman, a woman possessing a strength which is different from that of the ordinary run of mortals, a divine strength capable of fighting the evil which is present in history . . .

If we set ourselves to listen more to the faith of simple people in their relationship with Mary which expresses their need for survival and for a fuller life, we will understand much better that theology has to be poetry, helping us to live more richly, and that it has to be prophecy, denouncing all forms of religious pharisaism and every kind of injustice. Theology is finally a *Magnificat* sung by woman in the name of all the poor of the land who need bread, justice, liberty and love.

Mary is, today as yesterday, not only present in the individual struggles of each person, but is involved in the collective struggles for liberation in Latin America. She is with all those who need land to live on, with all those who campaign for better living conditions all round. Mary is an ally in the various campaigns for liberation and, in this sense, she is more than a model for women to imitate. She is the symbol, or rather, one of the symbols of the energy of a people in search of economic, cultural and religious autonomy and identity.

That is why, in the popular songs, she is called 'mother of the oppressed', 'ally of her people', 'liberator of us all'.

Ivone Gebara
The Month

Racial Justice Sunday
(2nd Sunday in September)

At the end of the road what a welcome awaited you! The whole village was there, all lined up, the older people at the back, the children in front. As soon as they saw you from afar they would ring the church bells and start coming in procession towards you singing, dancing and playing their flutes, horns and drums. This sound is electrifying and more than takes away all the aches and pains of the journey. They would meet you about half a mile from the village. All the children would come right up to you offering beautiful jungle flowers. Some of them garlanded you with the most exotic aromatic wild flowers. They would wash your hands and sometimes your feet. Sometimes they would pour oil on your hands and feet. Then they would make you sit in a chair all decorated with flowers and they would carry you into the village singing, dancing and drumming all round you in great excitement and joy.

This traditional Adibasi welcome has been one of the most enriching experiences of my life. All the hassles and problems along the way were somehow worthwhile just because they had led me to this tremendous welcome.

I often wonder if our life is not very similar to this. We are on the way to the Kingdom. The Kingdom is on the way towards us. How wonderful to get a welcome smile for every mile from all God's children. How wonderful even that I am covered with dust and bruised a bit from the way. I can then be washed and oiled.

John Shevlin
A World United

I t is in this way that the Church can become what Pope John XXIII called 'the village fountain' . . . It can become a place where the people of the village can stop by for clean water, for water that comes from afar, and brings with it tastes, echoes, tensions and passions of distant worlds. The village fountain is perhaps, as in some Byzantine places, the holy fountain where one can buy images of the mother of God and where all come, all the citizens, the sick, the rich and poor alike, pilgrims and traders, to be cured of their diseases, of their closures and their egoisms . . . We, in the Community of Sant'Egidio, like to be in harmony with this village fountain and we are content to be able to spend ourselves for this end.

Mario Marazziti
a Member of Sant'Egidio community

23rd week of the year

Hurrahing in harvest

S ummer ends now; now, barbarous in
beauty, the stooks arise
  Around; up above, what wind-walks! what lovely
    behaviour
  Of silk-sack clouds! has wilder, wilful-wavier
Meal-drift moulded ever and melted across skies?

I walk, I lift up, I lift up heart, eyes,
  Down all that glory in the heavens to glean our Saviour;
  And, éyes, heárt, what looks, what lips yet gave you a
Rapturous love's greeting of realer, of rounder replies?

And the azurous hung hills are his world-wielding shoulder
  Majestic – as a stallion stalwart, very-violet-sweet! –
These things, these things were here and but the beholder
  Wanting; which two when they once meet,
The heart rears wings bold and bolder
  And hurls for him, O half hurls earth for him off under
    his feet.

Gerard Manley Hopkins

G od of high and holy places
where I catch a glimpse of your glory,
above the low levels of life,
above the evil and emptiness which drags me down,
beyond the limits of my senses and imagination,
you lift me up.

In the splendour of a sunset,
in the silence of the stars,
in the grandeur of the mountains,
in the vastness of the sea,
you lift me up.

In the majesty of music,
in the mystery of art,
in the freshness of the morning,
in the fragrance of a single flower,
you lift me up.

Awe-inspiring God,
when I am lost in wonder
and lost for words,
receive the homage of my silent worship
but do not let me be content to bear your
   beauty and be still.
Go with me to the places where I live and work.
Lift the veil of reticence behind which I hide.
Give me the courage to speak of the things
   which move me,
with simple and unselfconscious delight.
Help me to share my glimpses of glory
until others are drawn to your light.

Jean Mortimer
in *SPCK Book of Christian Prayer*

Exaltation of the Holy Cross,
14 September

Today, in the left-hand aisle of the church of Sant'Egidio, in the popular district of Trastevere, in Rome, you can see a wooden cross. We found it some time ago, thrown away by the roadside. One can hardly call it a cross because it lacks the transversal branch, the arms. Today, only the central body, the trunk, of the cross remains. It even conveys an expression of suffering. We call it 'the Christ without arms', 'the powerless Christ', 'the Christ of weakness'. For us it symbolizes the call to transform the world through the weakness of the cross, without resorting to powerful means.

Mario Marazziti
a member of Sant'Egidio community

The tree is my eternal salvation. It is my nourishment and my banquet. Amidst its roots, I cast my own roots deep. Beneath its boughs I grow. Flying from the burning heat, I have set up my tent in its shadow and have found there a resting place, fresh with dew.

I flower with its flowers. Its fruits bring perfect joy, fruits which have been preserved for me since time began, fruits which now I freely eat. This tree is food, sweet food for my hunger and a fountain for my thirst; it is clothing for my nakedness; its leaves are the breath of life.

If I fear God, this is my protection; if I stumble, this is my staff; this is the prize for which I fight, the reward of my victory. This is my straight and narrow path; this is Jacob's ladder, where angels go up and down, and where the Lord himself stands at the top.

This Tree, vast as heaven itself, rises from earth to the skies, a plant immortal, set firm in the midst of heaven and earth, base of all that is, foundation of the universe, support of this world of humanity, binding force of all creation, holding within itself all the mysterious essence of human beings. Secured with the unseen clamps of the Spirit, it is so adjusted to the divine that it may never bend nor warp. Its foot rests firmly on earth, yet it towers to the topmost skies and spans with its all-embracing arms the boundless gulf of space between.

Jesus was All and in all, filling it with himself. He stripped himself naked for battle against the powers of the air. With him two thieves were stretched out, bearing within themselves the marks of those two people, the marks of those two human minds.

When the cosmic combat came to an end, the heavens shook, the stars well nigh fell from the sky, the light of heaven was for a time extinguished, rocks were split asunder, the entire world was all but shattered. But great Jesus breathed forth his divine soul and said, 'Father, into your hands I commend my Spirit.'

Then while all things shuddered and heaved in earthquake, reeling for fear, his divine soul ascended and gave life and strength to all. Again was creation still, as though this divine crucifixion and extension had everywhere unfolded and spread, penetrating all things, through all and in all. The indivisible had become divided so that all may be saved, and the world below might not remain ignorant of the coming of its God.

attrib. St John Chrysostom

Home Mission Sunday
(3rd Sunday in September)

Above all the gospel must be proclaimed by witness. Take a Christian or a handful of Christians who, in the midst of their own community, show their capacity for understanding and acceptance, their sharing of life and destiny with other people, their solidarity with the efforts of all for whatever is noble and good. Let us suppose that, in addition, they radiate in an altogether simple and unaffected way their faith in values that go beyond current values, and their hope in something that is not seen and that one would not dare to imagine. Through this wordless witness these Christians stir up irresistible questions in the hearts of those who see how they live: Why are they like this? Why do they live in this way? What or who is it that inspires them? Why are they in our midst?

Such a witness is already a silent proclamation of the Good News and a very powerful and effective one. Here we have an initial act of evangelization. The above questions will perhaps be the first that many non-Christians will ask, whether they are people to whom Christ has never been proclaimed, or baptized people who do not practise, or people who live as nominal Christians but according to principles that are in no way Christian, or people who are seeking, and not without suffering, something or someone whom they sense but cannot name. Other questions will arise, deeper and more demanding ones, questions evoked by this witness which involves pressure, sharing, solidarity, and which is an essential element, and generally the first one, in evangelization . . .

Let us therefore preserve our fervour of spirit. Let us preserve the delightful and comforting joy of evangelizing, even when it is in tears that we must sow. May it mean for us – as it did for John the Baptist, for Peter and Paul, for the other Apostles and for a multitude of splendid evangelizers all through the Church's history – an interior enthusiasm that nobody and nothing can quench. May it be the great joy of our consecrated lives. And may the world of our time, which is searching, sometimes with anguish, sometimes with hope, be enabled to receive the Good News not from evangelizers who are dejected, discouraged, impatient or anxious, but from ministers of the gospel whose lives glow with fervour, who have first received the joy of Christ, and who are willing to risk their lives so that the Kingdom may be proclaimed and the Church established in the midst of the world.

Pope Paul VI
Evangelii Nuntiandi:
evangelization in the modern world

24th week of the year

The last six years afforded me much time and food for thought. I came to the conclusion that the human race is not divided into two opposing camps of good and evil. It is made up of those who are capable of learning and those who are incapable of doing so. Here I am not talking in the narrow sense of acquiring an academic education, but of learning as the process of absorbing those lessons of life that enable us to increase peace and happiness in our world.

Aung San Suu Kyi

I take these to be the seven great facts and doctrines concerning God – his richness; his double action, natural and supernatural; his perfect freedom; his delightfulness; his otherness; his adorableness and his prevenience. These seven facts, vividly apprehended, will, even singly and how much more if seen conjointly, each penetrating and calling forth the others, bring much depth and breadth, much variety and elasticity into our prayer.

This, however, only if we understand plainly that there is no occasion whatsoever for us to constrain ourselves *positively* on these points. I mean that, though a Christian's prayer will suffer in its Christianity, if it consciously and systematically excludes, still more if it denies, any of these facts, yet no one soul, at any one period of its spiritual life, will feel equally attracted to them all.

It will be quite enough – indeed it will be the only wise course – if each particular soul, at any one period of its growth, attends positively, affirmatively, and lovingly to two or three, or even to but one of these facts. Thus not any one soul, but the society of souls, the Church of Christ, will simultaneously apprehend and apply all these facts and truths. The Church's several constituents and organs will supplement each other, and will, collectively, furnish a full perception and a full practice of these great facts of God.

Baron von Hügel
The Life of Prayer

St Matthew,
21 September

The feast which Levi gave to our Lord on his conversion is such a cheerful type to me of the Christian life. It is a festival of joy and gratitude for a conversion. We are sinners forgiven; *there* is a reason for perpetual praise. A feast represents a forgiven sinner's whole course; he is welcomed home, and he has brought more joy to heaven than there was before. His sorrow for sin is not a mortified, humiliated, angry disgust with himself. It is a humble, hopeful sorrow, always 'turning into joy'. So if his very sorrows are the material of joy, his life may be represented by the feast which Levi the publican gave to Our Lord, who had forgiven and called him.

'But I am unworthy of joy; I am willing to work and suffer if need be as a sinner. I don't look for joy.' That is a sentiment true for a pagan, but it contradicts the whole Creed of the Catholic Church. 'I believe in the Holy Catholic Church, the communion of saints, the forgiveness of sins.' So our life ought to be full of the joy of grateful love; the remembrance of sin means the remembrance of the love that called us out of our sins and forgave us the whole debt.

And besides, Levi made him a great feast. It is not that we are to be cheerful for our own gratification, but our life is to be full of praise and thanksgiving, singing and making melody in our hearts to the Lord, for the honour of Jesus. Levi made *him* a feast. Our habitual joy is due to God, and honours God; and our joy means not a reflection of the joy of God, but is the very joy of God ... If we are sinners forgiven, we ought to behave as forgiven, welcomed home, crowned with wonderful love in Christ, and so cheer and encourage all about us, who often go heavily because we reflect our gloom upon them instead of our grateful love, hope, confidence.

Father Congreve
Spiritual Letters

Our first step is the sociableness, the communicableness of God; he loves holy meetings, he loves the communion of saints, the household of the faithful: *deliciae eius*, says Solomon, 'his delight is to be with the sons of men', and that the sons of men should be with him. Religion is not a melancholy: the Spirit of God is not a damp: the Church is not a grave: it is a fold, it is an ark, it is a net, it is a city, it is a kingdom, not only a house but a house that hath many mansions in it.

John Donne
Eighty Sermons

Henri Nouwen,
21 September

It seems indeed important that we face death before we are in any real danger of dying and reflect on our mortality before all our conscious and unconscious energy is directed to the struggle to survive. It is important to be prepared for death, very important; but if we start thinking about it only when we are terminally ill, our reflections will not give us the support we need . . . Once you have reached the top of the mountain, it does not make much difference at which point on the way down you take a picture of the valley – as long as you are not in the valley itself . . .

Befriending death seems to be the basis of all other forms of befriending. I have a deep sense, hard to articulate, that if we could really befriend death, we would be free people. So many of our doubts and hesitations, ambivalences and insecurities, are bound up with our deep-seated fear of death, that our lives would be significantly different if we could relate to death as a familiar guest instead of a threatening stranger . . . Fear of death often drives us into death, but by befriending death we can face our mortality and choose life freely.

But how do we befriend death? . . . I think love – deep, human love – does not know death . . . Real love says, 'Forever'. Love will always reach out toward the eternal. Love comes from that place within us where death cannot enter. Love does not accept the limits of hours, days, weeks, months, years, or centuries. Love is not willing to be imprisoned by time.

The same love that reveals the absurdity of death also allows us to befriend death. The same love that forms the basis of our grief is also the basis of our hope; the same love that makes us cry out in pain also must enable us to develop a liberating intimacy with our own most basic brokenness. Without faith, this must sound like a contradiction. But our faith in Jesus, whose love overcame death and who rose from the grave on the third day, converts this contradiction into a paradox, the most healing paradox of our existence.

Henri Nouwen
A Letter of Consolation

Henri Nouwen died on 21 September 1996

Harvest Festival
(Sunday between
22 and 28 September)

God, bless thou thyself my reaping,
Each ridge, and plain, and field,
Each sickle curved, shapely, hard,
Each ear and handful in the sheaf.
  Each ear and handful in the sheaf.

Bless each maiden and youth,
Each woman and tender youngling,
Safeguard them beneath thy shield of strength,
And guard them in the house of the saints,
  Guard them in the house of the saints.

Encompass each goat, sheep and lamb,
Each cow and horse, and store,
Surround thou the flocks and herds,
And tend them to a kindly fold,
  Tend them to a kindly fold.

For the sake of Michael head of hosts,
Of Mary fair-skinned branch of grace,
Of Bride smooth-white of ringleted locks,
Of Columba of the graves and tombs,
  Columba of the graves and tombs.

Reaping blessing
*The Sun Dances: Prayers and Blessings
from the Gaelic*

L ord, your harvest is the harvest of love;
 love sown in the hearts of people;
love that spreads out
like the branches of a great tree
covering all who seek its shelter;
love that inspires and recreates;
love that is planted in the weak and the weary,
the sick and the dying.
The harvest of your love is the life that reaches
through the weeds of sin and death
to the sunlight of resurrection.
Lord, nurture my days with your love,
water my soul with the dew of forgiveness,
that the harvest of my life might be your joy.

Frank Topping
in *SPCK Book of Christian Prayer*

T he seed is Christ's, the harvest his; may we be stored
 within God's barn.
The sea is Christ's, the fish are his; may we be caught within
God's net.
From birth to age, from age to death, enfold us, Christ,
within your arms.
Until the end, the great rebirth, Christ, be our joy in
Paradise.

Traditional Gaelic prayer

25th week of the year

There is a story of a man who prayed earnestly one morning for grace to overcome his besetting sin of impatience. A little later he missed a train by half a minute and spent an hour stamping up and down the station platform in furious vexation. Five minutes before the next train came in he suddenly realized that here had been the answer to his prayer. He had been given an hour to practise the virtue of patience; he had missed the opportunity and wasted the hour. There are also many stories of men who have similarly missed trains which have been wrecked, and who ascribe their escape to Providence . . .

In all probability all the events which led up to all these men missing their various trains could be adequately accounted for in terms of the interaction of natural law, human freedom and divine grace. But at every point within the interaction God sees what are its possibilities for good, and the man who shares his enlightenment and his power and gives himself to make that good come true has found the meaning of that moment and his 'special providence'. The gates of the future are indeed open, the universe is in the making. But only if made aright can the making stand.

Leonard Hodgson
Essays in Christian Philosophy

The day itself is blessed by God. Doesn't this mean that everything that it contains, everything that happens to us during it, is within the will of God? Believing that things happen merely by chance is not believing in God. And if we receive everything that happens and everyone who comes to us in this spirit, we shall see that we are called to do the work of Christians in everything.

Every encounter is an encounter in God and in his sight. We are sent to everyone we meet on our way, either to give or to receive, sometimes without even knowing it. Sometimes we experience the wonder of giving what we did not possess, sometimes we have to pay with our own blood for what we give.

We must also know how to receive. We must be able to encounter our neighbour, to look at him, hear him, keep silence, pay attention, be able to love and to respond whole-heartedly to what is offered, whether it be bitterness or joy, sad or wonderful. We should be completely open and like putty in God's hands. The things that happen in our life, accepted as God's gifts, will thus give us the opportunity to be continually creative, doing the work of a Christian.

Metropolitan Anthony of Sourozh
Creative Prayer

Sunday for Older People
(Sunday nearest 1 October)

If I might only love my God and die!
But now he bids me love him and live on,
Now when the bloom of all my life is gone,
The pleasant half of life has quite gone by.
My tree of hope is lopped that spread so high;
And I forget how summer glowed and shone,
While autumn grips me with its fingers wan,
And frets me with its fitful windy sigh.
When autumn passes then must winter numb,
And winter may not pass a weary while,
But when it passes spring shall flower again:
And in that spring who weepeth now shall smile,
Yes, they shall wax who now are on the wane,
Yea, they shall sing for love when Christ shall come.

Christina Rossetti

I remember that one of the first people who came to me for advice when I was ordained was an old lady who said: 'Father, I have been praying almost unceasingly for fourteen years, and I have never had any sense of God's presence.' So I said: 'Did you give him a chance to put in a word?' 'Oh well,' she said, 'no, I have been talking to him all this time, because is not that prayer?' I said: 'No, I do not think it is, and what I suggest is that you should set apart fifteen minutes a day, sit and just knit before the face of God.'

And so she did. What was the result? Quite soon she came again and said: 'It is extraordinary, when I pray to God, in other words when I talk to him, I feel nothing, but when I sit quietly, face to face with him, then I feel wrapped in his presence.'

Metropolitan Anthony of Sourozh
Creative Prayer

Alone in my little hut in the forest
I have prepared for death.
Without moving I have been on a long journey
Towards my heavenly home.

I have trodden down my evil passions,
Stamped upon anger and greed.
I have cast aside jealousy and fear,
Leaving them by the wayside.

At times my pace has been bold and fast
Along the gospel way.
At times I have crawled on bended knee
Crying for forgiveness.

Now my journey is almost finished,
My creator comes to fetch me.
Alone I came to my hut in the forest,
And alone in death I shall leave it.

Anon. (Celtic)

26th week of the year

How easy, Lord, it is for me to live with you.
How easy it is for me to believe in you.
When my understanding is perplexed by doubts
or on the point of giving up,
when the most intelligent men see no further
than the coming evening, and know not
what they shall do tomorrow,
you send me a clear assurance
that you are there and that you will ensure
that not all the roads of goodness are barred.

From the heights of earthly fame I look back
in wonder at the road that led
through hopelessness
to this place whence I can send
mankind a reflection of your radiance.

And whatever I in this life may yet reflect,
that you will give me;
And whatever I shall not attain,
that, plainly, you have purposed for others.

                              Alexander Solzhenitsyn

Give me my scallop-shell of quiet,
My staff of faith to walk upon,
My scrip of joy, immortal diet,
My bottle of salvation.
My gown of glory, hope's true gauge,
And thus I'll make my pilgrimage.

And by the happy blissful way
More peaceful pilgrims I shall see.
They have shook off their gowns of clay
And go apparelled fresh like me.
From thence to heaven's bribeless hall,
Where no corrupted voices brawl,
No conscience molted into gold,
Nor forged accusers bought and sold,
No cause deferred, nor vain-spent journey.
For there Christ is the King's Attorney,
Who pleads for all without degrees
And he had angels, but no fees.

And when the grand twelve million jury
Of our sins with sinful fury
'Gainst our souls black verdicts give,
Christ pleads his death, and then we live.

Sir Walter Raleigh
Before his execution in 1618

C hange your hearts . . .
Unless we change our hearts we are not converted.
Changing places is not the answer.
Changing occupations is not the answer.
The answer is to change our hearts.
And how do we change?
By praying.

Mother Teresa of Calcutta

St Teresa of Lisieux,
1 October

Some time ago I was watching the flicker of a tiny night-light. One of the sisters, having lit her own candle in the dying flame, passed it round to light the candles of the others. And the thought came to me: 'Who dares glory in their own good works? It needs but one faint spark to set the world on fire.'

We come in touch with burning and shining lights, set high on the candlestick of the Church, and we think we are receiving from them grace and light. But from where do they borrow their fire?

Very possibly from the prayers of some devout and hidden soul whose inward shining is not apparent to human eyes – some soul of unrecognized virtue, and in her own sight of little worth: a dying flame!

What mysteries we shall one day see unveiled! I have often thought that perhaps I owe all the graces with which I am laden to some little soul whom I shall know only in heaven.

Only love can enlarge my heart. Jesus, I desire to run until that glorious day when I follow you to your Kingdom, singing the canticle of love. God has given me a clear insight into the deep mysteries of love. If only I could express what I know, you would hear heavenly music; but I can only stammer like a child, and if the words of Jesus were not my support, I would be tempted to hold my peace.

Eternal Word, Saviour! You are the Divine Eagle whom I love. You came into this land of exile, willing to suffer and to die, in order to carry every single soul into the very heart of the Trinity – love's eternal home.

You returned to your realm of light, and still remain hidden here to nourish us with Holy Communion. Forgive me if I tell you that your love reaches even to madness. My trust can know no bounds.

My folly lies in the hope that your love will accept me, and in my confidence that the angels and saints will help me to fly to you.

As long as you will it, I shall remain with my gaze fixed on you, for I long to be fascinated by your divine eyes, to be a prey to your love.

I am filled with the hope that one day you will swoop down upon me and bear me away to the source of all love ... that you will plunge me into its glowing abyss.

St Teresa of Lisieux
By Love Alone: daily readings

St Francis of Assisi,
4 October

Canticle of the furnace

L ove has cast me in a furnace:
He has pierced my heart,
And my body has fallen to the ground
The arrows fired
From his bow of love,
Have struck me,
He has turned peace into war.
I am dying of sweetness.

Love has cast me in a furnace:
The darts which he threw
Were lead-covered stones,
Each one weighing
Thousands of pounds:
They rained on me, like thick hail;
I was unable to count them;
Not one missed its mark.

Love has cast me in a furnace:
He never missed me once;
Such was his good aim.
I was lying on the ground.
My limbs could not assist me;
My body was broken;
I had no more feeling
Than a dead man.

Love has cast me in a furnace:
Not on account of death,
But because of joy:
After my body recovered
I became so strong,
That I could follow the guides,
Who conducted me
To the gates of heaven.

Canticle of love – part one

Love of loves,
Why have you so wounded me?
My heart, torn from its dwelling
Is consumed with love.
It is on fire, it burns, it finds no resting place:
It cannot escape, because it is chained:
It is consumed, like wax in the fire;

Dying, it lives: its languor is sweet:
It prays for power to escape,
And finds itself in a furnace.
Alas, where will I be led
By this terrible faintness?
It is death to live like this:
Such is the stifling heat of this fire.

Canticle of peace

Happy are those who endure in peace
By you, Most High, they will be crowned.

St Francis of Assisi
from *The Mirror of Perfection*
cantata by Richard Blackford

Harvest Fast Day
(1st Friday of October)

In the end the soil was glad that I had come to be, and held me firmly in its arms, like a nurse, while I grew. And the water fed my roots and the sun ripened my green into gold and the wind caressed me, and the miller looked upon what had come to be, and saw that it was good. And as I flourished in the field, I listened to the miller's silent meanings ...

And even as I grew in stature and in understanding, I knew that the grain that was swelling and ripening in me would be for the feeding of many; that my grain would have to die, that theirs might live again.

On a summer day the miller walked slowly through the field. The wind made waves through my standing, swaying height, and whispered its summer song. And the love of the miller swept over me, and he said:

'Do you hear the children crying, through the wind?' And I said:

'I hear the children crying. I will go. Let it be done to me, what must be done.'

I felt the stab of pain as he plucked me from the stalk, and cast me far away, into the barren empty field, where the children cried.

'Unless you fall into their ground and are buried deep in their earth, you cannot yield the food that will end their crying.'

And when the time was accomplished, I came to birth in the empty field. I was born out of emptiness into the stony ground. I cried, with the hungry children and I was hungry too. I was bent by the winds that flattened them and bruised by their hurts and heartaches ...

And always, in the distance, on the hillside, I would listen to the miller's words, carried on the winds:

'Where time is not and place has no meaning, you are with me, and they shall be so too. Go out and call them home, to the Harvest Supper.'

Margaret Silf
The Miller's Tale

M ay you, Lord, be for us a moon of joy and happiness. Let the young become strong and
the grown man keep his strength.
Let the pregnant woman be delivered, and the woman who
has given birth suckle her child.
Let the stranger reach the end of his journey, and those who
remain at home live safely in their houses.
Let the flocks that travel to feed
in the pastures return satisfied.
May you, Lord, be a moon of harvest and of calves.
May you be a moon of restoration and of good health.
Amen.

An African prayer

J esus, you often went hungry with your apostles; we thank you for the opportunities you give us of being able to provide food for those who have none and thus discover your presence in them.

Jesus, you said anyone giving a glass of water to a thirsty person in my name gives it to me; we thank you for the chance of being able to provide water for communities that previously had none.

Jesus, you often had no decent clothes and were hounded

by the authorities as a vagabond; we thank you for being able to help some of your brothers and sisters who suffer the same fate today in many parts of the world.

Jesus, you taught us to look for you in the sick, the imprisoned and the stranger; help us to reach out to those in our own society who are lonely, old, ill, refugees.

Jesus, you taught us that we do not live by bread alone but by every word that comes from the mouth of God; help us remember that the poor have spiritual needs as well as material and that we need to show them you are the Way, the Truth and the Life.

Jesus, help us to look at our world with all its divisions and injustices, not through the eyes of the wealthy and powerful, but through the eyes of the exploited and oppressed peoples who live in the poorer countries.

Jesus, help us to understand that the so-called debt of the poor countries to the wealthy has already been cancelled many times in high interest payments and is an unjust millstone round the necks of nations struggling to survive; may we do all we can to work for its total abolition as a fitting and Christian way of celebrating the jubilee year of 2000.

Jesus, as we continue to help the poor, show us how many of their problems originate in our own countries, whose wealth and high standards of living are often both the result and the cause of their poverty.

Jesus, help us to understand that to give is better than to receive; to support the poor in their struggle for justice is better than to give; and to commit ourselves directly in our own country to the struggle for a more just world, with a balanced distribution of resources and opportunities, is the greatest help we can give.

Jesus, we too are poor and in need; help us to find in the faces of the poor we serve your own face, your own presence and strength.

Michael Campbell-Johnston

God himself brought our race together into communion. He earlier shared his own goods and placed his own Logos as a common possession at the disposal of all. He made all things for all. All things are thus common to all and the rich may not claim more than their share.

To say, 'It is in my power, I have more than enough, why not enjoy it,' is neither human nor social. It is rather proper to charity to say, 'It is in my power, why not share with the needy?' For the one who is perfect is the one who fulfils the commandment, 'You shall love your neighbour as yourself?'

This is true enjoyment and riches stored up. But that which is given out for the satisfaction of foolish desires is reckoned as loss not as expenditures. For I know that God has given us the power to make use of things, but only to the extent necessary; and the use is intended to be common to all.

It is contemptible that one lives in luxury while the majority are needy. How much more glorious it is to benefit many than to live sumptuously! How much wiser it is to spend money on people than on gold and precious stones! How much more useful it is to adorn ourselves with friends than with lifeless objects! Whom will property benefit so much as showing kindness will?

In the gospel, the Lord clearly calls that rich man a fool who is filling up his barns and saying to himself, 'You have many goods stored up for many years. Eat. Drink. Make merry.' He says, 'This very night your life will be required of you. The things you have stored up, whose will they be?'

St Clement of Alexandria
Pedagogus

I slept and I dreamt that life was all joy
I woke and I found that life was all service
I served and I found that service was joy.

Rabindranath Tagore

The best part of the exchange had to be the people we met and the friends we made. Almost everywhere we went we were greeted by screaming warriors brandishing spears – an old tradition to scare away enemies – and then presented with garlands of flowers. When Solomon Islanders say, 'Make yourself at home,' they mean it: everything they have is yours.

Lisa Hartwell
After going to the Solomon Islands
as part of a youth exchange

Lord God, we ask you to forgive us our sins, to enlighten our imagination, so that we can share more equally the gifts you have left for all of your children, so that creation may join us in praising your name. Amen.

Oscar Romero

O God, to those who have hunger give bread, and to us who have bread give the hunger for justice.

Latin American Grace

27th week of the year

One method of meditation that many people find useful is to rest the mind lightly on an object. You can use an object of natural beauty that invokes a special feeling of inspiration for you, such as a flower or a crystal. But something that embodies the truth, such as an image of Buddha, or Christ, or particularly your master, is even more powerful.

If your mind is able to settle naturally of its own accord, and if you find you are inspired simply to rest in its pure awareness, then you do not need any method of meditation. However, the vast majority of us find it difficult to arrive at that state straight away. We simply do not know how to awaken it, and our minds are so wild and so distracted that we need a skilful means or method to evoke it.

By 'skilful' I mean that you bring together your understanding of the essential nature of your mind, your knowledge of your various, shifting moods, and the insight you have developed through your practice into how to work with yourself, from moment to moment. By bringing these together, you learn the art of applying whatever method is appropriate to any particular situation or problem, to transform that environment of your mind.

Everything can be used as an invitation to meditation. A smile, a face in the subway, the sight of a small flower growing in the crack of cement pavement, a fall of rich cloth in a shop window, the way the sun lights up flower pots on a windowsill. Be alert for any sign of beauty or grace. Offer up every joy, be awake at all moments, to 'the news that is always arriving out of silence'.

Slowly, you will become a master of your own bliss, a chemist of your own joy, with all sorts of remedies always at hand to elevate, cheer, illuminate, and inspire your every breath and movement.

In the ancient meditation instructions, it is said that at the beginning, thoughts will arrive one on top of another, uninterrupted, like a steep mountain waterfall. Gradually, as you perfect meditation, thoughts become like the water in a deep, narrow gorge, then a great river slowly winding its way down to the sea, and finally the mind becomes like a still and placid ocean, ruffled by only the occasional ripple or wave.

Sogyal Rinpoche
Glimpse after Glimpse:
Daily Reflections on Living and Dying

Mechthild of Magdeburg,
8 October

God asks the soul what it brings

GOD:
Thou huntest sore for thy love,
  What bring'st thou me, my Queen?

SOUL:
Lord! I bring thee my treasure;
It is greater than the mountains,
Wider than the world,
Deeper than the sea,
Higher than the clouds,
More glorious than the sun,
More manifold than the stars,
It outweighs the whole earth!

GOD:
O thou! image of my divine Godhead,
Enobled by my humanity,
Adorned by my Holy Spirit –
What is thy treasure called?

SOUL:
Lord! it is called my heart's desire!
I have withdrawn it from the world,
Denied it to myself and all creatures.
Now I can bear it no longer.
Where, O Lord, shall I lay it?

GOD:
Thy heart's desire shalt thou lay nowhere
But in mine own Divine Heart
And on my human breast.
There alone wilt thou find comfort
And be embraced by my Spirit.

SOUL:
Fish cannot drown in the water,
Birds cannot sink in the air,
Gold cannot perish
In the refiner's fire.
This has God given to all creatures
To foster and seek their own nature.
How then can I withstand mine?
    I must to God –
My Father through nature,
My Brother through humanity,
My Bridegroom through love,
His am I for ever!
    Think ye that fire must utterly slay my soul?
Nay! Love can both fiercely scorch
And tenderly love and console.
Therefore be not troubled!
Ye shall still teach me.
When I return
I will need your teaching
For the earth is full of snares.

Then the beloved goes into the lover, into the secret hiding place of the sinless Godhead ... And there, the soul being fashioned in the very nature of God, no hindrance can come between it and God.

Mechthild of Magdeburg
The Revelations of Mechthild of Magdeburg

28th week of the year

The pattern of redemption isn't a straight line, or even a wavy line. It isn't even a circle, because each time we re-connect to our 'beginnings', the connection is different, and the circle is re-drawn in a new and different way.

This pattern, which sounds so mysterious when we attempt to describe it in words, is actually as simple, and as beautiful, as the earth itself.

On the surface, and above, there is the weather, constantly changing, yet each kind of weather bearing its own gifts – some welcome, some less so. Sometimes the weather is extreme and 'out of order', sometimes it is moderated and balanced. In its unreliability it feels just like us, and our moods and feelings.

Then there is the layer of top-soil, just underneath our 'weather' and very much influenced by it, but more stable, and carrying the godseed for germination and growth. This is our heart-soil where God is growing his Kingdom.

And under the soil, the bedrock. Whenever we go deep, in prayer, or in relationship with God and with each other, or into the mystery and meaning of things, we will eventually come up against this hard rock. It can feel like the solid door of a locked room. There is no way out: no way in. So dark it is, that we don't even rightly know whether we are trying to get in (to a treasure chamber), or out (of a prison cell). Maybe both. Yet God is the bedrock, just as he is in our weather and our soil. The rock is his unwavering holding of us, the solid foundation without which we would sink into the quicksand. But it is also the hard rock that shatters us when we fall upon it, and which breaks us open, as it broke God himself upon the Cross.

And because that rock opens up, from time to time, in our inner vision – glimpse-wise and terrifyingly – as it did when Jesus uttered 'It is completed!', and as it does for us sometimes in the dreadful movements of our inner earthquakes, or in silent, secret shafts of burning light that occasionally streak through prayer or dream – because of these we know that beneath the bedrock is an ever-blazing fire. This feels like the molten centre of ourselves, the source of our passion and energy. Like our surface weather, it is sometimes wild and disordered, sometimes creative and life-giving.

This same inner fire is also the fire of God at the heart of all his creation. Sometimes we dread it, because it has the aspect of the flames of hell. Sometimes we long for it, because it seems to be alight with the very splendour of God's eternal presence and the radiance of heaven. This same fire, surely, licks our own hearts too, sometimes rising to reproach and consume us, sometimes seeming to transfigure us and our whole view of the world.

Margaret Silf
Landmarks: an Ignatian journey

St Teresa of Avila,
15 October

This secret union takes place in the deepest centre of the soul, which must be where God himself dwells, and I do not think there is any need of a door by which to enter it. The Lord appears in the centre of the soul, not through an imaginary, but through an intellectual vision (although this is a subtler one than that already mentioned), just as he appeared to the apostles, without entering through the door, when he said to them: '*Pax vobis*'. This instantaneous communication of God to the soul is so great a secret and so sublime a favour, and such a delight is felt by the soul, that I do not know with what to compare it, beyond saying that the Lord is pleased to manifest to the soul at that moment the glory that is in heaven, in a sublimer manner than is possible through any vision or spiritual consolation. It is impossible to say more than that, as far as one can understand, the soul (I mean the spirit of this soul) is made one with God, who, being likewise a Spirit, has been pleased to reveal the love that he has for us by showing to certain persons the extent of that love, so that we may praise his greatness. For he has been pleased to unite himself with his creature in such a way that they have become like two who cannot be separated from one another: even so he will not separate himself from her.

We might say that union is as if the ends of two wax candles were joined so that the light they give is one: the wicks and the wax and the light are all one: yet afterwards the one candle can be perfectly well separated from the other and the candles become two again, or the wick may be withdrawn from the wax. But there it is like rain falling from the heavens into a river or a spring; there is nothing but water there and it is impossible to divide or separate the water belonging to the river from that which fell from the heavens. Or it is as if a tiny streamlet enters the sea, from which it will find no way of separating itself, or as if in a room there were two large windows through which the light streamed in; it enters in different places but it all becomes one.

Perhaps when St Paul says: 'He who is joined to God becomes one spirit with him,' he is referring to this sovereign marriage, which presupposes the entrance of His Majesty into the soul by union.

St Teresa of Avila
Interior Castle

World Mission Sunday
(penultimate Sunday in October)

In its first centuries Christianity had a special power of its own which we desperately need to rediscover. At that time it was a matter of developing a truly Christian spirit. What happened in those early days of the Church? If we re-read the Acts of the Apostles we will find the example of the Apostle Philip baptizing the representative of the Queen of Ethiopia before that functionary had what we would today consider an elementary notion of Christian doctrine. It is important to realize that these early Christians knew absolutely nothing about such things as papal infallibility, but they knew what it was to be a Christian. At any rate, it is through them that Christianity has come down to us rather than the spiritism that the masses of Brazilian Christians pass on to their children.

We have lost the force of early Christians. Our words do not express Christianity, but merely express the fact that our social structures have Christian trimmings. And in Latin America, the very words we use in evangelization have been corrupted; try to speak of charity, poverty, or the afterlife, and you will be told, 'Go away; we know all about your Christianity!'

Unfortunately, they do know. Every word of the Christian message has been used to support the status quo of Christendom, but Christianity itself has been compromised by this attempt to maintain control of the masses, preserving Christian institutions by political means or through alliances with social conservatism. All this is justified on the basis that without this economic power and political influence it would be impossible to preach Christianity to the masses, but this only means that it would be impossible to maintain the social machine as a 'machine to make Christians'. How can we talk of Christianity with words that will reach human beings, with words that are not betrayed by these realities? In Latin America, more than elsewhere, the concern to guard Catholic institutions by every possible means has compromised the very words by which Christianity must be expressed.

The choice has still to be made to distinguish between what is authentically Christian and what is not. I believe that the pressure of reality is going to force Latin America and the Church to come to a decision. It is precisely at the moment where earthly kingdoms disappear around us that the Kingdom of Christ really begins. I believe that in this truth lies the hope for Latin America.

Juan Luís Segundo
'The Future of Christianity in Latin America'

29th week of the year

I had joined the monastery looking for a purifying discipline and I certainly found it. Gradually I began to like it. The pseudo-sophistication of adolescence fell away and I was greatly simplified. The mechanism of punctuality, of being summoned by bells, of fulfilling certain tasks by a certain time, became a pleasure. I realized that I could live any disciplined life, however hard: that discipline was easy.

Had we just had the rigid structure, we would soon have tired of it: it was monotonous and sometimes humiliating. In fact Father Alban's novitiate was very positive: he taught us a love of prayer and the desire to live a life wrapped up in God. I heard for the first time consciously of the love of God, about the ever-presence of God and the way every thought could be a means to forget oneself and one's fears and make one aware of him. To an outsider all that may seem very abstract and pointless, but to me the depth of commitment, a common experience we all shared, is one of the most valuable and mean-ingful of my whole life. Prayer is not just a state of suspended animation, like a cow asleep on its feet, nor a form of athletic trick by which one achieves in some way a stretching of the person: what is so hard for an outsider to understand, so hard for someone who lives for his activities to believe in, is that prayer is positive at all. Yet it is like a drug: it brings you to know a new world; not a drug like LSD which kills experience and finally man himself, but like love for a young wife or like writing poetry. Prayer gives you experience. Thus it was that in this year 1946 I began reading the simple manuals of prayer: Grou, Boylan and Merton, authors who treated of method and technique, like those little red military drill books that drill sergeants carried around. We quickly passed on to the masters:

Teresa of Avila, John of the Cross and – for me the most satisfying of all – the English Mystics. My Odyssey was made in an English ship. The Downside of the time was no sentimental place; its prayer too was a form of intellectual exercise, not an emotional experience. Part of the Downside folklore runs as follows:

Monk: Father Abbot, I thought I really ought to inform you: I am having visions.
Abbot: Oh no, no, Father; we definitely don't have visions at Downside.

Fabian Glencross
in *A Touch of God:*
eight monastic journeys

30th week of the year

God created a world of immense beauty, from the smallest flower to the most precious of gems, full of colour and wonder for our pleasure and for God's pleasure. What imagination to bring into being such a riot of beauty! 'In the beginning was the imagination of God' – it is not too loose a translation, I think, of the Greek word *Logos* (John 1).

What a risk God took in creating humans, the fruit of his imagining! 'Then God said: Let us make humankind in our image, according to our likeness.' We were created out of love, to be loved, but with the freedom to make our own response and, when we went wrong, what a risk God took, in Christ, to show us who it is who loves us.

For all our faults we still bear the image of God, and God entrusted to us the creative gift of imagination. It can release in us a whole flood of ideas giving us the ability to look beyond our own situation, to extend our understanding and to help us discover the new. God has put that ability to imagine in each and every one of us.

Alfred de Vigny said: 'The true God, the mighty God, is the God of ideas.' Our imagination gives us a window through which we can see more of God . . .

In August, the Fourth UN World Conference on Women takes place in Beijing. Women will be taking imaginative action by bringing ribbon banners from every corner of the world to 'Weave the World Together', with messages of hope, reconciliation and peace, to link diverse heritages to a common future . . .

If ever we needed to exercise our imagination it is now, with increasing pressures and stress in our lives, questions about declining standards, and the problem of dwindling congre-

gations. It is all too easy to become pessimistic and to forget
the power of the Holy Spirit – that spirit which was seen in
such an imaginative way, as wind and fire and understandable
language, to those women and men all those years ago; that
dynamic spirit which still lives.

Declining is not inevitable; new life and growth are possible.
Problems must not be allowed to cloud our imagination – we
need it all the more! New problems are often new opportunities
if we only have the imagination to grasp them. This is the time
for audacious imagination, and for displaying passion about
the good news we have to share.

Stella G. Bristow
Methodist Conference

All Saints,
1 November

B efore ever any of God's creatures longs for holiness, God
himself longs for every single one of his creatures to be
holy. The ground of love, as St John says, lies not in our love
for God but in his having loved us from the beginning. Of all
the truths that we have to try to realize in our undertaking,
none is more vital than this . . .

It was not until I found myself in the world of Islam that I ever
realized how one might long for God in a way analogous to the
way that a human lover longs for the beloved when separated
from him. The notion of serving God I was familiar with, as of
doing his will or fulfilling one's duty, and thereby loving him. But
the realization that the call to holiness is the echo of God's longing for each one of us, or that our search begins, continues and
ends in longing, only came to me when I heard the voice of Islam.

It was in the deep darkness of a bitingly frosty January
morning in the Holy Land, near Nazareth. As I lay shivering
with cold, waiting for the break of dawn, in the hostel high
above the town, I suddenly heard the cry of the muezzin from
the mosque hundreds of feet below: '*Allahu akhbar* – God is
great – prayer is better than sleep.' Those words I had heard
many times before, but this time they arose out of another
world and were addressed to another world. The cry came out
of a heart that would never rest content with earthly satisfac-
tions. It pierced the thick darkness and stillness of the early
hours, echoing and re-echoing around the hills in which Nazareth is cupped. The cry was sustained for some quarter of an
hour; and even when it ceased and silence fell upon Nazareth
once more, the message continued to reverberate within me:

only One can satisfy longing of such depth and intensity. No
creature can do so, but only the Creator.

The call which I heard in Nazareth is not a call of the same
type that we humans experience through the urge for food,
say, or for drink or sex. Such urges can be satisfied, in an
earthly way, by food and drink and sex. But the longing for
holiness is a call to absolute union with the Holy One and
comes from beyond this earth. So it can only be satisfied from
beyond.

Donald Nicholl
Holiness

D ear God, creator of women in your own image,
    born of a woman in the midst of a world half women,
carried by women to mission fields around the globe,
made known by women to all the children of the earth,
give to the women of our time
   the strength to persevere,
   the courage to speak out,
   the faith to believe in you beyond
   all systems and institutions
so that your face on earth may be seen in all its beauty,
so that men and women become whole,
so that the Church may be converted to your will in
   everything and in all ways.

We call on the holy women
who went before us,
channels of Your Word
in testaments old and new,
to intercede for us
so that we might be given the grace
to become what they have been
for the honour and glory of God.

Saint Esther, who pleaded against power for the liberation
of the people. – *Pray for us.*
Saint Judith, who routed the plans of men and saved the
community,
Saint Deborah, laywoman and judge, who led the people of
God,
Saint Elizabeth of Judea, who recognized the value of
another woman,
Saint Mary Magdalene, minister of Jesus, first evangelist of
the Christ,
Saint Scholastica, who taught her brother Benedict to
honour the spirit above the system,
Saint Hildegard, who suffered interdict for the doing of
right,
Saint Joan of Arc, who put no law above the law of God,
Saint Clare of Assisi, who confronted the Pope with the
image of woman as equal,
Saint Julian of Norwich, who proclaimed for all of us the
motherhood of God,
Saint Thérèse of Lisieux, who knew the call to priesthood in
herself,
Saint Catherine of Siena, to whom the Pope listened,
Saint Teresa of Avila, who brought women's gifts to the
reform of the Church,
Saint Edith Stein, who brought fearlessness to faith,
Saint Elizabeth Seton, who broke down boundaries between
lay women and religious by wedding motherhood and
religious life,
Saint Dorothy Day, who led the Church to a new sense of
justice.

Mary, mother of Jesus, who heard the call of God and
answered,
Mary, mother of Jesus, who drew strength from the woman
Elizabeth,
Mary, mother of Jesus, who underwent hardship bearing
Christ,

Mary, mother of Jesus, who ministered at Cana,
Mary, mother of Jesus, inspirited at Pentecost,
Mary, mother of Jesus, who turned the Spirit of God into
  the body and blood of Christ, pray for us. Amen.

Joan Chittister
A Litany of Women for the Church

All Souls,
2 November

C aptains and leaders of the dread hosts of heaven
    enthroned on high,
Ministers of the divine glory,
Michael and Gabriel the chief commanders,
Who serve the Master with all the spiritual powers:
Make intercession, without ceasing, for the world,
Asking that we may receive forgiveness of our sins
And grace and mercy in the day of judgement.

Hymn for the Feast of the Holy Angels
in the Orthodox Church

W hen anyone prays, the angels that minister to God and
    watch over mankind gather round about him and join
with him in his prayer. Nor is that all. Every Christian – each
of the 'little ones' who are in the Church – has an angel of his
own, who 'always beholds the face of our Father which is in
heaven' (Matthew 18:10), and who looks upon the Godhead
of the Creator. This angel prays with us and works with us,
as far as he can, to obtain the things for which we ask.

'The angel of the Lord,' so it is written, 'encamps beside
those who fear the Lord and delivers them' (Psalm 33:8), while
Jacob speaks of 'the angel who delivers me from all evils'
(Genesis 48:16): and what he says is true not of himself only
but of all those who set their trust in God. It would seem, then,
that when a number of the faithful meet together genuinely for

the glory of Christ, since they all fear the Lord, each of them will have, encamped beside him, his own angel whom God has appointed to guard him and care for him. So, when the saints are assembled, there will be a double Church, one of men and one of angels.

Origen

Today or tomorrow, when we stand by the graves, or when our heart must seek distant graves, where perhaps not even a cross stands over them any longer; when we pray, 'Lord, grant them eternal rest, and may perpetual light shine upon them'; when we quietly look up towards the eternal homeland of all the saints and – from afar and yet so near – greet God's light and his love, our eternal homeland; then all our memories and all our prayers are only the echo of the words of love that the holy living, in the silence of their eternity, softly and gently speak into our heart. Hidden in the peace of the eternal God, filled with his own bliss, redeemed for eternity, permeated with love for us that can never cease, they, on their feast, utter the prayer of their love for us: 'Lord, grant eternal rest to them whom we love – as never before – in your love. Grant it to them who still walk the hard road of pilgrimage, which is none the less the road that leads to us and to your eternal light. We, although silent, are now closer to them than ever before, closer than when we were sojourning and struggling along with them on earth.'

Karl Rahner
The Eternal Year

At the heart of the Christian faith is the conviction that, when death is accepted in a spirit of faith, and when one's

whole life is oriented to self-giving so that at its end one gladly
and freely surrenders it back into the hands of God the Creator
and Redeemer, then death is transformed into a fulfilment.
One conquers death by love – not by one's own heroic virtu-
ousness, but by sharing in that love with which Christ accepted
death on the Cross. The Christian is one who believes that
when he has united his life and his death with Christ's gift of
himself on the Cross, he has not merely found a dogmatic
answer to a human problem and a set of ritual gestures which
comfort and allay anxiety: he has gained access to the grace
of the Holy Spirit.

Therefore he lives no longer by his own forfeited and fallen
existence, but by the eternal and immortal life that is given
him, in the Spirit, by Christ. He lives 'in Christ'.

What then 'comes after death' is still not made clear in terms
of 'place of rest' (a celestial cemetery?) or a paradise of reward.
The Christian is not concerned really with a life divided
between this world and the next. He seeks the Face of God,
and the vision of him who is eternal life (John 17:3).

Thomas Merton
Conjectures of a Guilty Bystander

I f you believe that prayers for the living are a help to them,
why should you not pray for the dead? Life is one, for as
St Luke says: 'He is not the God of the dead but of the living'
(20:38). Death is not an end but a stage in the destiny of man.

The love which our prayer expresses cannot be in vain; if
love had power on earth and had no power after death it would
tragically contradict the word of Scripture that love is as strong
as death (Song of Songs 8:6), and the experience of the Church
that love is more powerful than death, because Christ has
defeated death in his love for mankind.

Prayer for the dead

31st week of the year

Death is the touchstone of our attitude to life. People who are afraid of death are afraid of life. It is impossible not to be afraid of life, with all its complexity and dangers, if one is afraid of death. This means that to solve the problem of death is not a luxury. If we are afraid of death we will never be prepared to take ultimate risks; we will spend our life in a cowardly, careful and timid manner. It is only if we can face death, make sense of it, determine its place and our place in regard to it, that we will be able to live in a fearless way and to the fullness of our ability. Too often we wait until the end of our life to face death, whereas we would have lived quite differently if only we had faced death at the outset . . . If only we realized whenever confronted with a person that this might be the last moment either of his life or of ours, we would be much more intense, much more attentive to the words we speak and the things we do.

Only awareness of death will give life this immediacy and depth, will bring life to life.

Metropolitan Anthony of Sourozh

As they were keeping the evening vigil in the church where Wilfrid's remains rested, certain of the less watchful brethren standing outside saw a sign appear in the sky. They kept quiet about it till the next morning. When the rest heard about it, they were deeply grieved and murmured to each other that it had been kept back from them because of their sins. Their honesty was soon rewarded. When the feast that ended the solemnities was over, the whole assembly went out of doors in the twilight to sing compline. Suddenly a wonderful white arc shone out before them in the heavens, encircling the entire monastery. Apart from the lack of colour it looked exactly like a rainbow.

We worshipped and praised the Lord for this sign, the Lord who is wondrous in his saints, for we clearly saw that he was with us, building a wall of protection around his chosen vineyard. Our conviction was borne out in every event that rose to affright us.

Eddius Stephanus
Life of Wilfrid

Remembrance Day
(2nd Sunday in November)

Why these bitter words of the dying, O brethren, which they utter as they go hence? I am parted from my brethren. All my friends do I abandon and go hence. But whither I go, that understand I not, neither what shall become of me yonder; only God who hath summoned me knoweth. But make commemoration of me with the song: Alleluia.

But whither now go the souls? How dwell they now together there? This mystery have I desired to learn, but none can impart aright. Do they call to mind their own people as we do them? Or have they forgotten all those who mourn them and make the song: Alleluia.

We go forth on the path eternal, and as condemned, with downcast faces, present ourselves before the only God eternal. Where then is comeliness? Where then is wealth? Where then is the glory of this world? There shall none of these things aid us, but only to say oft the psalm: Alleluia.

If thou hast shown mercy unto man, O man, that same mercy shall be shown thee there; and if on an orphan thou hast shown compassion, the same shall there deliver thee from want. If in this life the naked thou hast clothed, the same shall give thee shelter there, and sing the psalm: Alleluia.

Youth and the beauty of the body fade at the hour of death, and the tongue then burneth fiercely, and the parched throat is inflamed. The beauty of the eyes is quenched then, the comeliness of the face all altered, the shapeliness of the neck destroyed; and the other parts have become numb nor often say: Alleluia.

With ecstasy are we inflamed if we but hear that there is light eternal yonder; that there is paradise, wherein every soul of righteous ones rejoiceth. Let us all, also, enter into Christ, that all we may cry aloud thus unto God: Alleluia.

Funeral Ikos
Part of the Greek funeral sentences
for the burial of priests

L ooking beyond this life, my first prayer, aim and hope is that I may see God. The thought of being blest with the sight of earthly friends pales before that thought. I believe that I shall never die; this awful prospect would crush me, were it not that I trusted and prayed that it would be an eternity in God's presence. How is eternity a boon unless he goes with it?

And for others dear to me, my one prayer is that they may see God.

John Henry Newman

H eavenly Father,
you are the giver of life,
and you share with us
the care of the life that is given.
Into your hands we commit in trust the developing life
that we have cut short.
Look in merciful judgement on the decision that we have
made,
and assure us in all our uncertainty that your love for us can
never change. Amen.

Prayer by Bishop Peter Firth, proposed to the
Church of England's General Synod in 1979
but not accepted

Jesus, we remember that before you came into your Kingdom you went through the darkest time you knew on earth. Today we have come here to consider some of the deepest, darkest feelings human beings can go through. We thank you for whatever experience we may have had of brokenness and darkness that brought us here today. We thank you because you can transform everything, and you are calling us to go back into the darkness and meet those people who are still there.

It is time to feel in us the life, the love and the hope that we have received from you: the power of your resurrection shining into the darkness.

We thank you because the light is always brighter in the darkness. We offer our lives and the rest of this day to you. Amen.

Prayer by a counsellor

Mary of Bethlehem and Nazareth,
   wife of Joseph;
virgin mother of the Son of God made man: woman of
   sorrows,
model of faith, you are our mother,
living now in the joy of the presence of God.
You watch over each one of us with gentleness, compassion
   and tenderness.
We entrust all people hurt by abortion to your motherly
   care.
May your unfailing love console our sisters and brothers.
and be for them a source of healing and joy.
   Holy Mary, pray for us all.

Prayer for all those hurt by abortion,
adapted from a Canadian prayer

There is a sound of weeping in the world:
    It is women, weeping for their children.
They refuse to be consoled because their children are no
    more.
The sorrow they have shown shall have its reward, says the
    Lord.
Wipe away their tears, for their children will be returned to
    them.

Prayer for women hurt by abortion,
based on Jeremiah 31:15–17
all from *Prayer After Abortion*
ed. Althea Hayton

32nd week of the year

In the spring of 1994, Pat Smith began sharing in the life of St Francis House. Unfortunately, life in the army, followed by many rather solitary years living and drinking on the streets, meant that the communal life at St Francis House would make unrealistic demands on Pat. In the end, after just two months, it was all too much. The shared life, the struggle to stay dry and the nightmares and memories of several tours of duty in Northern Ireland became intolerable and we parted company with feelings of anger, fear and distress at the house for some time afterwards.

A year later in June this year, Pat, not yet fifty years old, was buried following a sudden and fatal heart attack while staying at the Simon House hostel in the centre of Oxford.

For all the difficult times associated with Pat's stay at St Francis House, the most lasting memory for me is how the birth of a very sick child was able to break down barriers caused by lingering feelings of fear, anger and distrust. That child, our son James, revealed the Jesus in Pat that had been difficult for me to see for so long. Within days of Jamie's birth, Pat became Mena's most faithful visitor. Not a fit man, Pat would walk the two miles to the hospital, often in hot summer sunshine, to enquire on this tiny infant's progress . . . As Jamie's condition improved and his condition was no longer life-threatening, Pat's visits stopped, and the cycle of drinking began once again.

Pat's mind seemed tortured, scarred by life in war-stricken Belfast . . . The violence and death he witnessed as a soldier did not allow him to find that inner peace which he seemed at times to desire more than anything else. However, now he has passed from this life to the next, I am hopeful that the peace that passes all understanding, the peace of Christ, will now be his for eternity. For in loving James he revealed a humanity far more valuable than the inhumanity bred of war and life on the streets.

Clive Gillam
St Francis House Newsletter

The only thing the sun produces is light; if there is shade it does not come from the sun but from something that gets in the way of the sun. That is how it is with God: the only thing he produces is life; everything which hinders or weakens life comes from the other side, from our weakness, our sin, our limitation. What God does is strengthen our weakness with his resurrection power.

I thank God for this growing certainty, yet it does not in any way lessen my desire to go on living with you, or to go on struggling for life, which I love more than ever.

Yes, there have been times when I have felt a hole in my stomach, times when a question rises up from within: why me? But at root this question goes on blaming God for what is happening. And then I slip into the realization, which comes from the depths of my faith, that it is not God who sends us death, but rather God is the one who is with us in our death, at our side, so that we may live it through with faith and gracefulness, with deep hope, even with deep joy.

Carlos Bravo Gallárdo

St Margaret of Scotland,
16 November

While Margaret was still in the flower of youth, she began to lead a life of great strictness, to love God above all things, to occupy herself with the study of the Holy Scriptures and to exercise her mind therein with joy. Keen penetration of intellect was hers to understand any matter whatever it might be; tenacity of memory to retain many things; and a graceful facility of language to give expression to her thoughts.

While therefore she meditated in the law of the Lord day and night, and, like another Mary sitting at his feet, she delighted to hear his word, it came about that by the desire of her friends more than her own – rather by the appointment of God – she was married to Malcolm, son of Duncan, the most powerful King of the Scots . . .

What could be more compassionate than her heart? What more gentle to the needy? Not only would she give her goods to the poor, but if she could, she would have freely given herself. She was poorer than any of her paupers, for they, having nothing, desired to have, but she was anxious to dispose what she had. When she walked or rode out in public, crowds of poor people, orphans and widows, flocked to her as they would to a most beloved mother, and none of them ever left her without being comforted. And when all she had brought with her for the use of the needy had been distributed, she used to receive from her attendants and the rich who accompanied her their garments and anything else they had with them at the time, to bestow upon the poor, so that no one might ever go away from her in distress. Nor did those who were with her take this ill; they rather strove among themselves to offer her what they had, since they knew for certain that she would pay them the double of what they had given . . .

It was the custom to bring three hundred poor people into the royal hall, and when they had been seated round it in order, the King and Queen came in, and the doors were shut by the servants, for with the exception of the chaplains, certain religious, and a few attendants, no one was permitted to witness their almsgivings. The King on the one side, and the Queen on the other, waited upon Christ in the person of his poor, and with great devotion served them with food and drink, which had been specially prepared for this purpose.

Turgot, Bishop of St Andrews
Saint Margaret

St Elizabeth of Hungary,
17 November

I've agreed to write a radio script about St Elizabeth. It must be made clear that she was a flame leaping upwards – swift, swift – like all who reach perfection early – rushing towards the peak, consuming herself and everything she touched. But the spark came from the apostolic 'movement of poverty', as yet darkly smouldering – or, more correctly, from its Franciscan climax. That such a thing should exist: a poverty *movement*! an ideal of poverty, catching thousands in its sway. And not just from 'below' either, as self-assertion of the populace, but rather flaming down from above in Francis, Clare, Elizabeth and their like . . .

Ludwig's death was the decisive test as to whether her yearning for poverty was 'idealism', i.e. a passing whim, or serious – so serious that it could even replace the foundation which had been torn out of her life. She passed the test. From then on – no longer borne by her husband – she 'foundered', but indeed, in this wreck, reached a new foundation for her life. She was exactly the same age as Little Thérèse when she died. What a difference! Elizabeth's lightning directness, impulsive, unselfconscious, beside the perpetual reflection of Thérèse, for ever bent over her interior life, straining to catch every breath, every changing shade of her ego.

Would Elizabeth as much as dare even to *think* of herself as 'the heart of the Church', let alone put this into words? Yet in her 'the Heart of Jesus overflowed into the Church', as Peterson puts it. But Elizabeth was far from being a product of the poverty movement! She wasn't even primarily roused and inspired by it – with her it is all much less conscious, earlier, almost instinctive, like a homing bird. It began already in the little girl in the Wartburg, a little wild creature, half-imprisoned, taking the WORD seriously all the same, not the word of book learning (certainly she must have lived in the Wartburg as though in a dream-cave), but rather the image, the crucifix, and the daily picture of the beggars at the castle gate in whom she, gifted with insight, recognized the Lord. It matured with the heart of the girl in love, the bride, the young wife – all without conscious thought, the way her love grew – blossoming into awareness in her encounter with the Franciscans: 'This is what I always meant.'

Ida Friederike Görres
Broken Lights: diaries and letters 1951–19

E lizabeth's ruthless charity was, in terms of real social benefits, negligible. But it helped to spark off the political revolution that led to the fall of feudalism and the rise of the towns and cities, and so shaped modern history. Yet all she saw was the face of Christ in the sick and starving.

Rosemary Haughton
Elizabeth's Greeting

Prisoners' Sunday
(3rd Sunday in November)

I spread the magnificent loot on my bed and quickly worked out how I would enjoy it. It consisted of four pages from the magazine section of the weekend paper – three pages of advertisements and a back page of crossword puzzles, chess and stamp news. How lucky I was. There were no less than three crossword puzzles. Here was a week's reading material at least. One crossword puzzle every other day, and in between a page of advertisements. Every day for a week I had something to look forward to. I read the Births and the Marriages, and even the Deaths. So the world had not stood still. I read the Cars for Sale and the We Want to Swop columns. For one glorious week I dipped into my treasure, each day carefully restoring it to its hiding place under the mattress or in my clothes. Special savour was given to the crossword puzzles by the fact that I had to fill them in with a pin and marmite.

Herman Váldez
Diary of a Chilean concentration camp

Prison is not necessarily a place of correction, nor do we all sit and sort ourselves out to come out reformed with positive and constructive ideas. For some, unfortunately, it is a place of further education to more sophisticated and complicated crime. Two wrongs have never made one right. For those let down and for those unjustly thrown behind bars it is even an opportune period to plot revenge against 'the enemy'. Let me tell you something. The enemy who let you down or unjustly caused your suffering is best judged and punished by God almighty. If we are

Christians we are told to love our enemies. They may be mistaken in their dealings, but for the unjust there is only one greater power who delivers the ultimate vengeance. My own experience as a prisoner has been that the Holy Spirit helped me as a Christian to be aware that praying for revenge was shameful; and I started to pray, 'Forgive them Lord, for they know not what they do.' What a victory! The just God must have given up on the man who was responsible for my imprisonment and many more – he was actually shot by his own men. I never wished his death; why it happened is inexplicable. But the Lord stopped him from causing further injustice in his own way at his own time.

> *The Prisoner's Lantern: meditations by a*
> *Christian prisoner in Ethiopia*

Jesus said, 'If any man will come after me, let him deny himself, and take up his cross' (Luke 9:23). The first thing a Christian has to do is to deny himself. Everything else follows afterwards. If you take up your cross and have not denied yourself, the sacrifice you bring will only tend to magnify you, make you proud, and destroy your soul.

There is a legend about a dove that, pursued by an eagle, took refuge in Moses' bosom. The eagle demanded the surrender of its prey, arguing that God himself ordained that one creature should live by the sacrifice of another. Moved by its argument but concerned for the dove, Moses gave an equivalent amount of flesh from his own bosom, then freed the dove.

> Richard Wurmbrand
> *The Total Blessing*

O God our Father, we pray for those in prison who are innocent of charges laid against them. Keep them from bitterness and despair, we beseech you. May the truth of their position be established and may your standards of justice prevail in our courts.

Lord, I am waiting for you. I know now that it is not for

lesser joys and lesser relief that I wait impatiently. It is you I need above all. Come to me and set me free, from my worries; from my regrets; from my false desires; from my captivity to self-seeking and self-pleasing.

Your service is perfect freedom. Lord, make me your servant that I may be truly free.

I do not know how you can deliver me, Lord, but you are the only just and loving God. Give me the Holy Spirit who will free me from bondage – whatever my bondage, whether behind iron bars or not behind bars.

The Prisoner's Lantern: meditations by a
Christian prisoner in Ethiopia

B elieve me, it was often thus
  In solitary cells, on winter nights
A sudden sense of joy and warmth
And a resounding note of love.
And then, unsleeping, I would know
Someone is thinking of me now
Petitioning the Lord for me.
My dear ones, thank you all
Who did not falter, who believed in us!
In the most fearful prison hour
We probably would not have passed
Through everything – from start to end –
Our heads held high, unbowed.
Without your valiant hearts
To light our path.

Irina Ratushinskaya
quoted in *The Lion Prayer Collection*

Lord Jesus,
you experienced in person
torture and death
as a prisoner of conscience.
You were beaten and flogged
and sentenced to an agonizing death
though you had done no wrong.
Be now with prisoners of conscience
throughout the world.
Be with them in their fear and loneliness,
in the agony of physical and mental torture,
and in the face of execution and death.
Stretch out your hands in power
to break their chains.
Be merciful to the oppressor and the torturer
and place a new heart within them.
Forgive all injustice in our lives
and transform us to be
instruments of your peace,
for by your wounds we are healed.

Amnesty International

The greatest miracle of all is prayer. I have only to turn my thoughts to God and I suddenly feel a force bursting into me; there is new strength in my soul, in my entire being . . . The basis of my whole spiritual life is the Orthodox liturgy, so while I was in prison I attended it every day in my imagination . . .

At the central point of the liturgy . . . I felt myself standing before the face of the Lord, sensing almost physically his wounded, bleeding body. I would begin praying in my own words, remembering all those near to me, those in prison and those who were free, those still alive and those who had died.

More and more names welled up from my memory . . . the

prison walls moved apart and the whole universe became my residence, visible and invisible, the universe for which that wounded, pierced body offered itself as a sacrifice . . . After this, I experienced an exaltation of spirit all day – I felt purified within.

Not only my own prayer helped me, but even more the prayer of many other faithful Christians. I felt it continually, working from a distance, lifting me up as though on wings, giving me living water and the bread of life, peace of soul, rest and love.

Anatoli Levitin
(USSR)

As we closed our doors this morning, and walked freely through the church door, other doors slammed behind other people and they do not know if or when they will be open again; doors in prison cells and torture chambers; doors separating families; doors in labour camp units. Let us ask Christ, who came to set all men free, to enable us to experience his freedom and to bring that freedom to others.

Pax Christi
Prayer for prisoners of conscience

You come through thick stone walls, armed guards and bars: you bring me a starry night and ask about this and that. You are the Redeemer. I recognize you. You are my way, my truth and my life. Even my cellar blooms with stars, and peace and light pour forth. You sprinkle beautiful words on me like flowers: 'Son, what are you afraid of? I am with you!'

Viktoras Petkus
(Lithuania)

33rd week of the year

I have been to Taizé only once and that was about 25 years ago. Père Schutz spoke to us on several occasions. I can remember just five words of what he said, and they have come back to me again and again. 'For me,' said Fr Schutz, 'prayer is waiting.'

There is much in Scripture to support those words. 'The Lord is good to those who wait for him,' says Jeremiah. 'They that wait for the Lord shall renew their strength,' writes Isaiah. 'I waited patiently for the Lord, and he heard my cry,' from the Psalms. And more than 2,000 years later, and moving beyond the Bible to St John of the Cross, we read that in prayer we are to learn to rest in loving waiting upon God.

And so, when the time for silence comes, I ask you to take up your position for prayer (and sitting is usually best for most of us), and then, having asked the help of the Holy Spirit, to be content to wait, patiently, expectantly, lovingly, longingly. Try to realize this is all that you can do for yourself. God must do the rest. See yourself as the parched earth looking upwards waiting patiently for the rain to fall. You can only wait . . .

This period of waiting is sure to be demanding. And you will find yourself asking: 'Is it any use? Am I really praying?' And here are words of comfort. And they come from St Augustine. 'Your very desire is itself your prayer; if your desire is continued, so is your prayer also. Whatever you are doing, if you are desiring to pray, you are praying. If you do not wish to cease from prayer, do not cease from desire.' And these words are true, the intention or the desire *is* prayer whether we are speaking of vocal prayer, eucharistic prayer, office prayer, Jesus prayer, rosary prayer or, as now, the prayer of the silence of the heart before God . . .

Undoubtedly in this period of waiting, waiting, we are sometimes taken hold of. The parched earth is rewarded with a
shower of rain. St Antony the Great says that he prays best
who does not know he is praying. Watch a group of children
at play. They are so engrossed in their game that they do not
know they are playing . . .

These showers of rain, as it were, come and go, and the
parched earth cannot determine their time or intensity. So, too,
these periods of which I have spoken depend on God and not
on us. They may be waited for, but not sought, least of all
striven after: striving would be in vain.

Prayer is waiting, intending, desiring God. Prayer, we might
say, is a holding on to God, until waiting, waiting, waiting,
we move into the knowledge that we are being held.

Robert Llewelyn
Taizé Service, Norwich Catholic Cathedral
24 November 1995

Youth Sunday
(Sunday before Advent)

I like youngsters

G od says: I like youngsters, I want people to be like them.

I want only children in my kingdom; this has been decreed from the beginning of time.

I like little children because my likeness has not yet been dulled in them.

So, when I gently lean over them, I recognize myself in them.

I like them because they are still growing, they are still improving.

But with grown-ups there is nothing to expect any more.

They will no longer grow, no longer improve.

They have come to a full stop.

I am ready to give you again the beautiful face of a child, the beautiful eyes of a child . . .

For I love youngsters, and I want everyone to be like them.

Michel Quoist
Prayers of Life

G od is a shoulder to cry on, support yourself on him.
God is a joker, laugh with him.
God is peace, relax in her.

God is a father, sit on his lap.

God is a bird, shelter under her wings.

God is a builder, work with him.

God is love, care with her.

God is a defender of justice, stand up with him for what is right.

God is creation, create with her.

God is a mother, love with her.

God is a child, marvel with him.

God is good, do not condemn yourself by her.

God is a tree, stand tall and straight with him.

God is a friend, trust in her.

God is a wind, you can't see him, but he can be felt.

God is creation, rejoice in it.

God is part of you, and you are part of God.

Laugh with and at and love yourself.

Oliver

a prayer by a Year II student, written at

St Cassian's Retreat Centre

Christ the King
(Sunday before Advent)

To see Christ is to see God and all of humanity. This mystery has evoked in me a burning desire to see the face of Jesus. Countless images have been created over the centuries to portray the face of Jesus. Some have helped me to see his face; others have not. But when I saw Andrew Rublev's icon of Christ, I saw what I had never seen before and felt before, I knew immediately that my eyes had been blessed in a very special way...

One of the more remarkable qualities of this Christ icon is that the iconographer has portrayed a slight movement. The shoulders and upper chest are painted at a three-quarters angle, while the face, eyes, nose and lips are set fully facing us. Thus we see Jesus turning towards us. The longer we pray before the icon, the more deeply we will feel this movement. It seems as if Jesus is moving forward but then notices us, turns towards us and looks us directly in the face.

I am reminded of the encounter between Jesus and Peter after Peter's denials: 'The Lord turned and looked straight at Peter, and Peter remembered what the Lord had said to him' (Luke 22:61)... As we look at Rublev's Saviour we can understand Peter's tears better. We feel them in ourselves. They are tears of both repentance and gratitude for so much love...

The Christ by Rublev looks directly at those who observe him and confronts them with his penetrating eyes. They are large, open eyes with an owlish quality, accentuated by big brows and deep, round shadows. They are not severe or judgemental, but they see all that is. They form the true centre of the icon. One could say, 'Jesus is all eyes'. His penetrating look brings to mind the words of the psalmist:

'O Lord, you search me and you know me, you know my
    resting and my rising,
you discern my purpose from afar.
You mark when I walk or lie down, all my ways lie open to you.
O where can I go from your spirit, or where can I flee from
    your face?' (Psalm 139:1–3,7) . . .

The One who sees unceasingly the limitless goodness of God came to the world, saw it broken to pieces by human sin and was moved to compassion. The same eyes that see into the heart of God saw the suffering hearts of God's people and wept (John 11:36). These eyes, which burn like flames of fire penetrating God's own interiority, also hold oceans of tears for the human sorrow of all times and all places. That is the secret of the eyes of Andrew Rublev's Christ.

Henri Nouwen
America magazine

F riendship with the poor makes us friends of the eternal king. Love of that poverty establishes kings, even on this earth, and kings not of earth but of heaven. This is evident because while the future heavenly kingdom may be promised to others, it is promised here and now to the poor and those who suffer tribulation; it is the abiding Truth who says, 'Blessed are the poor in spirit, for theirs is the kingdom of heaven' – 'even now they have a right to the kingdom'.

Not only are they kings, but they make others sharers in the kingdom, as Christ teaches us in St Luke when he says, 'Make friends for yourselves by means of unrighteous mammon, so that when it fails they may receive you into the eternal habitations.' These 'friends' are the poor, thanks to whose merits those whom they help enter into dwellings of glory, especially if they are poor of their own free will. According to St Augustine these are the little ones of whom Christ says, 'Anything you did for one of the least of these, you did for me.'

In this way the excellence of poverty becomes evident. Poverty does not think it worthwhile to heap up treasures out of dung or base earth, but, with the full power of its love, buys that precious treasure in the field of holy Church, whether it be Christ himself or his spiritual gifts, from which he is never separated.

To appreciate the true utility of poverty, how far it really has a place among the means suitable to gain our final end, one should reflect on the many sins from which we are preserved by holy poverty, since it does away with the stuff of which they are made, *quia non habet unde suum paupertas pascat amorem*. It slays pride, that worm of the rich, and cuts out those infernal leeches of excess and gluttony, and of so many other sins. And should we fall, through weakness, it helps us to get up quickly, because there is none of that amorous attachment which, like glue, binds the heart to the earth and to the things of the earth, and leaves no freedom to get up again, to come to one's senses and to turn to God. Poverty makes it easier in every case to hear better the voice, i.e. the inspiration, of the Holy Spirit, removing any obstacles in its way. It also makes prayers more effective in the sight of God, 'The Lord heard the prayer of the poor.' It speeds us along the way of the virtues like a traveller relieved of every burden. It frees us from that slavery common to so many of the great of this world, in which '*all things obey or serve money*'.

Polanco
(Secretary to Ignatius of Loyola)
Letter to members of the Society of Jesus, 1547
in *Iñigo:*
Letters personal and spiritual

I read how Edward the First ingeniously surprised the Welsh into subjection, proffering them such a prince as should be:

1. The son of a king.
2. Born in their own country.
3. Whom none could tax for any fault.

The Welsh accepted the conditions, and the king tendered them his son Edward, an infant, newly born in the castle of Carnarvon.

Do not all these qualifications mystically centre themselves in my Saviour?

1. The King of heaven saith unto him, Thou art my Son, this day have I begotten thee.
2. Our true countryman, real flesh, whereas he took not on him the nature of angels.
3. Without spot or blemish, like to us in all things, sin only excepted.

Away then with those wicked men who will not have this king to rule over them. May he have dominion in and over me. Thy Kingdom come. Heaven and earth cannot afford a more proper prince for the purpose, exactly accomplished with all these comfortable qualifications.

Thomas Fuller
Good Thoughts in Worse Times (1647)

When for the thorns with which I long, too long,
    With many a piercing wound,
My Saviour's head have crown'd,
I seek with garlands to redress that wrong:
Through every garden, every mead,
I gather flow'rs (my fruits are only flow'rs),
Dismantling all the fragrant towers
That once adorn'd my shepherdesse's head:
And now, when I have summ'd up all my store,
Thinking (so I myself deceive)
So rich a chaplet thence to weave

As never yet the King of Glory wore:
Alas! I find the Serpent old,
That, twining in his speckled breast,
About the flowers disguis'd, does fold
With wreaths of fame and interest.

Ah! foolish man, that would'st debase with them,
And mortal glory, Heaven's diadem!
But Thou who only could'st the Serpent tame,
Either his slipp'ry knots at once untie,
And disentangle all his winding snare;
Or shatter too with him my curious frame
And let these wither – so that he may die –
Though set with skill, and chosen out with care:
That they, while thou on both their spoils dost tread,
May crown thy feet, that could not crown thy head.

Andrew Marvell

O King of glory and Lord of valours, who hast said,
'Be of good cheer, I have overcome the world': be thou
victorious in us thy servants, for without thee we can do nothing. Grant thy compassion to go before us, thy compassion to
come behind us: before us in our undertakings, behind us in
our ending. And what more shall we say but that thy will be
done; for thy will is our salvation, our glory, and our joy.

Alcuin

Acknowledgements

The editor and publishers are grateful for permission to use the extracts which make up this book. For ease of reference they are listed by month, with full details given only for the first reference, any subsequent one being referred back to the month of first usage, or, if within the same month (see above).

Every effort has been made to trace copyright holders, but where we have been unsuccessful, sources are marked (source unknown).

November

St Augustine (source unknown)
Report of Seventh Interecclesial Assembly of basic ecclesial communities, Margaret Hebblethwaite, *Base Communities: an introduction*, Geoffrey Chapman, 1993
William D. Miller, *Dorothy Day: a biography*, Harper & Row, New York 1982. Reprinted by permission of HarperCollins Publishers Inc.
C. S. Lewis, 'The Weight of Glory' in *Screwtape Proposes a Toast and other pieces*, HarperCollins Fount, 1965
Etty Hillesum, *Etty: a Diary 1941–43*, transl. Arnold J. Pomerans, Triad, Grafton Books, 1985, used by permission of Jonathan Cape

December

Gwen Vendley, quoted in Ana Carrigan, *Salvador Witness: The Life and Calling of Jean Donovan*, Simon and Schuster, New York, used by permission of the author, copyright © 1984 Ana Carrigan
Julian Filochowski, Letter to CAFOD Supporters, December 1995
Jesuit Refugee Service, statement made at Seven Fountains, Chiang Mai, Thailand 21 November 1985

St Bernard, Sermon for the First Sunday in Advent

A Carthusian, *The Prayer of Love and Silence*, Darton, Longman & Todd, London 1962

Jim Cotter, 'Praying with Mary', *By Heart for the Millennium*, Cairns Publications, Sheffield 1998, p. 14

Human Rights Day Service: Amnesty International UK

Out of the Darkness: paths to inclusive worship, Australian Council of Churches, Canberra 1986

Thomas Merton, *Seasons of Celebration*, Farrar, Straus and Giroux, New York 1965

Thomas Merton, *Conjectures of a Guilty Bystander*, copyright © 1966 by The Abbey of Gethsemani. Used by permission of Double-day, a division of Random House, Inc.

Ethiopian Prayer of the Covenant, CAFOD's prayer for Advent 1996

Marion Kim, Korea, prayer used by Christian Aid

Holli Ball, Christian Aid's prayer for Advent 1996, Christian Aid

Bishop Victor Guazzelli, homily on World AIDS Day, 1 December 1996

Oscar Romero, *The Violence of Love*, Plough Publishing House, 1998

Clive Sansom, 'The Witnesses: The Innkeeper's Wife' in *Poems 1951*, Penguin Books, 1951

St Augustine, *On the Gospel*

Kenneth Leech, 'Meanings of Christmas: A strange, persistent and defiant light', *The Independent*, 29 December 1992. By permission of the author.

St Ephraim the Syrian, in *SPCK Book of Christian Prayer*, SPCK, 1995

John Henry Newman, 'The Mystery of Godliness' in *Parochial and Plain Sermons V, VII*, The Fathers of the Birmingham Oratory

St Augustine, *Sermons on Christmas*

Oscar Romero (source unknown)

T. S. Eliot, *Murder in the Cathedral*, Faber & Faber, 1935.

John Henry Newman, 'The Mystery of Godliness' (see above)

T. S. Eliot, Chorus from 'The Rock', Faber & Faber

St Athanasius (source unknown)

Tissa Balasuriya, *Mary and Human Liberation*, Centre for Society and Religion, Sri Lanka 1990

John Henry Newman: 'The Mystery of Godliness' (see above)

Prudentius, *A Treasury of Early Christianity*, ed. Anne Fremantle

Pierre Claverie, Joachim Ruhuna, Christophe Munzihirwa (source unknown)

Michael Campbell-Johnston, 'Message of a massacre', *The Tablet*, 24/31 December 1994

Archibald Campbell Tait, *SPCK Book of Christian Prayer* (see above)

Anna Briggs, *Not Counting the Women and Children – a life of Josephine Butler*, copyright © Anna Briggs, Sea Change Theatre, Cambridge

Karl Rahner, 'Spiritual Balance-Sheet of a Year', *Everyday Faith*, Burns & Oates/Herder Ltd, 1968

Francis Brienen, in *SPCK Book of Christian Prayer* (see above)

M. Louise Haskins, *The Gate of the Year*

January

Pope John Paul II, prayer for the third year of preparation for the Great Jubilee, CAFOD

Millennium Prayer, Millennium Resolution, reproduced by kind permission of Churches Together in England, copyright © New Start 2000 Ltd

Jubilee prayer, St Michael's Parish, Liverpool 6

Prayer from the Litany of Reconciliation used daily in Coventry Cathedral

World Council of Churches, Geneva, opening worship of the sixth assembly, Vancouver 1983

Prayer from Japan (source unknown)

Pope John Paul II, *Prayers and Devotions*, Viking

Ancient Ethiopian hymn from *Catholic Near East*

Thomas Merton, *Conjectures of a Guilty Bystander* (December)

Bede Griffiths, from his Christmas Message 'The Gifts of the Magi', 20 December 1986, Darton, Longman & Todd

Aloysius Pieris (source unknown)

Mary Grey (source unknown)

Jan Berry, in *SPCK Book of Christian Prayer* (December)

Johann Tauler (source unknown)

Hermann Hesse, *The Journey to the East*, Granada, 1972

Evelyn Waugh, *Helena*, used by permission of Peters, Fraser & Dunlop

St Maximus of Turin, St Ignatius of Antioch, St Peter Chrysologus,

Philip of Heraclea all from *The SPCK Book of Christian Prayer* (December)

Hilda Graef, *The Light and the Rainbow*, Longmans, 1959. Copyright Roman Catholic Archdiocese of Birmingham

St Hilda Community, *The New Women Included: a book of services and prayers*, SPCK, 1996

Final Declaration of the Swanwick meeting of the Inter-Church process, September 1987, *Churches Together in Pilgrimage*, BCC/CTS 1989, copyright © CTBI Publications

The Pilgrims' Prayer, copyright © 1987 CTBI Publications

St Bernard (source unknown)

Kate McIlhagga, *Encompassing Presence*, the Prayer Handbook for 1993, United Reformed Church

Richard Wurmbrand, *The Total Blessing*, SPCK/Triangle, 1995

Leonardo Boff, Sermon on the Mount of Corcovado, *Crie* No. 336, Lima

St Francis de Sales from *Introduction to the Devout Life*, Copyright © 1950 Harper & Brothers. Used by permission of Doubleday, a division of Random House, Inc.

St Angela Merici, *Counsels* and *Testament*

St Thomas Aquinas, *Adoro te devote*, transl. Gerard Manley Hopkins

St Thomas Aquinas, 'Prayer before a picture of Christ', *An Aquinas Reader*, Hodder & Stoughton

Jim McCartney, *Edges* magazine, Blackburn

David Blanchflower, *All Year Round*, British Council of Churches, 1987

Attributed to Nelson Mandela (source unknown)

Jim Cotter, 'I vow to you, my friends of earth', *Prayer in the Morning*, Cairns Publications, Sheffield 1989, p. 125

Mary Ward, quoted in Lavinia Byrne, *Mary Ward: A Pilgrim Finds Her Way*, Carmelite Centre of Spirituality, Dublin 1984

February

The Lives of the Saints from the 'Book of Lismore', ed. Whitley Stokes, Clarendon Press 1890

Timothy of Jerusalem, *Oratio in Symeonem*

Origen, *Hom. XV sur Luc.*

Pedro Arrupe, farewell speech to the Jesuits at the opening of the 33rd General Congregation

An Irish prayer, an Irish blessing, an Irish grace, from *Favourite Prayers*, Cassell, 1998

St Patrick, in *SPCK Book of Christian Prayer* (December)

St Gregory the Great, 'Dialogues' from *A Word in Season*, vol. iv, Augustinian Press, Villanova, PA, USA, 1991

Elaine Kennedy, *Edges* magazine, Blackburn, June-August 1998

Thomas Menamparampil, *A Path to Prayer*, St Paul's, Mumbai, Bombay 1992

Edward Taylor (source unknown)

Max Müller (source unknown)

Christina Rossetti (in the public domain)

Jonathan Sacks, 5 July 1994, on the launch of tthe RE syllabuses

Mother Teresa of Calcutta, *Mother Teresa: Jesus, the Word to be spoken*, HarperCollins Fount, 1987

Cardinal Basil Hume, Westminster Cathedral, 28 February 1997, funeral homily for Michael Hollings

Forbes Robinson, *Letters to his Friends*, 1904

March

D. Gwenallt Jones, from the *Oxford Book of Welsh Verse in English*, Oxford, 1979

Alison Evans, Columban lay missionary

The Women's Creed (source unknown)

Julia Esquivel, *Threatened with Resurrection*, The Brethren Press, 1982

Joan Smith, *Celebrating Women: the new edition*, ed. Hannah Ward, Jennifer Wild, Janet Morley, SPCK, 1995; USA & Canada: Morehouse Publishing, Harrisburg, PA

Archbishop Nguyen Van Thuan, *Five Loaves and Two Fish*, Tinvui Media, CA 1998

'The Martyrdom of Perpetua', *A Lost Tradition: Women Writers of the Early Church*, Patricia Wilson-Kastner, in the series *Visionary Women*, ed. Monica Furlong, Arthur James, Alresford 1996

George Herbert, *The Temper*

Pierre Teilhard de Chardin, *Le Milieu Divin* and *Letters to Léontine Zanta*, HarperCollins 1957 and 1969

Sylvia Sands, 'Stations of the Cross'

Richard Rolle, *The Fire of Love*

R. W. Barbour, *Thoughts*, 1900

St John of the Cross, 'The Dark Night', from *The Collected Works*, transl. Kavanaugh and Rodriguez, ICS Publications, Washington 1991

Michel Quoist, in *Hodder Book of Christian Prayers*, Hodder & Stoughton, 1986

Kathy Galloway, in *SPCK Book of Christian Prayer* (December)

Jim Cotter, 'We grieve and confess', 'We have injured your love', from *Prayer at Night's Approaching*, Cairns Publications, Sheffield 1997, pp. 24–25, p. 4

Prayers for peace in Northern Ireland, composed by Pax Christi (Ireland) and the Fellowship of Reconciliation

Michael Woodward, 'Epiphany at the Bay of Bengal', the *Merton Journal*

Michael Ramsey, *To Believe is to Pray*, Cowley Publications, Oxford 1996

Clare Brennan, from an address in Exeter College Chapel, Oxford, 7 February 1996

Ben Okri, Dom Helder Camara, Satish Kumar, *They shall not rob us of hope . . .* (AFOD, 1992). Ben Okri extract used by permission of Jonathan Cape

Fabian Glencross in *A Touch of God: eight monastic journeys*, ed. Maria Boulding, SPCK 1982

Barbara d'Arcy, 'Lord you are the light of the world' from *The Trampled Vineyard: worship resources on housing and homelessness*, CHAS and Unleash, 1992

Terence Morris, from an address in Winchester Cathedral, 28 December 1997, copyright © Terence Morris 1997

Kevin Kelly, from a sermon in Liverpool Metropolitan Cathedral, 24 March 1981

Althea Hayton, *Prayer in Pregnancy*, Wren Publications, St Albans, 1996

Guerric of Igny (source unknown)

St Ephraim: A homily on the nativity, in Brock, *The Harp of the Spirit*, Augustinian Press, Villanova, PA, USA, and also in *A Word in Season*, 1991 (February)

Damian Lundy, *The Sower* magazine

Peter Windram, *Priest*, published privately 1992

April

Edwina Gateley (source unknown)

John Shevlin, copyright © John Shevlin 1992

Marguerite d'Oingt (source unknown)

John Donne, 'An Hymn to God the Father'

Metropolitan Anthony of Sourozh, *Creative Prayer*, Darton, Longman & Todd, 1987

Martin Luther King: adaptation copyright © The Catholic Community of Portadown, July 1998

Richard MacKenna, *God for Nothing*, Churchman Publishing, Worthing, 1984

Mother Teresa of Calcutta, *A Simple Path*, Rider, 1995

Jim Frazer, 'Sunday Worship' from Ballywillan Presbyterian Church, BBC Radio 4, 16 August 1998

Dietrich Bonhoeffer, quoted in *A Third Testament* by Malcolm Muggeridge, HarperCollins/BBC, 1977

Andrew of Crete, quoted in *From the Fathers to the Churches*, Vol. II, from the Divine Office, used by permission of A. P. Watt on behalf of The Hierarchies of England, Wales, Ireland and Australia, and in the USA by permission of GIA, Chicago, Ill. HarperCollins, 1983

Orthodox hymn for Palm Sunday (source unknown)

Luis Espinal, quoted in *Base Communities: an introduction* (November)

Pablo Galdámez, from *Faith of a People*, English transl. copyright © 1986 Orbis Books, Maryknoll, New York, 1986

Pope John XXIII quoted in *John XXIII: Pope of the Council*, Peter Hebblethwaite, Geoffrey Chapman, 1984

John Henry Newman, *Parochial and Plain Sermons* (December)

Count Leo Tolstoy, *What I Believe*, transl. Aylmer Maude, from John Baillie, *A Diary of Readings*, Oxford University Press, 1955, 1981, 1994

Mother Teresa of Calcutta (source unknown)

Luigi Santucci, *Wrestling with Christ*, transl. Bernard Wall, HarperCollins, 1972. By permission of Barbara Wall.

John Fletcher, letter to Henry Brooke

Luigi Santucci, *Wrestling with Christ* (see above)

George Herbert (source unknown)

St Hilda Community, *The New Women Included* (January)

Ernesto Cardenal, transl. John Griffiths, *Psalms*, Sheed & Ward, 1981

Thomas Greenan, *Give Sorrow Words: poems from El Salvador*, Scottish Catholic International Aid Fund, Glasgow 1995

Elie Wiesel, *Night*, Andrew Wadsworth, in *Words are not enough: a resource pack for Christian Worship on the theme of torture*, copyright © Medical Foundation for the Care of Victims of Torture, 1998

Banned radio advertisement, Amnesty International

George Herbert, 'The Agonie'

St Ignatius of Loyola, in *SPCK Book of Christian Prayer* (December)

St Hilda Community, *The New Women Included* (January)

A client of the Medical Foundation for the Care of Victims of Torture (see above)

Dorothee Soelle, *Celebrating Resistance: the way of the Cross in Latin America*, Mowbray, 1993

Walter Raleigh (in the public domain)

Julia Esquivel, *Threatened with Resurrection* (March)

St Augustine, *Confessions 13, 35–37*, transl. Maria Boulding, Hodder & Stoughton, 1997

Francis Kilvert, *Diary*, 16 April 1876

St Augustine, *Sermons 241, ii, 1*

Sedulius Scottus, 'Easter Sunday' in *Celtic Christianity: ecology and holiness*, ed. Christopher Bamford and William Parker Marsh, Floris Books, Edinburgh, 1986, reprinted by permission of Floris Books

Damian Lundy, 'New Daytime Dawning, breaking like the Spring', Kevin Mayhew, Stowmarket

Lancelot Andrewes (source unknown)

Karl Barth, in *SPCK Book of Christian Prayer* (December)

Alexander Carmichael, *The Sun Dances: Prayers and Blessings from the Gaelic*

Brother Roger Schutz, from *Prayer: seeking the heart of God*, with Mother Teresa of Calcutta, HarperCollins Fount, 1992

George Herbert, 'Easter'

St Romanos the Melodist, 'On the Resurrection' from *On the Life of Christ*, transl. Archimandrite Ephrem Lash, AltaMira Press, Walnut Creek, CA 94596

St Hilda (source unknown)

Dietrich Bonhoeffer, *A Testament of Hope*, ed. Geoffrey B. Kelly and F. Burton Nelson, HarperCollins, San Francisco 1990

St Manchan, *Threshold of Light: prayers and praises from the Celtic tradition*, ed. A. M. Allchin and Esther de Waal, Darton, Longman & Todd, 1986

Edwina Gateley (source unknown)

Victor Hugo (source unknown)

Thomas Berry (source unknown)

Robert McAffee Brown (source unknown)

St Francis of Assisi (source unknown)

Richard Rolle, *The Fire of Love*, transl. Clifton Wolters, Penguin Books, 1972

St Thomas à Kempis, *The Imitation of Christ*, transl. Betty Knott, HarperCollins Fount, 1963

C. S. Lewis, *Letters to Malcolm: Chiefly on Prayer*, HarperCollins Fount

Maria Petyt (source unknown)

William Wordsworth, *Tintern Abbey*

St Catherine of Siena, letter to Br Raymond of Capua, OP

George Appleton, in *Reflections from a Life of Prayer*, SPCK, 1995

May

A Celtic Miscellany, Penguin Classics

Carlo Carretto, *Letters from the Desert*, transl. Rose Mary Hancock, Darton, Longman & Todd, 1972

Pope John Paul II, *Gift and Mystery*, Doubleday / Catholic Truth Society

Pierre Teilhard de Chardin, *Hymn of the Universe*, HarperCollins Fount, 1965

Yevgeny Yevtushenko, quoted in Donald Nicholl, *Triumphs of the Spirit in Russia*, Darton, Longman & Todd

Sheldon Vanauken, *A Severe Mercy*, Hodder & Stoughton, 1977

Ernesto Cardenal, *Psalms*, transl. John Griffiths, Sheed & Ward, 1981

Philip Jebb in *A Touch of God* (March)

Julian of Norwich in *Showings*, ed. Edmund Colledge and James Walsh, SPCK, 1978

St Augustine, *Sermon on the anniversary of his episcopal ordination* 340, 1

St Clement of Alexandria, transl. Elizabeth Barrett Browning

Karl Rahner, *Prayers for a Lifetime*, T. & T. Clark, Edinburgh 1986

Thomas Aquinas (source unknown)

Thomas Traherne, from *Centuries*, in the public domain

Pierre Teilhard de Chardin (source unknown)

St Hilda Community, *The New Women Included* (January)

Susanna Wesley, quoted in *Hearts Aflame*, ed. Michael McMullen, SPCK, 1995

St Cuthbert, from a letter

Henry Suso, *Meditations*, Mowbray, 1993

Michel Quoist, 'There are two loves only', *Prayers of Life*, Gill & Macmillan, Dublin

Miriam Therese Winter, *Woman Wisdom*, © Medical Mission Sisters, 1991, p.274. Reprinted by permission.

St Francis of Assisi, *Absorbeat*, transl. Benen Fahy OFM

Bernard Shaw, *St Joan*, Longman, 1991, © 1951, 1957, 1991, The Public Trustee as Executor of the Estate of Bernard Shaw

'The Trial of Joan of Arc', quoted by Marina Warner in the series *Visionary Women* ed. Monica Furlong, Arthur James, Alresford 1996, with thanks to the Folio Society for use of extracts from the translation by W. S. Scott of the Orleans Manuscript published by the Society in 1956

Papal Decree 1894 introducing cause of Joan's canonization

Janet Morley, *All Desires Known*, SPCK, 1992

Phoebe Willetts, *Celebrating Women: the new edition* (March)

Sr Elaine MacInnes, from a talk to the Alister Hardy Institute, 8 November 1997, with thanks to the Religious Experience Research Centre, Westminster College, Oxford

June

Aboriginal prayer read in Westminster Abbey, 20 April 1997

William Temple (source unknown)

Rex Chapman (source unknown)

St Augustine, *Sermon on the Ascension*

Mozarabic Sacramentary (source unknown)

Doreen Alexander, Michael Galvin and Peter W. A. Davison, taken from *Dare to Dream: a prayer and worship anthology from around the world*, ed. Geoffrey Duncan, HarperCollins Fount, 1995

John Dalrymple, *Longest Journey: notes on Christian maturity*, Darton, Longman & Todd, 1979

Emile Cammaerts, *The Laughing Prophet: the seven virtues and G. K. Chesterton*, Methuen, 1937

Jürgen Moltmann, 'Pentecost and Theology of Life', The Lambeth Lecture, Kings College, London, 11 January 1996

Pierre Teilhard de Chardin, *Hymn of the Universe*, (May)

Jan van Ruysbroeck, *The Adornment of the Spiritual Marriage*, E. P. Dutton, 1916

Eric Milner-White (source unknown)

Nikos Kazantzakis (source unknown)

Paul Florensky (source unknown)

Janet Morley, *All Desires Known* (May)

Cardinal Basil Hume, *Basil in Blunderland*, Darton, Longman & Todd, 1997

St Augustine, *The Confessions* (April)

St John of the Cross, *Poems*, tr. E. Allison Peers, Anthony Clarke, 1974

Church of Scotland, *Book of Common Order*, St Andrew Press, Edinburgh

Derek Webster, *Our Time Now*, Kenelm Press, 1997

St Patrick from *The Lorica (Breastplate)*

John V. Taylor, *The Go-Between God*, SCM Press, 1972

William Johnston, *Christian Mysticism Today*, HarperCollins, 1984

Metropolitan Anthony of Sourozh, *Creative Prayer* (April)

Richard McIlkenny (source unknown)

Paula Fairlie in *A Touch of God* (March)

Peter Levi, 'Sermon on St Thomas More', Church of the Holy Redeemer, Chelsea, *The Tablet*, 24 August 1968

Elizabeth Goudge, *God So Loved the World*, Hodder & Stoughton, 1951

Hans Urs von Balthasar, *The von Balthasar Reader*, ed. Medard Kehl and Werner Löser, T. & T. Clark Ltd, Edinburgh 1982

Donal Neary, *Lighting the Shadows: reflections and prayers for young people*, Veritas, Dublin 1995

St Francis de Sales (source unknown)

St Aelred, Sermon 16, 298–301 in *A Word in Season* volume IV (February)

Sr Vandana, written in India for *The Tablet*

July

Frank Topping, *An Impossible God* (adapted)
Ida Friederike Görres, *Broken Lights: diaries and letters 1951–59*, transl. Barbara Waldstein-Wartenberg, Burns & Oates, 1964
Jim Cotter, *Prayer at Night's Approaching*, pp. 18–19 (March)
Dorothy Day, from *Selected Writings*, ed. Robert Ellsberg, copyright © 1983, 1992 Robert Ellsberg and Tamar Hennessey, Orbis Books, Maryknoll, New York 1992
Thomas Merton, a letter to Amiya Chakravarty
Hebrew Morning Service, Oscar Wilde, John Donne, Eastern Church, Old Breton all from *God of a Hundred Names*, ed. Barbara Greene & Victor Gollancz, 1962
St Augustine, *Confessions* (April)
Cardinal Basil Hume, from an address to the Parliamentary Christian Fellowship, 10 July 1996
Ancilla Dent, 'Ecology, Faith, Stewardship', an address given at the Kent Christian Ecology Group day, at Minster Abbey, Kent, July 1993
Lancelot Andrewes, *English Sermons: Mirrors of Society*, ed. Christine d'Haussy, Presses Universitaires du Mirail, 1995
Fr Seraphion of Mount Athos, adapted by Fr Jan Bereza OSB
Michel Quoist, *Prayers of Life* (May)
St Ignatius of Loyola, from *Iñigo: letters personal and spiritual*, ed. Joseph A. Munitiz, Iñigo Enterprises, Oxford 1995

August

Anthony de Mello, *Sadhana: a way to God*, Gujarat Sahitya Prakash, Gujarat, 1978
Metropolitan Anthony of Sourozh, *Sacrament and Image: Essays in the Christian Understanding of Man*, ed. A. M. Allchin, Fellowship of SS Alban and Sergius 1967
Maggie Ross, *The Fountain and the Furnace*, Paulist Press
Jordan of Saxony, *Nine Ways of Prayer*, Humbert of Romans, Prayer to St Dominic, all copyright Blackfriars, Oxford
John M. Oesterreicher, *Walls are Crumbling*, Devin-Adair Co., New York 1952

Walter Nigg, *Francis of Assisi*, transl. William Neil, Mowbray, 1975

Florence Nightingale in Rosemary Hartill, *Florence Nightingale: Letters and Reflections*, in the series *Visionary Women* (May)

Gaelic Prayer from *The Sun Dances* (April)

George Every, 'The End of the Age'

Dorothee Soelle, *Celebrating Resistance* (April)

Society of Jesus, General Congregation 32

Pedro Arrupe, in Jean-Claude Dietsch, *Pedro Arrupe: itinéraire d'un jésuite*, Le Centurion, Paris 1982

St Bernard of Clairvaux, *On the Love of God*, transl. Terence L. Connolly

John O'Donohue, *Anam Cara: spiritual wisdom from the Celtic world*, Bantam Press, 1997

St Augustine, *Confessions* (April)

Angela Tilby, 'Thought for the Day', BBC Radio 4, 13 May 1996

St Augustine, *Confessions* (see above)

The Story Books of Little Gidding (1631–32)

Note on desk of Diana, Princess of Wales (source unknown)

Cardinal Basil Hume, from a meditation broadcast after the death of Diana, Princess of Wales

Derek Webster, *Our Time Now* (June)

Menander (source unknown)

September

Gerard W. Hughes, *God of Surprises*, Darton, Longman & Todd; USA: Cowley Publications, 28 Temple Place, Boston. MA 02111; *cowley@cowley.org*; 1–800–225–1534

Mother Teresa of Calcutta, *A Gift for God*, HarperCollins Fount, 1975

Ivone Gebara, *The Month*, August/September 1987

John Shevlin, *A World United*, Steyl Press, 1992

Mario Marazziti, from a talk given in London, copyright © Mario Marazziti

Gerard Manley Hopkins, 'Hurrahing in Harvest'

Jean Mortimer, in *SPCK Book of Christian Prayer* (December)

Mario Marazziti (see above)

Acknowledgements

423

St John Chrysostom (attributed) (source unknown)
Pope Paul VI, *Evangelii Nuntiandi: evangelization in the modern world*, 8 December 1975, used by kind permission of The Catholic Truth Society
Aung San Suu Kyi, opening address to NGO Forum, Beijing 1995
Baron von Hügel, *The Life of Prayer*, Dent, 1927
Father Congreve, *Spiritual Letters*, 21 September 1884
John Donne, *Eighty Sermons*
Henri Nouwen, *A Letter of Consolation*, Harper & Row, New York 1982
Reaping blessing from *The Sun Dances* (April)
Frank Topping, in *SPCK Book of Christian Prayer* (December)
Trad. Gaelic Prayer (source unknown)
Leonard Hodgson, *Essays in Christian Philosophy*, 1930
Metropolitan Anthony of Sourozh, *Creative Prayer* (April)

October

Christina Rossetti (in the public domain)
Metropolitan Anthony of Sourozh, *Creative Prayer* (April)
Anonymous Celtic prayer (source unknown)
Alexander Solzhenitsyn (source unknown)
Sir Walter Raleigh, 1618 (source unknown)
Mother Teresa of Calcutta (source unknown)
St Teresa of Lisieux, *By Love Alone: daily readings*, ed. Michael Hollings, Darton, Longman & Todd 1986
St Francis of Assisi, from *The Mirror of Perfection*, cantata by Richard Blackford
Margaret Silf, *The Miller's Tale*, Avon Books, London, 1996
An African prayer used by CAFOD
Michael Campbell-Johnston, 'Jesus, you often went hungry . . .' copyright © *The Tablet* 1997
St Clement of Alexandria, *Pedagogus II 12, 119–120, 125*
Lisa Hartwell (source unknown)
Rabindranath Tagore (source unknown)
Oscar Romero (source unknown)
Latin American grace (source unknown)
Sogyal Rinpoche, *Glimpse after Glimpse: Daily Reflections on Living and Dying*, Rider Books, 1995

Mechthild of Magdeburg, Lucy Menzies, *The Revelations of Mechthild of Magdeburg or the Flowing Light of The Godhead*, Longman Green
Margaret Silf, *Landmarks: an Ignatian journey*, Darton, Longman & Todd, 1998
St Teresa of Avila, *Interior Castle*, transl. E. Allison Peers
Juan Luís Segundo, 'The Future of Christianity in Latin America' reprinted from *Cross Currents*, Summer 1963
Fabian Glencross in *A Touch of God* (March)
Stella G. Bristow, extract from Vice-Presidential Address to the Methodist Conference, Bristol 1995

November

Donald Nicholl, *Holiness*, Darton, Longman & Todd, 1981
Joan Chittister, *A Litany of Women for the Church*
Hymn for the Feast of the Holy Angels in the Orthodox Church
Origen, from *Seasons of the Spirit*, SPCK, London 1984
Karl Rahner, *The Eternal Year*, Burns & Oates, London, 1964
Thomas Merton, *Conjectures of a Guilty Bystander* (December)
Prayer for the dead (source unknown)
Metropolitan Anthony of Sourozh, *Seasons of the Spirit* (see above)
Eddius Stephanus, *Life of Wilfrid*
Funeral Ikos, transl. by Isabel Hapgood
John Henry Newman, Letter, February 1880
Bishop Peter Firth, a counsellor, a Canadian prayer and a prayer based on Jeremiah 31:15–17, taken from Althea Hayton, *Prayer After Abortion*, Wren Publications, St Albans, 1997
Clive Gillam, *St Francis House Newsletter*, The Catholic Worker Movement, Oxford
Carlos Bravo Gallardo, letter to friends
Turgot, Bishop of St Andrews, *St Margaret*, by Iain Macdonald, Floris Books, Edinburgh 1993. Reprinted by permission of Floris Books
Ida Friederike Görres: *Broken Lights* (July)
Rosemary Haughton, *Elizabeth's Greeting*, Constable 1968
Herman Váldez, *Diary of a Chilean concentration camp*, Victor Gollancz, 1975

The Prisoner's Lantern: meditations by a Christian prisoner in Ethiopia, 1988 Keston Institute, 4 Park Town, Oxford OX2 6SH, website: http://www.keston.org

Richard Wurmbrand, *The Total Blessing* (January)

The Prisoner's Lantern (see above)

Irina Ratushinskaya, Amnesty International, Anatoli Levitin, Pax Christi, Viktoras Petkus, from *The Lion Prayer Collection*, Mary Batchelor, Lion 1992

Robert Llewelyn, from the Taizé Service, Norwich Catholic Cathedral, 24 November 1995

Michel Quoist, 'I Like Youngsters', *Prayers of Life* (May)

Oliver, prayer written at St Cassian's Retreat Centre, 15 November 1995

Henri Nouwen, *America* magazine, v. 154, 11 January 1986. All rights reserved. Reproduced with permission of America Press, Inc., 106 W. 56th Street, New York, NY 10019

Polanco, Letter to Members of the Society of Jesus, 7 August 1547, in *Iñigo* (July)

Thomas Fuller, *Good Thoughts in Worse Times*, 1647

Andrew Marvell (source unknown)

Alcuin (source unknown)

Index

Names in italics are Feastdays; names in roman are authors

Index 427